NANCY BERMEO

ORDINARY PEOPLE IN EXTRAORDINARY TIMES

The Citizenry and the Breakdown of Democracy

ORDINARY PEOPLE IN EXTRAORDINARY TIMES

ORDINARY PEOPLE IN EXTRAORDINARY TIMES

THE CITIZENRY AND THE BREAKDOWN OF DEMOCRACY

Nancy Bermeo

PRINCETON UNIVERSITY PRESS

PRINCETON AND OXFORD

LIBRARY OF CONGRESS CATALOGING-IN-PUBLICATION DATA

BERMEO, NANCY GINA, 1951–

ORDINARY PEOPLE IN EXTRAORDINARY TIMES : THE CITIZENRY AND
THE BREAKDOWN OF DEMOCRACY / NANCY BERMEO

P.   CM.

INCLUDES BIBLIOGRAPHICAL REFERENCES AND INDEX.

ISBN 0-691-08969-8—ISBN 0-691-08970-1 (pbk.)

1. CIVIL SOCIETY. 2. DEMOCRACY. 3. AUTHORITARIANISM. 4. ALLEGIANCE.
5. GOVERNMENT, RESISTANCE TO. 6. CRISES. 7. ELITE (SOCIAL SCIENCES)
8. SOUTH AMERICA—POLITICS AND GOVERNMENT—CASE STUDIES. I. TITLE.

JC337.B47 2003

306.2—DC21   2002035472

BRITISH LIBRARY CATALOGING-IN-PUBLICATION DATA IS AVAILABLE.

THIS BOOK HAS BEEN COMPOSED IN SABON TYPEFACE

PRINTED ON ACID-FREE PAPER. ∞

WWW.PUPRESS.PRINCETON.EDU

PRINTED IN THE UNITED STATES OF AMERICA

1   3   5   7   9   10   8   6   4   2

For Richard, Ben, Sam, and Nick

WITH LOVE

CONTENTS

FIGURES

TABLES

ACKNOWLEDGMENTS

Before beginning I should state that my argument has benefited greatly from the advice and assistance of many people in many different countries. I am indebted to Jeremy Adelman, Astrid Arrarás, Eleanor Bermeo, Sarah Bermeo, Sheri Berman, Larry Diamond, Stephan Haggard, Luis E. González, Megan Kennedy, Atul Kohli, José Miguens, Charles Myers, Valeria Palanza, Paul Sigmund, Alfred Stepan, and Michael Wallerstein. I am especially grateful to Ugo Amoretti, Michael Bernhard, and Amelie von Zumbusch, who contributed to this project in innumerable ways, and to the German Marshall Fund for funding an early stage of this research. My deepest debt is to my husband, Richard Thypin, whose wisdom and kindness remain both boundless and inspirational, even as we enter our third decade together.

PART I

OUR LITERATURE AND INTERWAR EUROPE

WHAT ROLE DO ORDINARY PEOPLE play in the making of popular government? What role do they play in its collapse? The scholarly community has given a great deal of attention lately to the drama of democratization, but the spotlight has fallen most often on political elites. Though there can be little doubt that professional politicians, interest group leaders, and military officials play key roles in the creation and the maintenance of any democratic state, the role of ordinary people deserves close attention too. This is true first and most obviously because democracy is supposedly "rule by the people," but it is also true because much of what elites attempt to do is conditioned by their judgments of how ordinary people will behave.

The ordinary people who stand in the foreground of this study are simply citizens. Some might call them "the masses" or "the public," but both terms have connotations of singularity that do a disservice to the heterogeneity of the group. The term "people" draws our attention to the individuality of the group's membership and the adjective "ordinary" underscores the fact that they have no extraordinary powers vis-à-vis the states in which they live. They are neither politicians nor military officers. They spend most of their lives in personal endeavors—earning money, supporting families, and pursuing whatever leisure activities their social status allows. They are the people who compose the vast majority of the citizenry in virtually every country in the world. Their sheer force of numbers makes them worthy of close attention—but what is most interesting about ordinary people is what they do in extraordinary times. What do they do when times get hard? How often do they abandon the normally exhausting pursuit of private security and comfort and take actions that contribute to forming a new political landscape with a new political regime? How often are they moved to defend democracy and how often do they embrace dictatorship instead?

These are timely but extremely difficult questions. They present us with two challenges. First, though ordinary people are ubiquitous in the world around us, they are often hard to find in social science studies of regime change. This is due in part to the weighty role of elites (and to our own elitism), but it is also the result of the fact that we usually rename people when we study them in a systematic way. They are there throughout our work but often disassembled. When ordinary people leave the private sphere and enter the texts of social scientists, they typically do so as "voters," as "demonstrators," and as "members" of public associations. They become part of what is often called "civil society." Reassembling ordinary people from an array of partial identities and abstractions is our first challenge.[1]

Our second and more serious challenge is to evaluate two competing visions of how ordinary people behave in the drama of democracy's construction and consolidation. In one vision, ordinary people seem heroic. Either as single actors challenging dictatorship through individual acts of resistance or as members of associations nurturing democracy in civil society, common citizens appear in some of our literature as democracy's salvation. In a second set of works, ordinary people seem much less noble. As members of groups, they can demand too much of democracy and erode its capacity to perform and survive. As individuals, ordinary people can be democracy's fickle friends. In times of crisis, they will abandon democratic parties and support polarized parties instead. Rather than being democracy's salvation, ordinary people can be democracy's undoing.

Evaluating these competing perspectives requires a sustained empirical analysis of what ordinary people are doing as democracies move from situations of crisis to situations of collapse. If we are to understand the extent to which ordinary people are (or are not) responsible for democracy's undoing, we must analyze the connections between citizen action and regime breakdown. How were ordinary people acting when democracies fell on hard times? Since I obviously cannot analyze all political action, I have chosen to answer this question through the study of electoral behavior, strikes, demonstrations, and acts of violence. There are other forms of political participation, of course, but these are certainly among the most important, and they link up with my larger research questions in direct ways. Voting and taking collective action are essential elements of democratic citizenship. These activities are also essential to the fate and quality of democratic regimes because political and military leaders judge the risks of democracy by looking at how ordinary people use the freedoms that democracy affords. Political activity takes place in many spheres, but streets, factories, farms, and polling places are uniquely important because of the role they play in the calculations of political elites.

Examining the role of ordinary people in the breakdown of any single democracy requires a narrative of regime change that puts ordinary citizens in the role of protagonists. Formulating even tentative conclu-

---

[1] Happily, the disassembled version of the ordinary citizen is not universal. Sidney Tarrow, Juan Linz, and Alfred Stepan all make reference to "ordinary people" or "ordinary citizens" as important actors in their recent books. See Sidney Tarrow, *Power in Movement* (New York: Cambridge University Press, 1994), 1; and Juan Linz and Alfred Stepan, *Problems of Democratic Transition and Consolidation: Southern Europe, South America, and Post-communist Europe* (Baltimore: Johns Hopkins University Press, 1996), 8.

sions about democracies *in general* requires multiple historical narratives. This book is thus a comparative political history. It tells the untold stories of actors who have never received the attention they deserved. Its first empirical section deals with interwar Europe and history's first set of failed democracies.[2] Its second empirical section examines a set of failed democracies in South America in the 1960s and 1970s. The geographical and temporal sweep of the histories related here is broad, but the commonalties are deep and multiple.

It is in the tracing of these commonalties that the book accomplishes its central task, for the stories of seemingly diverse people separated in time and space yield general lessons of substantial theoretical and political importance. These lessons challenge much of our common wisdom about how ordinary people react to political crisis and about how and when moments of crisis develop into full-blown dramas of regime change.

The strengths of previous scholarship on democratic decline and collapse are many. Thus, though my arguments here have a critical bent, they use previous work as a foundation rather than a foil. Giovanni Sartori's work on polarization provides the bedrock for much of my thinking. He does us great service by pointing out a simple truth: when political actors group themselves in opposite and distant ideological camps, they vacate the middle ground where cooperation is most likely and leave democracy vulnerable to collapse. The histories I analyze here confirm this insight. Yet they also have forced me to think harder about the connection between polarization, regime change, and the actions of ordinary people. For Sartori (and many others), ordinary people are the masons of polarization. They use their votes, one by one, to create distant and uncooperative political blocks. I show that this vision is accurate in only a small minority of cases and that mass defections to extremist parties are rare. Where support for extremist parties does rise, it is often the result of either an expansion of the franchise or the mobilization of nonvoters. Those who have attributed the breakdown of democracy to popular defections have mistaken changes in the composition of the electorate for changes of mind and heart.

In pointing this out, I do not deny the basic utility of the polarization model. I argue instead that the model suits some political actors better than others. Political elites and the leaders of groups in civil society

---

[2] Here and throughout this book, I use the term *democracy* in a narrow sense to connote electorally competitive regimes. I am aware that most of these systems are not fully democratic and that electoral competition was limited in some of these states, but open competition for political office distinguishes all of these systems from dictatorships and makes them worthy of study as a group.

often do polarize, and their polarization often does contribute mightily to the breakdown of democracy. Close analysis of the chronologies of regime change led me to understand that polarization is not a single process but a set of processes unfolding with different sets of actors, in different spheres, and with different degrees of intensity. Polarization can take place in private spheres or in public spheres, and the distinction is highly consequential for our understanding of the role of ordinary people. *Private polarization* involves changes in voting preference and changes in public opinion. These changes are private in the sense that they are manifest in relatively private spaces—in the ostensibly secret act of voting and the ostensibly anonymous act of responding to a questionnaire. *Public polarization* is much more visible. It takes the form of mobilizations and countermobilizations in the public space of plazas, streets, taverns, factories, and farms.

The political preferences of ordinary people are best assessed in private space, for the vast majority of ordinary people never mobilize in public space. Those who do use public space become, by their very actions, "extraordinary." Whether they are so extraordinary that they no longer represent the majority of their fellow citizens is an empirical question with an answer that varies from case to case.

All but a few of the seventeen cases I analyze here fall into two categories. There was either no significant polarization in either private or public space, or there was polarization in public space alone. In the former set of cases, the blame for the breakdown of democracy lay wholly with political elites. In the latter set of cases, where public polarization ran high, the responsibility for democratic breakdown lay with elites as well. Sometimes, their own democratic convictions were so weak that they used public polarization as a rationalization for creating their own authoritarian regime. Other times, they allowed public polarization to grow violent and to threaten both the public order and the military as an institution. When the military was threatened, democracy was doomed.

In both sets of cases, parliamentary and military elites conflated public and private polarization, mistaking the actions of some for the will of the many. Popular support for alternatives to dictatorship went either unrecognized or unexploited by elites. The histories that follow are, thus, stories of leadership failure. They are prefaced in chapter 1, with an overview of our current thinking about ordinary people, political crisis, and the consolidation of democracy. The remainder of the book explores the strengths and limitations of our current thinking with evidence from seventeen cases of democratic breakdown and three cases of democratic survival.

1

HEROES OR VILLAINS?

IMAGES OF CITIZENS AND CIVIL SOCIETY

IN THE LITERATURE ON DEMOCRACY

TELEVISION MAKES IT EASY to find and disseminate heroic images of ordinary people in the dramas of democratization. The vision of a solitary Chinese dissident standing bravely in front of a rolling tank in Tiananmen Square is not easily forgotten. Nor is it easy to forget the images of thousands of other people who faced down forces of coercion in different parts of the world: frail-looking Philippine nuns protecting ballot boxes for the People's Power Movement, burly Polish workers occupying shipyards in the name of Solidarity, and determined Argentine mothers marching defiantly in the Plaza de Mayo in the name of missing children and lost rights. These images have their counterparts in most stories of democratization. They testify to the ubiquity of courage and to the depth of the longing for liberty.

These images also help explain our current fascination with an abstraction called "civil society." Like most abstractions, this term means different things to different people. I use it as shorthand for the networks of formal and informal associations that mediate between individual actors and the state. These networks may function for good or for evil. For me the term "civil" conveys location rather than approbation.[1] Yet there can be little doubt that these networks facilitate the heroic actions we see on film, for they draw individuals out of private worlds and into public spaces. They also offer the fellowship, resources, and reinforcement that make acts of defiance seem feasible. The names of the ordinary people who act heroically are not widely known—but the networks they pass through are named and remem-

---

[1] "Civil society" is a neutral term for me, though I recognize that it is a normatively positive political goal for many others. Philippe Schmitter discusses the negative and ultimately anti-democratic elements of civil society in "Some Reflections about the Concept of Civil Society (in General) and Its Role in the Liberalization and Democratization of Europe (in Particular)," an unpublished manuscript presented at the conference "Civil Society before Democracy" at Princeton University, October 1996. Jan Kubik gives a helpful overview of the various meanings of the term in *Civil Society before Democracy*, ed. Nancy Bermeo and Philip Nord (New York: Rowman and Littlefield, 2000).

bered. Student organizations, church groups, trade unions, and women's groups have a salience in our literature that their individual members usually lack. It is not surprising that civil society became the "celebrity" of our recent democratic transitions.[2] Celebrity status requires a name, and the ordinary people who were often the real heroes of these transitions remain, for the most part, anonymous.

Whatever its origins, our contemporary reverence for civil society is profoundly connected with our current thinking on the durability and quality of democracy. This chapter opens with a brief discussion of these connections and then moves on to argue four related points: first, that civil society was cast in a much more ambiguous role in our recent past; second, that this ambiguous role was closely related to suspicions about ordinary people and their commitment to democracy; third, that these suspicions are reflected in our theories of party systems and voting; and finally, that these suspicions, and the theories they gave rise to, require reexamination.

Civil Society and Democracy

Civil Society as Salvation

Civil society is cast in a heroic role in a wide variety of works that deal with democratization. The role most easily connected with contemporary newsreels portrays civil society as a barrier to tyranny. Tocqueville writes that the growth of civil society's component institutions "should be regarded, not as the best, but as the *only* means of preserving freedom."[3] A broad spectrum of contemporary analysts agrees. We read that civil society is a necessary defense against the "monstrous state,"[4] that it provides "reservoirs of resistance to arbitrary or tyrannical action,"[5] and that without political associations, societies everywhere will be completely dominated by "the central power apparatus."[6] Civil society not only "lays down limits on the actions of the state,"[7] but

---

[2] Linz and Stepan, *Problems of Democratic Transition*, 9.

[3] Alexis de Tocqueville, *Democracy in America* (New York: Vintage Books, 1945), 341.

[4] Francisco Weffort, "Why Democracy?" in *Democratizing Brazil*, ed. Alfred Stepan (New York: Oxford University Press, 1989), 349.

[5] Philippe Schmitter, "Some Propositions about Civil Society and the Consolidation of Democracy" (unpublished manuscript, 1993), 24. Also in *Polis* (Moscow) vol. 5, no. 35 (1996) (in Russian).

[6] Seymour Martin Lipset, "Social Requisites of Democracy Revisited" (unpublished presidential address, American Sociological Association, 1993), 29–30.

[7] Edward Shils, "The Virtue of Civil Society," *Government and Opposition* 26, no. 1 (1991): 4. For similar views, see John Keane, "Introduction," in *Civil Society and the State*, ed. John Keane (New York: Verso, 1988), 61; and George Kolankiewicz, "The Reconstruc-

also counterbalances,[8] "penetrates," "fragments," and "decentralizes" state power.[9]

Another strand of argument presents civil society as the basis of good and effective government. According to this view, civil society provides state elites with "clear counsel" on "authentic," rather than contrived, needs.[10] It "presents authorities with more aggregated, reliable and actionable information"[11] and thereby plays "a central role in resolving problems of successful governance."[12] Strong civil societies "support progress towards . . . greater social and economic equality."[13] Strong civil societies "*expect* better government" and then "*get* it (in part because of their own efforts)."[14]

We connect civil society with good government because we believe that civic associations affect their individual members in salutary ways. Civil society is often portrayed as a school for the training of democratic citizens. It is the space which provides "the taste and habit of self-rule."[15] It is the place for citizens to learn the "civic manners" that make "opposition less rancorous."[16] The actual "experience of civil society . . . seems to work against intolerance and even materialism."[17] It is a place where citizens are able to relate themselves "effectively and meaningfully" to their political systems and thereby gain a sense of efficacy.[18] Participation in civic organizations "inculcates skills of cooperation as well as a sense of shared responsibility for collective endeavors."[19] It "quickens political awareness . . . dispels isolation and

---

tion of Citizenship: Reverse Incorporation in Eastern Europe," in *Constructing Capitalism*, ed. Kazimierz Z. Poznanski (San Francisco: Westview Press, 1992), 144.

[8] Dietrich Rueschemeyer, Eveline Huber Stephens, and John D. Stephens, *Capitalist Development and Democracy* (Chicago: University of Chicago Press, 1992), 6. The authors write that civil society provides a "counterweight to state power."

[9] Charles Taylor, "Modes of Civil Society," *Public Culture* 3, no. 1 (Fall 1990): 117.

[10] Michael Bernhard, "Civil Society and Democratic Transition in East Central Europe," *Political Science Quarterly* 108, no. 2 (1993): 314; and George Kolankiewicz, "The Reconstruction of Citizenship: Reverse Incorporation in Eastern Europe," in Poznanski, *Constructing Capitalism*, 142.

[11] Schmitter, "Some Propositions," 24.

[12] Joshua Cohen and Joel Rogers, "Secondary Associations and Democratic Governance," *Politics and Society* Special Issue 20, no. 4 (1992), 394.

[13] Rueschemeyer et al., *Capitalist Development and Democracy*, 10–11.

[14] Robert Putnam, *Making Democracy Work* (Princeton: Princeton University Press, 1993), 182.

[15] Taylor, "Modes of Civil Society," 115. This is a perspective Taylor shares with Montesquieu. It is part of what he calls the M-stream vision of civil society.

[16] Shils, "The Virtue of Civil Society," 13.

[17] Michael Walzer, "The Idea of Civil Society," *Dissent* 38, no. 2 (1991): 300–301.

[18] Gabriel Almond and Sidney Verba, *The Civic Culture* (Boston: Little, Brown, 1963), 245.

[19] Putnam, *Making Democracy Work*, 90. See also John A. Booth and Patricia Bayer Richard, "Civil Society and Political Context in Central America," in *Beyond Tocqueville: Civil*

mutual distrust,"[20] and "broadens the participants' sense of self, developing the 'I' into the 'We.' "[21] Democratically organized associations may "influence political behavior [even] more than underlying personal values, no matter how authoritarian."[22]

Having accorded civil society a role that is both positive and powerful, it makes sense that scholars would use their assessments of particular civil societies as bases for political projections. Civil society is now an "independent variable" of great importance. We read that the "weak civic traditions" of the formerly Communist regimes make their successful democratization highly problematic,[23] that the "flatness" of civil society in the Eastern European states creates grave problems for their elected politicians,[24] and that its "undeveloped, semi-atomized" nature provides a seedbed for dangerous populism.[25] Believing, along with Victor Perez-Diaz, that successful democratizations are possible *"only* if, and only to the extent that, a civil society or something like it, either predates the transition or becomes established in the course of it,"[26] scholars and policy makers now define the creation of civic associations in new democracies as an "urgent need."[27]

Our arguments about the dangers of civil society's weakness have their counterparts in arguments about the merits of "density." If sparse associational life is problematic for democracy, it makes sense to argue that dense organizational landscapes are beneficial. The argument for the merits of density takes many forms. We read that "a dense social

---

Society and the Social Capital Debate in Comparative Perspective, ed. Bob Edwards, Michael Foley, and Mario Diani (Hanover, N.H.: University Press of New England, 2001), 43.

[20] Putnam, *Making Democracy Work*, 89 and 138. Lipset makes a similar argument in "Social Requisites of Democracy Revisited," 31.

[21] Robert Putnam, "Bowling Alone: America's Declining Social Capital," *Journal of Democracy* 6, no. 1 (January 1995): 67.

[22] Seymour Martin Lipset, *Political Man* (Garden City, N.Y.: Anchor Books, 1960), 91.

[23] Putnam, *Making Democracy Work*, 183.

[24] Juan Linz and Alfred Stepan, "Political Identities and Electoral Sequences: Spain, the Soviet Union, and Yugoslavia," *Daedalus* 121, no. 2 (1992): 132.

[25] Jean Cohen and Andrew Arato, *Civil Society and Political Theory* (Cambridge: MIT Press, 1992), 69.

[26] Victor Perez-Diaz, *The Return of Civil Society* (Cambridge: Harvard University Press, 1993), 40.

[27] Hannan Rose, "From Command to Free Polities," *Political Quarterly* 64, no. 2 (April/June 1993): 165. For other statements on the urgency of reshaping civil society in former communist regimes, see Michael Bernhard, "Civil Society and Democratic Transition," 326; and Laurence Whitehead, "'Reform of State' and 'Regulation of the Market,'" *World Development* 21, no. 8 (1993): 14. Thomas Carothers critiques programs for funding civil society abroad in *Assisting Democracy Abroad: The Learning Curve* (Washington D.C.: Carnegie Endowment for International Peace, 1999).

infrastructure of secondary associations" is a requisite for improving "wages, skills, productivity and competitiveness,"[28] that "a dense network of secondary associations both embodies and contributes to effective social collaboration,"[29] that "the density of [civil society's] networks prevents radical polarization," and that the "growing organizational density of civil society" constitutes both "an underpinning for the political organization of subordinate classes" and an essential "counterweight to the overwhelming power of the state."[30] A dense civil society seems to have many merits. Indeed, it is hard to think of another political configuration that brings so much to so many. But, as is always the case in politics, the drama is more complicated as we move in closer and examine individual actors in greater depth.

Civil Society as Spoiler

The positive image I have sketched above is vivid in our contemporary literature and a composite of the work of some of the most (deservedly) influential scholars in the field of politics. Yet only a short while ago our literature portrayed civil society in a very different light. In the literature of the 1970s civil society is more often cast in an ambiguous role. The terms used to discuss civil society are different—scholars write of "interest groups," "class associations," and "popular organizations" instead—but the message in this older literature is very clear: an overly active society can harm democracy.

Rather than being portrayed as the possible savior of democracy, civil society is often cast in the role of spoiler: it is portrayed as sometimes asking too much—as spoiling the chances for democracy's survival. Almond and Verba's path-breaking study of the "civic culture" helped to lay the foundation for this ambivalent vision. The civic culture—the political culture particularly appropriate for democracy—is a "blend of activity and passivity."[31] It is one in which "there is political activity, but not so much as to destroy governmental authority; there is involvement and commitment, but they are moderated; there is political cleavage, but it is held in check."[32] The "intensity of the individu-

---

[28] Cohen and Rogers, "Secondary Associations and Democratic Governance," 395, synthesizing the work of others.

[29] Putnam, *Making Democracy Work*, 90.

[30] Walzer, "The Idea of Civil Society," 300; Rueschemeyer et al., *Capitalist Development and Democracy*, 77. See also p. 50.

[31] Almond and Verba, *The Civic Culture*, 369.

[32] Ibid., 360.

al's political involvement and activity" must be moderated for democracy to thrive.[33]

Throughout the sixties and seventies, the collapse of democracies *was* preceded by intense "political involvement and activity" on the part of organized students, peasants, and workers—so the carriers of this more ambivalent vision had little trouble making their case. In 1968, Samuel Huntington captured the ambiguities of popular participation in his theory of mass praetorianism. He drew a distinction between "institutionalized societies," in which the expansion of civil society *"reduces* tensions,"[34] and "praetorian societies," in which "the participation of new groups *exacerbates"* tensions.[35] In praetorian societies, people participate in politics more than ever before, but they have failed to cultivate the *"art* of associating together." The problem is not confined to the subordinate classes. In fact, "societies which have high levels of middle-class political participation have strong tendencies toward instability" as well.[36]

A broad range of scholars made the connection between a highly activist society and democratic instability. Even in works that focus on political elites, we read that elite links to the various elements of civil society are a major explanation for the shortcomings of elite behavior. Linz writes that alliances between political leaders and "the Church, the Vatican, Masonry, big business, or high finance" create suspicions and exacerbate crises.[37] He writes that "those identified with specific social interests," such as "the working class," "the trade unions," or "the Church," "are least able to give foremost consideration to the persistence of institutions," and their "unwavering commitment" to democracy *per se* "becomes extremely unlikely."[38] Linz never writes that the elements of civil society should not be allowed to organize, but he does imply that they should be kept at a distance from actual rulers—especially in times of crisis. Organization is fine, but direct connections with those in power is problematic.

Though he writes from a very different perspective, Guillermo O'Donnell in his seminal work on the origins of bureaucratic authoritarianism also casts civil society in an ambiguous role. Like nearly all of his colleagues at the time, O'Donnell does not use the term civil

---

[33] Ibid., 339.

[34] Samuel P. Huntington, *Political Order in Changing Societies* (New Haven: Yale University Press, 1968), 197–98.

[35] Ibid., 5.

[36] Ibid., 87.

[37] Juan J. Linz, *Crisis, Breakdown, and Reequilibration* (Baltimore: John Hopkins University Press, 1978), 68–69.

[38] Ibid., 53.

society itself, but he explicitly adopts the theory of mass praetorianism[39] and argues that "the pre-coup Argentine and Brazilian governments were *victimized* by" praetorian coalitions.[40] His explanation for the breakdown of democratic regimes is materialist, but it is the ensemble of organizations within civil society at a stage of "high modernization" that ultimately explains why bureaucratic authoritarian regimes emerge. When a certain stage of development allows even the base of society to get organized, the trouble begins. O'Donnell writes that when "the consumption and power participation preferences of the popular sector are high and are articulated with continuity and important *organizational* support," elected politicians in dependent economies face "a barely manageable schedule of political demands."[41] In their attempt to respond to the "very real" threats from the mobilized citizenry, "governments tended to adopt whatever policies best satisfied the sector that was most threatening at a given time, but the zero-sum conditions meant that each such policy decision raised new threats from other powerful sectors."[42]

The connection between the empowerment of organized sectors of society and ineffective policy-making is made quite explicitly by other scholars. Huntington explains that an "excess of democracy" and "increased popular participation" may erode a government's capacity "to deal with issues requiring subtle understanding and delicate handling."[43] Albert Hirshman provides a related cautionary message in his work on "voice"—his more elegant term for interest articulation. "Voice," he writes, "can be overdone: the discontent . . . could become so harassing that their protests would at some point hinder rather than help." In a passage which explicitly draws on the work of Almond and Verba he concludes, "[A] mixture of alert *and* inert citizens, or even an alternation of involvement and withdrawal, may actually serve democracy better than total, permanent activism or total apathy."[44] Likewise Linz argues that the problems of governance are made "particularly difficult" by the fact that democratic leaders depend on "party organization . . . middle-level cadres" and "leaders of special interest groups." The "increasing infiltration of interest groups at the grass-

---

[39] Guillermo A. O'Donnell, *Modernization and Bureaucratic-Authoritarianism* (Berkeley: Institute of International Studies, University of California, 1979), 143–44.

[40] Ibid., 74. He also states that they collaborated in praetorianism.

[41] Ibid. Emphasis added.

[42] Ibid., 143–44.

[43] Huntington, *Political Order*, 430–31.

[44] Albert Hirshman, *Exit, Voice, and Loyalty* (Cambridge: Harvard University Press, 1970), 31–32. There is a longer elaboration of the argument that "elites must be allowed to make decisions" on p. 32. The emphasis here is mine.

roots level by emerging leaders identified with . . . disloyal oppositions tends to further limit the political leadership's freedom of action in terms of system interests."[45] Linz's concept of "disloyal opposition" reminds us that some of the associations embodied in civil society may be openly opposed to democracy itself.

The portrait of civil society in these works from the 1960s and the 1970s is very different from the portrait we see most frequently today. Rather than associating civil society with the stabilization of democracy, or with good and efficient government, these earlier works emphasize an association with *ineffective* policy-making and *instability* instead.

This more ambivalent vision of civil society has backward and forward linkages. Tocqueville was quick to point out that unrestrained liberty of associations could be a source of advantage for some nations and a "cause of destruction" for others.[46] In more recent work, one can detect a certain caution about civil society on the Left. Rueschemeyer, Stephens, and Stephens, taking their cue from Gramsci, point out that the organizations of civil society may serve as conduits for the ideologies of the dominant classes;[47] Walzer reminds us that civil society "generates radically unequal power relationships," if left to itself;[48] and Cohen and Arato, quoting Juan Corradi, caution that the mobilization of civil society can have demobilizing consequences: "Fear of the regime can easily be replaced by society's fear of itself."[49]

Even if these undesirable scenarios are avoided, Philippe Schmitter points out that civil society "is not an unmitigated blessing for democracy" anyway. The policies that emerge from a robust civil society may be "biased, wrongheaded and too long in the making."[50] Sheri Berman argues persuasively that the "vigor of associational life" may serve to "undermine and delegitimize" the formal political structures on which democracy rests.[51] As Keith Whittington puts it, "Civil society may be as much a threat to democratic institutions as a support."[52]

[45] Linz, *Crisis, Breakdown, and Reequilibration*, 53.

[46] Tocqueville, *Democracy in America*, 256. He also argued that "the unrestrained liberty of association for political purposes is the privilege which a people is longest in learning to exercise" (pp. 202–3).

[47] Rueschemeyer et al., *Capitalist Development and Democracy*, 274.

[48] Walzer, "The Idea of Civil Society," 302.

[49] Cohen and Arrato, *Civil Society and Political Theory*, 617.

[50] Schmitter, "Some Propositions about Civil Society," 24–25; Cohen and Rogers, "Secondary Associations and Democratic Governance," 401–2.

[51] Sheri Berman, "Civil Society and the Collapse of the Weimar Republic," *World Politics* 49, no. 3 (April 1997): 414.

[52] Keith Whittington, "Revisiting Tocqueville's America: Society, Politics and Association in the Nineteenth Century," in Edwards et al., *Beyond Tocqueville*, 22. Edwards et al.

Cautions about civil society are thus still with us, even in some of the literature that celebrates the connection between democracy and dense associational life. Yet the existence of two distinct visions of civil society raises important questions with profound political implications. When does civil society present us with its most desirable visage? When does its opposite face appear? Translated into vernacular language, these abstract questions bring us back to the subject of ordinary citizens. When do ordinary people swell the ranks of anti-democratic groups and when do they support democratic groups instead? The vast literature on political authoritarianism gives us a number of leads on how these questions might be answered, and it is to this literature that we turn in our next section.

Suspect Citizens and Parties as Constraints

Much of the literature on authoritarianism casts the ordinary citizen in an ignoble role. Ordinary people are often depicted as somehow ill-suited for the freedoms and power that democracy affords. The sympathies of the authors who make these arguments vary, but their negative assessments are unmistakable. Their assessments are also unmistakably linked to the more negative visions of civil society summarized above, for if civic associations can work against democracy, it is logical that the individual actors who compose them be blamed.

Blame emerges from a variety of quarters and falls on a broad range of ordinary actors. Profound suspicions about the political wisdom of ordinary people date from at least the fifth century BC. Aristotle was deeply suspicious of the wisdom of the poor and thought that "superior individuals deserved superior political powers."[53] He and other Greek philosophers were often quoted by conservatives seeking to restrict the franchise, but suspicions were voiced outside of conservative circles as well. J. S. Mill lamented "the ignorance and especially the selfishness and brutality of the mass."[54] Proudhon argued that suffrage

---

conclude their collection with a reminder that associations "may limit members' connections with the wider community; they may include some and exclude others; they may serve selfish and/or antisocial as well as civic ends and they may battle one another furiously over the nature of the 'public good' " (p. 272).

[53] Aristotle, *The Politics* (Baltimore: Penguin, 1962), 121–22, 238–40. "If the majority, having laid their hands on everything, distribute the possessions of the few, they are obviously destroying the state" (pp. 121–22). Aristotle's distrust, however, was not limited to the less wealthy; he feared the power of tyrants and the rich for the same reasons. See Joshua Ober, *Mass and Elite in Democratic Athens* (Princeton: Princeton University Press, 1989), 295.

[54] Schmitter, "Some Propositions about Civil Society," 24–25; Cohen and Rogers, "Secondary Associations and Democratic Governance," 401–2.

for the uneducated was "the stumbling bloc of liberty" and not "an instrument of progress" at all. Beatrice Webb wrote (as late as 1884) that she could not comprehend the argument for universal suffrage or the related "democratic theory that . . . you produce wisdom" by "multiplying ignorant opinions indefinitely."[55]

In these and many other early arguments, ordinary people were suspect citizens because they lacked basic education. As education became more readily available, the poor judgment of the common man was attributed to ignorance of a more general sort, as well as isolation, frustration, and patterns of child rearing. The rise of Fascism produced strong incentives to understand what became known as the "authoritarian personality,"[56] but interest in the nexus between individual temperaments and political systems went far beyond students of psychology. Seymour Martin Lipset's award-winning study *Political Man* presents a highly influential perspective on the authoritarian potential of a whole range of classes. Coming to the "gradual realization that extremist and intolerant movements in modern society are more likely to be based on the lower classes" than on any other, Lipset was particularly concerned with "working class authoritarianism" and found its roots in "low education, low participation, . . . little reading, isolated occupations, economic insecurity and authoritarian family patterns."[57] He concluded that, "other things being equal," "the lower strata" "will be more attracted to an extremist movement than to a moderate and democratic one."[58]

Lipset's suspicions about ordinary people's political tendencies are not confined to the working class. He argues that "*each* major social stratum has both democratic and extremist expressions," and that for any stratum, extremist, authoritarian tendencies can be activated by "crisis" and "displacement."[59] In trying to discern which social group would destabilize the "conditions of the democratic order" in any particular case, Lipset concluded: "The real question to answer is which strata are most 'displaced' in each country? In some it is the new working class . . . in others, it is the small business-men and other relatively independent entrepreneurs. . . . In still others, it is the conservative and traditionalist elements."[60]

---

[55] Levin, *The Specter of Democracy*, 62–63. Webb later recanted her position.

[56] For early classics, see Theodor Adorno et al., *The Authoritarian Personality* (New York: Harper, 1950); and R. Christie and M. Jahoda, eds., *Studies in the Scope and Method of the Authoritarian Personality* (Glencoe, Ill.: Free Press, 1954).

[57] Lipset, *Political Man*, 87, 100–101.

[58] Ibid., 92.

[59] Ibid., 127, 116.

[60] Ibid., 136.

Lipset seems to have drawn his conclusions with reluctance. He takes care to emphasize both his personal commitment to democracy and his position as "a man of the left,"[61] but one senses that he does this precisely because he is the bearer of such bad news. According to his findings, ordinary people of many sorts are only conditionally committed to democracy. In times of crisis they cannot be trusted to resist the allure of authoritarianism unrestrained.

Though Lipset's conclusions did not go unchallenged,[62] they were mirrored in a broad range of studies that focused explicitly on the breakdown of democracy. Whether the theories found the roots of democratic failure in poor leadership, economic collapse, or flawed political structures, ordinary people were always a major medium through which cause became effect. Inadequate leaders rose to power with the votes of ordinary people. Economic problems went unsolved because popular ignorance and impatience constrained policy-makers. Political structures were deemed inadequate because they allowed popular passions too much latitude. Juan Linz synthesized the common wisdom in his seminal essay on the breakdown of democratic regimes, writing: The fall of the . . . system is usually the result of a shift in loyalty by citizens of weak commitment, by the apolitical, as a result of a crisis of legitimacy, efficacy or effectiveness. If these citizens had not shifted their allegiance, the previous rulers would have been able to resist the change."[63]

The scholars who drew these conclusions about "citizens of weak commitment" were generally not of weak commitment themselves.[64] On the contrary, the desire to maintain and consolidate electoral democracy despite the citizenry's alleged inadequacies led many scholars to focus on questions of institutional design. What sorts of political institutions could best constrain the popular tendencies that worked against democracy?

This question and others like it stimulated a wave of research and writing on political parties and party systems. Political parties became

---

[61] Ibid., xxi. For a more extended discussion of Lipset's commitment to democracy, see pp. xix–xxxvi.

[62] Alejandro Portes offers a compelling challenge in "Political Primitivism, Differential Socialization, and Lower-Class Leftist Radicalism," *American Sociological Review*, vol. 36, no. 5 (October 1971). See also S. Miller and Frank Riessman, "Working-Class Authoritarianism: A Critique of Lipset," *British Journal of Sociology* 12, no. 3 (September 1961).

[63] Linz, *Crisis, Breakdown, and Reequilibration*, 44.

[64] In a festschrift for Juan Linz, for example, Lipset writes that Linz "favored a classically liberal democratic Spain." Seymour Martin Lipset, "Juan Linz: Colleague—Student—Friend," in *Politics, Society, and Democracy: Comparative Studies*, ed. H. E. Chehabi and Alfred Stepan (Boulder: Westview Press, 1995), 3–4.

(and remain) one of the principal means of controlling the less desirable instincts of a suspect citizenry. Observing the association between weak parties and frail democracies in both interwar Europe and the Third World, a broad range of scholars forged a link between strong parties and viable democracies.

Samuel Huntington laid out a clear and influential argument for the remedial effects of political parties in 1968. As "parties develop strength," he wrote, they "become the buckle which binds one social force to another. . . . They create regularized procedures for leadership succession, . . . for the assimilation of new groups," and thus for "the basis of stability and orderly change."[65]

These are no mean achievements, and the reliance on parties as a primary means for counteracting the destabilizing forces in society is still very much with us. Lipset, who referred explicitly to the positive role of parties in *Political Man*, wrote much more recently that political parties are "the most important mediating institutions between the citizenry and the state," and that "having at least two parties with an *uncritically loyal* mass base comes close to being a necessary condition" for democratic stability.[66] Scott Mainwaring and Timothy Scully convey a similar message in their 1995 survey of party systems in Latin America: "The nature of parties and party systems shapes the prospects that stable democracy will emerge, whether it will be accorded legitimacy and whether effective policy-making will result." For these and many other authors, parties "shape" the prospects of political systems by shaping the messages that citizens get and send. Mainwaring and Scully state clearly, "Parties [make] it easier for citizens with little time and little political information to participate in politics." Parties "take positions on key issues rending society and, by so doing, put order into what would otherwise be a cacophony of dissonant conflicts. . . . The way [parties] shape the political agenda—*giving voice to certain interests and conflicts while simultaneously muting others*—enhances or diminishes prospects for effective government and stable democracy."[67] For all these authors, parties seem to exercise their positive role by being agents of constraint. Constraint is presumably needed because at least some citizens cannot be trusted either to recognize or to petition for the common good without guidance.

The literature on *party systems* suggests that parties themselves must be constrained and thus that ordinary people must be doubly harn-

[65] Huntington, *Political Order*, 405.

[66] Lipset, "Social Requisites of Democracy Revisited," 34–35.

[67] Scott Mainwaring and Timothy Scully, eds., *Building Democratic Institutions: Party Systems in Latin America* (Stanford: Stanford University Press, 1995), 2–3.

essed. Giovanni Sartori's model of polarized pluralism provides a highly influential argument to this effect. Drawn from the experience of democracies that failed, Sartori's message is that party systems (and party elites) must restrain the forces of polarity inherent in political democracies. If party systems fail to constrain both the ideological range and the number of parties in the national legislature, centrifugal forces will tear democracy apart.

The idea that societies contain "centrifugal forces" and that systemic breakdown is a result of unrestrained polarization is common throughout the literature, but Sartori's theory deserves special attention because of its wide acceptance and its detailed elaboration. Polarization, according to Sartori, is a "synthetic characteristic" of party systems, meaning it is the outcome of system characteristics. It exists when relevant anti-system parties sit "two poles apart" on the Left-Right spectrum, when mutually exclusive, bilateral oppositions flank the government, and when "centripetal" or "moderating drives" are discouraged by the existence of parties at the metrical center of the political spectrum. Under polarized pluralism, we see "the likely prevalence of centrifugal drives over centripetal ones, . . . the enfeeblement of the center [and] a persistent loss of votes to one of the extreme ends (or even to both.)"[68]

The connection between polarization and the breakdown of democracy is made most explicitly in an important article written by Sartori and Giacomo Sani. Sani and Sartori insist that "working democracy and polarization are inversely related," and "that the best single explanatory variable for stable versus unstable, functioning vs. non-functioning, successful versus immobile and easy versus difficult democracy is polarization."[69]

This vision of polarization is especially relevant to our puzzle about when ordinary people join the ranks of anti-democratic groups, because the flight to the poles of a political spectrum is often, if not always, seen as a challenge to democracy from the base.

How often is this story enacted? Does the polarization metaphor capture the drama of what actually transpires as democracies collapse? My answers are elaborated in the historical chapters that follow. Briefly put, they involve the following main points. Ordinary people often

[68] Giovanni Sartori, *Parties and Party Systems: A Framework for Analysis* (New York: Cambridge University Press, 1976), 132–34. Sartori's full definition of polarized pluralism involves three characteristics not mentioned above: ideological patterning, irresponsible oppositions, and the politics of outbidding (pp. 137–39).

[69] Giacomo Sani and Giovanni Sartori, "Polarization, Fragmentation and Competition in Western Democracies," in *Western European Party Systems*, ed. Hans Daalder and Peter Mair (Beverly Hills: Sage, 1983), 337.

play a peripheral role in the breakdown of democracy. In the cases where their role is more central, it is only partially captured by the polarization metaphor. We have often mistaken the polarization of select and relatively small groups in civil society for polarization in society as a whole. In the vast majority of the cases explored here, and in the majority of democracies that have broken down historically, voters did not polarize in the way predicted, nor did public opinion in general shift toward the anti-democratic poles of the Left-Right political spectrum. We must distinguish between the highly visible polarization of civic groups in public spaces and the less visible polarization of opinion expressed in elections and in polls. When we make these distinctions, we find that popular defection from democracy is not as common as some of the more tragic cases of democratic collapse have led us to believe. Our understanding of regime breakdown will improve with more careful analysis of who defects from democracy and how.[70]

---

[70] Ruth Collier has completed a compelling study of how important working-class mobilization has been in bringing about third-wave democracies. I look instead at the role of workers and others in bringing about dictatorship. See Ruth Berins Collier, *Paths toward Democracy: The Working Class and Elites in Western Europe and South America* (New York: Cambridge University Press, 1999).

2

ORDINARY PEOPLE AND THE BREAKDOWN
OF DEMOCRACY IN INTERWAR EUROPE

THE INTERWAR YEARS were a watershed for democracy and for democratic theory. Never before had so many citizens in so many nations been accorded so many formal rights. Yet, tragedy followed. In 1920, twenty-six out of twenty-eight European states were parliamentary democracies. By 1938, thirteen of these democracies had become dictatorships. This chapter is about why these regimes broke down and about the role that ordinary citizens played in the breakdown process.

As the preceding chapter made clear, suspicions about the political wisdom of ordinary people were voiced for centuries before World War I came to an end. However, there can be little doubt that the tragedy of interwar fascism intensified both cynicism and fear. Scholars who tried to explain mass support for anti-democratic movements often cast the ordinary citizen in an ignoble if not villainous role. The plotline that emerged from analyses of the interwar years would be repeated in other analyses of other breakdowns for years to come. Reduced to its basics, the story runs like this: citizens who are inexperienced in the use of democratic freedoms find themselves in new democracies during a time of economic scarcity. Democratically chosen leaders prove incapable of reducing the scarcity, but the untutored citizenry continues to overload the new regimes with excessive demands anyway. The gap between government performance and perceived scarcity continues to widen until, finally, the citizenry turns toward extremist parties and against democracy itself. Though the emphases of each storyteller vary substantially, the theme is usually the same: If citizens experience severe material scarcities in new democracies, they don't just get mad, they go mad. They abandon the political Center and actively support groups and movements that will destroy the democracy that gave them the freedom to make demands in the first place.

This tragic story has been documented with compelling evidence. Indeed, the story's basic logic seems so convincing that we have begun to hear it repeated in fearful forecasts about the voting public in parts of Eastern Europe and Latin America. Though there can be little doubt that economic dislocation did help to drive millions of ordinary people into the ranks of Fascist movements in the interwar years, both the context in which the story unfolded and the dynamics of the story itself need to be more clearly specified.

It is wrong to reduce the role of ordinary people in all the failed democracies to a story of collective madness induced by scarcity. The rise of Fascism and the fall of the interwar democracies are not synonymous processes. In fact, using the cases of Fascist victory as a base for generalizations about the breakdown of democracy can be highly misleading. If we look beyond the relatively well-known cases of Italy and Germany to the whole set of ill-fated interwar democracies, we formulate very different answers to our opening questions. We learn that popular support for unambiguously anti-democratic parties varied greatly within the democracies that collapsed, and that the citizenry played a much more peripheral role in the dismantling of democracy than the Fascist cases would lead us to believe. We also learn that economic performance failures are not consistently powerful predictors of either democracy's decline or the growth of anti-democratic support among ordinary people. The evidence for this argument is taken from the study of the regimes listed on table 2.1.

Popular Support for Anti-democratic Parties

Discussions of fascism in Italy and Germany bring to mind images of thousands of uniformed supporters parading past vast and cheering crowds. There can be little doubt that spectacular demonstrations of mass support, captured frequently on film, reflect an important aspect of the fascist reality. But a broad, comparative lens shows that only a small fraction of European adults were willing to pay the costs of formal membership in anti-democratic organizations of the Right.[1] Before democracies were toppled and freedom of association was curtailed, Fascist parties—parties that placed an enormous value on active mobilization—succeeded in mobilizing only a small fraction of the European citizenry.

Even the most popular movements on the continent were quite small in formal terms. In Austria, on the eve of the Dollfuss takeover, less than 4 percent of the adult population was associated with either the

---

[1] I define these as parties that publicly condone the violent defiance of elected governments. I confine most of my analysis here to right-wing, anti-democratic groups because, with the possible exception of Poland, all the democratic regimes studied here fell to the Right.

TABLE 2.1
The Survival of Parliamentary Regimes in Europe's Interwar Years

Survivors[a]	Casualties[b]	Basic Chronology for Casualties	
		First Post-War Election	Initiation of Authoritarian Regime
Belgium	Austria	Feb. 1919	Mar. 1933
Denmark	Bulgaria	Aug. 1919	June 1923
Czechoslovakia*	Estonia	Apr. 1919	Mar. 1934
Finland*	Germany	Jan. 1919	Jan. 1933
France	Greece	Nov. 1926	Aug. 1936
Iceland	Italy	Nov. 1919	Oct. 1922
Ireland*	Latvia	Apr. 1920	May 1934
Luxembourg	Lithuania	May 1920	Dec. 1926
Netherlands	Poland	Jan. 1919	May 1926
Norway	Portugal	Mar. 1919	May 1926
Sweden	Romania	Nov. 1919	Feb. 1938
Switzerland	Spain	June 1931	July 1936
United Kingdom	Yugoslavia	Nov. 1920	Jan. 1929

[a] Smaller survivors (e.g. Iceland, Luxembourg) are not discussed in the text.
[b] Hungary is left off the casualty list because it never succeeded in having fully free national elections. Turkey and the USSR are excluded because I am using a narrow definition of Europe.
* Surviving democracy founded after WWI.

Heimwehr or the Austrian Nazis.[2] In Germany on the eve of the Weimar Republic's last free election, Nazi membership rolls included slightly over 2 percent of German adults.[3] In Italy, party membership before the March on Rome (i.e., before the party had access to the spoils of office) reached only 332,000—less than 1 percent of the Italian population as a whole.[4] The comparable figure for Romania was under 2 percent. These were probably the largest movements in Europe.

[2] On Austria, see Gerhard Botz, "Changing Patterns of Social Support for Austrian National Socialism," in *Who Were the Fascists?* ed. Stein Ugelvik Larsen, Bernt Hagtvet, and Jan Petter Myklebust (New York: Columbia University Press, 1980).

[3] M. Rainer Lepsius, "From Fragmented Party Democracy to Government by Emergency Decree and Nationalist Takeover: Germany," in *Europe*, ed. J. Linz and A. Stepan (Baltimore: Johns Hopkins University Press, 1978), 70.

[4] Renzo De Felice, *Mussolini il Fascista*, vol. 1, *La Conquista del Potere, 1921–1925* (Turin: Einaudi, 1966), 8–11.

I use the word probably because of the ambiguities of the Spanish case and the difficulty of classifying the heterogeneous groups that eventually took up arms against the Republic in the Civil War. Since the Republican government was freely elected, we might argue that everyone who supported the Nationalist cause was fundamentally anti-democratic. This would amount to nearly 50 percent of the adult population. But comparing this figure to the figures for Fascist membership cited above would mean equating the choice of party in peacetime with the choice of sides in a civil war, and this is highly problematic. If we consider only the membership of the CEDA (the collection of parties that supported Franco and the rebellious officers) we get a smaller but still substantial percentage of the population, but this would mean ignoring the range of opinion within the CEDA, and overlooking the distinction between disloyal and semiloyal opposition.[5] What we can conclude with certainty is that Spain's official Fascist party—the Falange de las JONS—attracted very little support before the onset of the Civil War. Stanley Payne estimates that the party had fewer than ten-thousand adherents in 1936 and concludes that it was "the smallest and the weakest of the independent forces in Spanish politics."[6] Given the choice between joining an unambiguously anti-democratic party like the Falange and a semiloyal group like the CEDA, an overwhelming majority of Spaniards chose the latter. In Spain, as in the rest of Europe, ordinary people eschewed membership in explicitly Fascist groups.

Membership figures are hard to verify, but looking across all the European cases, there is no obvious relationship between the formal size of Fascist groups and the likelihood of democratic survival. Nations such as France and Belgium, where anti-democratic parties attracted a comparatively large percentage of the citizenry, weathered the interwar years with their democracies intact. Yet nations such as Portugal and Poland, with comparatively weaker Fascist groups, collapsed into dictatorship.

Given that most of the citizens who supported extremist movements were likely to avoid the costs of membership in the first place, votes are

---

[5] These terms were coined by Juan Linz, and I have used them as he does. A disloyal opposition is one that makes "blanket attacks on the political system rather than on particular parties or actors" and attacks on the government and system parties with "disruptive purposes." A semiloyal opposition may work with disloyal parties and manipulate the political system, but has no "intent to overthrow the system or change it radically." Linz acknowledges the ambiguity in both of these terms, reminding us that the "boundary between disloyalty and loyalty becomes confusing for many participants." Linz, *Crisis, Breakdown, and Reequilibration*, 29–32.

[6] Stanley Payne, *Falange* (Stanford: Stanford University Press, 1965), 81, 279.

a more accurate indicator of overall movement support. Yet, ordinary people were also reluctant to vote for Fascists in the vast majority of cases. By this measure, too, the anti-democratic Right was weaker than the poor record of democracy would lead us to expect.

In Italy, vote support for the anti-democratic Right was never close to majoritarian. The Fascist Party had 6 percent of the assembly seats at the time of the March on Rome. The total for all three of the right-wing parties that might have been considered anti-democratic was at most 12 percent.[7] In Austria, the maximum was just over 9 percent.[8] In Germany, a near majority of the electorate did vote for anti-democratic, right-wing parties on the eve of Hitler's rise to power, but we reach this conclusion only if we include votes for four anti-democratic parties of the Right.[9] Not even in the German case do we find a single authoritarian party voted into office with a majoritarian electoral mandate. Only a third of the German people actually voted for the Nazi Party in Weimar's last free election. *Fewer* Germans were voting Nazi in this last election than in the previous contest some months before.

In none of the other European states did Fascist or other anti-democratic right-wing parties (individually or combined) come close to winning the loyalty of a majority of the electorate. The Nazi Party was extraordinarily popular in the German case, but the conclusions we might reach from studying the collapse of Weimar cannot be extended to other regimes.

In a majority of regimes that broke down, only a small fraction of ordinary people used party membership or votes to petition for an anti-democratic regime change. This generalization holds for parties on the anti-democratic Left as well.

Did mass actors exert other sorts of direct pressure on these doomed democracies? Were ordinary citizens sending strong signals through other means? We need careful event-analysis to answer with much conviction, but the data we do have suggest that pressures from below were neither as direct nor as constant as one would expect. Admittedly, strike rates rose in almost all these states in the aftermath of World War I. With inspiration from the Bolshevik revolution and a rapid expansion of trade-union freedoms, the rise in the strike rate is unsurprising.

---

[7] I give seat figures here because the parties were in a coalition. No vote figures are available.

[8] The maximum reached was in the 1930 elections, when the National Socialists gained 3 percent and the Fatherland Block obtained 6.2 percent of the votes. Thomas T. Mackie and Richard Rose, *The International Almanac of Electoral History* (London: Macmillan, 1974), 31.

[9] These are the Nazis, the Hanoverian People's Party, the German National People's Party, and the Bavarian People's Party.

TABLE 2.2
Industrial Disputes and the Rise of Dictatorship

Country	Trends in Strikes Rates in Two Years prior to Regime Change	
	As Measured by Number of Strikes	As Measured by Number of Strikers
Austria	Decline	Decline
Bulgaria	—	—
Estonia	Rise	Decline
Germany	Rise	Decline after Rise
Greece	—	—
Italy	Sharp Decline after Rise	Sharp Decline after Rise
Latvia	—	—
Lithuania	—	—
Poland	Decline	Decline
Portugal	Sharp Decline after Rise	—
Romania	Decline after Rise	Decline
Spain	Decline[a]	—
Yugoslavia	Rise	Decline after Rise

Sources: Brian R. Mitchell, *European Historical Abstracts 1750–1988;* Tönu Parming, *The Collapse of Liberal Democracy and the Rise of Authoritarianism in Estonia* (London: Sage Publications, 1975); Kathleen Schwartzman, *The Social Origins of Democratic Collapse* (Lawrence: University Press of Kansas, 1989); Juan Linz, "From Great Hopes to Civil War: The Breakdown of Democracy in Spain," in Linz and Stepan, *Europe.*

[a] There was a sharp rise in 1936, before the outbreak of the civil war, but in the two years prior to regime change, strikes declined.

But, as table 2.2 illustrates, the number of individuals engaging in strike activity was generally *decreasing* in the years immediately prior to democratic collapse. The image of workers striking relentlessly until the moment of regime collapse is apparently mythical.

The Specifics of Regime Breakdown

When we look at the individual histories of each of the regimes that collapsed, it becomes clear that the citizenry often played a peripheral role in the breakdown of democratic government. With few exceptions, the interwar regimes broke down either because political elites deliberately chose to disassemble them, or because political elites unwittingly took actions that led to the regime's collapse. This argument is best sustained with a chronological review of the whole series of failed democracies. Chronological analysis is essential because political elites in different states paid careful attention to one another. What happened in a neighboring state was often analyzed as a model to be duplicated, a forecast of things to come—or a fate to be avoided. Elite actions can only be understood if seen in temporal and geographic context.

Beginning with the Bolsheviks

The interwar years would have been dramatically different if they had not begun with the Bolshevik revolution. The successful left-wing assault on Russia's first elected assembly proved inspirational for many and horrifying for many more. Was the Bolshevik victory to be duplicated throughout Europe?

The events in Hungary in 1919 suggested precisely this, for there a provisional government abandoned power to the Bolsheviks before free elections were even held.[10] A coalition of left-wing Social Democrats and Communists, assisted by thousands of armed soldiers making their way home from the Russian front, assumed control of the state after Michael Karolyi proved unable to defend Hungarian territory from Romanian, Czech, and Yugoslavian occupation.[11] The regime the Left established was replaced by a right-wing dictatorship in a matter of months, so this was ultimately a failed revolution, but there were many revolutionary attempts in other states. These attempts also failed completely—and relatively quickly—but they could always be constructed as proof of a constant threat and justification for preemptive actions of all sorts.

ITALY

The hopes and fears inspired by the Bolsheviks' success played an important role in the breakdown of Italian democracy in 1922.[12] The Italian citizenry was mobilized rapidly and comparatively densely into Red and anti-Red camps; there can be little doubt that the transition

---

[10] For more on the Kun regime and its aftermath, see Andrew Janos, *The Politics of Backwardness in Hungary* (Princeton: Princeton University Press, 1982); and C. A. Macartney, *Hungary: A Short History* (Chicago: Aldine, 1962).

[11] I am indebted to Michael Bernhard of Pennsylvania State University for clarification of how and why the Karolyi government fell.

[12] António Gramsci drew a parallel between Nitti and Kerensky and optimistically hoped the Italian case would mirror the Russian one. See Christopher Seton-Watson, *Italy from Liberalism to Fascism: 1870–1925* (London: Methuen, 1967), 560.

to dictatorship was greatly affected by the extra-parliamentary activity of both groups. The fact that the postwar democracy began, not just with massive labor mobilizations, but with the seizures of factories and farmland as well, helps to explain why the democratic regime disintegrated in less than three full years: Mussolini was spectacularly successful in using the specter of Red revolution as a means of mobilizing support for a counteroffensive.

Yet, despite the success of mass mobilization in Italy, it would be wrong to place the blame for the fall of Italian democracy with its ordinary citizens. As our previous discussion made clear, Mussolini had nothing close to a popular mandate. Mussolini gained power because the reigning political elite invited him to rule. The invitation process had two stages. In the first, Liberal prime minister Giovanni Giolitti made the grave mistake of giving the Fascists an air of legitimacy by inviting the party onto the electoral lists of the National Block.[13] In the second and fatal stage, King Victor Emmanuel asked Mussolini to form a government. As S. J. Woolf reminds us, the Fascist March on Rome was "unnecessary" because Mussolini was called to power "in a more or less constitutional manner" by the king himself.[14]

The king's action was not a response to the petitions of the mobilized masses, but rather a reflection of the serious inadequacies of Italy's most powerful state officials. A close reading of events forces us to recognize that many of Italy's politicians simply neglected their obligations when the battle lines were drawn. Giolitti, the Liberal leader who had given the Fascists an air of legitimacy in the first place, resigned from the government and simply stayed outside of Rome during the entire period of crisis, behaving "with an utter unconcern for the piazza or public opinion."[15] Facta, the Liberal leader who took his place, submitted the resignation of his cabinet on the night of the infamous March on Rome—and simply went home to bed! Marshal Diaz, the nation's commander in chief, refused to commit his officers to the defense of the regime when the king asked whether he could depend on the military to repel Mussolini's advance.[16] Yet, the whole March on

---

[13] The Block was a coalition of diverse parties united only in their opposition to socialism. It included the Liberals, Nationalists, Democrats, and Social Reformists. Fascists were made to seem more respectable by their appearance on what was essentially a mainstream party list. See Farneti, "Social Conflict, Parliamentary Fragmentation, Institutional Shift, and the Rise of Fascism: Italy," in Linz and Stepan, *Europe*, 23.

[14] S. J. Woolf, "Italy," in *European Fascism*, ed. S. J. Woolf (London: Weidenfeld and Nicolson, 1968), 39.

[15] Alexander De Grand, *The Hunchback's Tailor: Giovanni Giolitti and Liberal Italy from the Challenge of Mass Politics to the Rise of Fascism* (Westport, Conn.: Praeger, 2001), 251.

[16] For more details see Adrian Lyttelton, *The Seizure of Power: Fascism in Italy, 1919– 1929* (London: Weidenfeld and Nicolson, 1973). The coercive forces of the Italian state

Rome was "a bluff" that could have easily been prevented had the state's armed forces offered resistance.[17]

Throughout the interwar period, the deputies of the national assembly distinguished themselves by their absence during votes of confidence and key debates. A full 31 percent of all parliamentary deputies missed the vote of confidence in the last Facta government. The rate of absenteeism during the last years of Italy's democracy varied between 21 and 45 percent and increased steadily from February 1922 until the regime collapsed.[18]

BULGARIA

The breakdown of the democracy in Bulgaria followed on the heels of the breakdown in Italy, and there, too, political elites played the dominant role in the process. Free elections in 1919 had brought the peasant-based Agrarian National Union to power and its leader, Stamboliski, endeavored to promote the welfare of his constituency through a variety of progressive reforms. The redistribution of property was not a prominent item on Stamboliski's agenda because the nation's land-tenure system was fairly egalitarian even before the peasant party came to power.[19] Thus, there were no spontaneous property seizures, as there had been in Italy. But there were three threats of a different nature that triggered the assault on the elected government. The first threat was to King Boris of Bulgaria and his entourage, who were menaced by Stamboliski's unrestrained republicanism. The second threat was to a heterogeneous set of opposition-party politicians who found themselves shut out of power when the expansion of the franchise enabled a nation of peasants to elect a vibrant peasant party. The third and most important threat was to the military. This emerged when Stamboliski railed against military adventurism, argued that the funds that went to the military could be better used elsewhere, and signed a treaty cutting the armed forces from 850,000 to 20,000 men. The enraged Bulgarian military elite formed a Military League, which eventually engi-

---

were rarely if ever used against fascist groups. Many army officers and enlisted men sympathized with the squads, but even politicians such as Giolitti believed that the "fascist phenomenon could be dealt with only politically" and not through police or military force. De Grand, *The Hunchback's Tailor*, 239.

[17] The characterization is Adrian Lyttelton's. The point about the military is made there and in S. J. Woolf, "Italy."

[18] Farneti, "Social Conflict," 30–31.

[19] Hugh Seton-Watson, *Eastern Europe between the Wars*, 3d ed. (Hamden, Conn.: Archon Books, 1962), 243, writes that Bulgaria had a "healthier property structure in agriculture than any other state in Eastern Europe."

neered the breakdown through an armed coup. Royalist and opposition politicians joined the coup coalition.

The Bulgarian people themselves played a most peripheral role in the events leading to the breakdown of the regime. Indeed, the immediate catalyst for the coup was a highly intellectualized parliamentary debate about orthography. Stamboliski sought to simplify Bulgaria's alphabet and spelling in order to facilitate a massive literacy campaign. Members of the Bulgarian Academy of Sciences plus a range of conservative parties used the parliamentary debates on language policy to question Stamboliski's patriotism and to forge a dictatorial coalition from a diverse range of nationalist partners.[20] There was no popular mobilization around these language issues, nor around the other principal issues that divided regime elites.[21]

POLAND

The collapse of the Polish, Portuguese, and Lithuanian democracies in 1926 was also very much the result of the incapacities and infighting of political elites. All three of these democracies were assaulted by factions of their own military establishments.

Poland's democracy fell in May 1926 to military forces grouped around the charismatic character of Jozef Pilsudski. Pilsudski had become a national military hero during Poland's struggle for independence. He is thus one of the few coup-makers in the interwar period who had a broad popular following before seizing power. But Pilsudski was dramatically different from Mussolini and other movement entrepreneurs. He organized no political party and no civilian organization, he led no popular movement, and he even forbade "his followers to organize a conspiratorial network within the army."[22]

Poland was in domestic turmoil when Pilsudski assumed power. A turbulent Parliament had produced fourteen different cabinets in less than eight years, and a weak currency and high unemployment had caused demonstrations and even riots in the weeks before the coup. However, the 1926 coup was primarily "the result of conflict in the army" and of conflict "between the civilian government and Pilsudski

---

[20] See Marin Pundeff, *Bulgaria in American Perspective* (New York: Columbia University Press, 1994), 83.

[21] For an outstanding study of Bulgaria, see John D. Bell, *Peasants in Power* (Princeton: Princeton University Press, 1977).

[22] Joseph Rothschild, *Pilsudski's Coup d'Etat* (New York: Columbia University Press, 1966), 361.

himself."[23] Pilsudski's principal concerns lay with policies related to the armed forces and to foreign affairs more generally. Though his seizure of power was certainly facilitated by public frustration with a fractious Parliament, citizen support for anti-parliamentary parties did not rise over time.[24] Poland's peasantry and working class were "unmoved" by the "revolutionary appeals of communism,"[25] and those who were attracted to the extremist Right probably felt represented by the reigning coalition anyway. Parties on the Left backed Pilsudski's coup after it was set in motion, and the Socialist union that controlled the railways tipped the military balance in Pilsudski's favor by refusing to transport troops loyal to the government at a key moment during the coup itself. But Pilsudski was not carried to power by an anti-democratic movement from below. Quite the contrary, his backers "still had confidence" in his "democratic inclinations"[26] and he seems to have not wanted to seize power through violent means. He organized what he intended to be an "armed demonstration" against "a government notoriously indifferent to the moral interests of the state and the army," expecting that he could force the president into simply dismissing a newly named cabinet. When the president refused and asked his army to use force to counter Pilsudksi's demonstration, fighting ensued. Pilsudski's forces won, and he was thrust into power. Pilsudksi was reportedly surprised and intensely embarrassed that the coup took place at all.[27] "Never greatly interested in the complexities of domestic politics," he was provoked into action by personal rivalries with government leaders and by what he saw as Poland's failure in foreign affairs.[28]

---

[23] Antony Polonsky, *Politics in Independent Poland: 1921–1939* (Oxford: Clarendon, 1972), 128.

[24] For an excellent discussion of the institutional reasons for Poland's domestic troubles and for the data illustrating that extremist parties were not amassing support, see Michael Bernhard, "Institutional Choice and the Failure of Democracy: The Case of Interwar Poland," *East European Politics and Societies* 13, no. 1 (Winter 1999): esp. 46 and 60.

[25] Norman Davies, *Heart of Europe: A Short History of Poland* (Oxford: Oxford University Press, 1984), 124.

[26] Rothschild cites a book written by a Socialist leader named Ignacy Daszynski. See Rothschild, *Pilsudski's Coup d'Etat*, 19. Rothschild is convinced that these assessments were legitimate and that Pilsudski's long-term goals for Poland were "ultimately those of a free, law abiding and pluralistic democracy" (p. 362). Those who believed in his democratic proclivities seem to have been at least partially right, for he held fairly competitive elections in 1928. See Jeffrey Kopstein and Jason Wittenberg, "Lessons from the First Wave for the Third Wave: The Social Bases of Radicalism in Interwar Eastern Europe" (unpublished paper, APSA, September 2001).

[27] Rothschild, *Pilsudski's Coup d'Etat*, 361.

[28] Polonsky, *Politics in Independent Poland*, 139.

LITHUANIA

The breakdown of democracy in neighboring Lithuania was also the result of a military coup. There, as in Poland, the regime change was initiated by military officers who feared how a new government would deal with the armed forces and with foreign policy more generally. In Lithuania, the catalyst for the coup was the May 1926 electoral victory of a moderately leftist coalition of Peasant Populists and Social Democrats. The Christian Democrats had dominated Lithuanian politics since the war's end, and conservatives in the military and in the society at large feared that the new government would immediately succumb to pressures from the neighboring Bolshevik government in Russia. The new government did little to allay these fears, for it fired key military officers, cut military spending, and signed a nonaggression pact with the Soviet Union.[29] Shortly after the pact was signed, a small group of military men and Nationalist politicians burst into a session of parliament and demanded control of the state. The elected government was so surprised that it offered no resistance.

The coup was not entirely a military affair, for it was supported from its very beginning by civilians associated with the Nationalist Party. But this was not a movement party, as Mussolini's had been. It had not run candidates in elections until the year of the coup itself and had then won only three of the nation's eighty legislative seats. It was a small, highly intellectualized group, headed by the dean of the social sciences (!) at the University of Kaunas.[30] Though the citizenry of Lithuania was not wholly silent on the eve of the coup, protest activities were generally small and focused. The left-leaning regime had allowed the Polish minority the right to establish some Polish-speaking schools, and this had stirred popular demonstrations against Polonization. The government had also allowed leftists of all sorts more freedom of assembly and speech. The Communist Party, which had been banned, made use of these new freedoms and became visible in public space again in marches and demonstrations.[31] This provoked Nationalist countermarches, but they seem to have been confined almost exclusively to small groups of university students, and not the mass of the

---

[29] Albertas Gerutis, *Lithuania: 700 Years* (New York: Maryland Books, 1969), 220.

[30] Georg von Rauch, *The Baltic States: The Years of Independence* (London: C. Hurst, 1974), 120.

[31] See Royal Institute of International Affairs, *The Baltic States* (London: Oxford University Press, 1938) for a good overview of the period; and Leonas Sabaliunas, *Lithuania in Crisis: Nationalism to Communism, 1939–1940* (Bloomington: Indiana University Press, 1972), 7. Smetona, the coup-maker who would rise to the presidency, describes the period as one in which "dark mobs" "insisted on a Bolshevik government." Sabaliunas, *Lithuania in Crisis*, 8.

citizenry.[32] With fewer than 22,000 industrial workers in the entire nation, the threat from a revolutionary proletariat on the Left was minimal.[33] As von Rauch aptly put it, "The army was the only power factor of any consequence."[34]

PORTUGAL

The breakdown of Portuguese democracy provides us with especially interesting material because Portugal is often categorized as one of the "most fascist" regimes of the interwar period.[35] This leads us to expect that the coup was the culmination of high levels of popular mobilization. Yet this breakdown, like so many others, was the result of a fairly small coup-coalition based on a factionalized military. The coalition was composed of military leaders, small conservative parties, social Catholics, and fringe groups of integralists and fascists.[36] The coup was announced on May 28 in the northern city of Braga by General Gomes da Costa (a hero from the First World War).[37] He marched south to Lisbon with almost no military opposition, and the elected government merely resigned. The whole process was so lacking in drama that the newspapers offered interviews with the general as he proceeded south. He emphasized that the movement was an "exclusively military one, neither conservative nor radical" and that the armed forces had taken action only because "the majority" of the civilian politicians had shown themselves to be a "discredit to the country."[38]

There can be little doubt that the coup was welcomed by sectors of Portuguese society. Large landowners had been suspicious of democracy from its beginning, and industrialists had long complained of the democracy's inability to maintain order.[39] The legitimacy of the regime had waned considerably with the urban middle classes that had

---

[32] Gerutis, *Lithuania*, 219.

[33] Rauch, *The Baltic States*, 127.

[34] Ibid., 120.

[35] Peter Merkl cites this common wisdom in a highly informative article in the Stein Larsen volume. Peter Merkl, "Comparing Fascist Movements," in Larsen et al., *Who Were the Fascists?*, 761.

[36] António Costa Pinto, *Salazar's Dictatorship and European Fascism* (New York: Columbia University Press, 1995), 141.

[37] H. V. Livermore, *A New History of Portugal* (Cambridge: Cambridge University Press, 1966), 330.

[38] A. H. de Oliveira Marques, *História de Portugal* (Lisbon: Palas Editores, 1981), 258–59.

[39] Kathleen Schwartzman, *The Social Origins of Democratic Collapse* (Lawrence, Kansas: University of Kansas Press, 1989), 37–39.

once been its base of support,[40] and even the working class seems to have been divided in its loyalties, as illustrated by the fact that the General Confederation of Labor took no public position on the coup for five days.[41]

This said, we should not conclude that the breakdown of Portuguese democracy was actually brought on by public pressures or social movements. António Costa Pinto reports that there were "no traces whatsoever" of rural mobilization "by the anti-republican reaction,"[42] and that "the only players" on the streets of urban Portugal in 1926 "were the military."[43] Politically, there was little to fear from radical workers parties—or from left-wing mobilization in general.[44] From 1925 on, right-wing attempts to organize militias were made "redundant" because "disorder prevailed" not on the "streets but within parliament and government."[45]

Fascism as a popular movement simply never took off. References to Fascism or to the milder dictatorship of Primo de Rivera in neighboring Spain remained confined to "the Geographical Society."[46] In Portugal, as in so many other places, ordinary people were reluctant to take direct action against a democratic regime.

YUGOSLAVIA

The state of Yugoslavia did not even exist when the Portuguese Republic fell. It was called the Kingdom of Serbs, Croats, and Slovenes. The fact that some form of parliamentary government endured there until 1929 is remarkable because some of the country's elected political elite showed little commitment to even the most rudimentary principles of democracy and civility. The regime's breakdown took the form of a coup led by King Alexander, who acted independently of any political party in an effort to impose order on a system racked by instability and violence. Cabinets changed an average of twice a year, the Croat Peasant Party (one of the largest in the nation) simply refused to participate in parliamentary sessions for months at a time, and political leaders stormed in and out of state buildings brandishing lethal weapons

---

[40] Marques, *História de Portugal*, 256.

[41] Schwartzman, *The Social Origins of Democratic Collapse*, 43. The confederation eventually came out in opposition and called a general strike.

[42] Costa Pinto, *Salazar's Dictatorship*, 146.

[43] Ibid., 135.

[44] Schwartzman, *The Social Origins of Democratic Collapse*, 183.

[45] Costa Pinto, *Salazar's Dictatorship*, 145.

[46] Ibid., 135.

of all sorts.[47] During the last months of the regime, a Serbian M.P. shot and killed five Croatian M.P.s on the floor of the parliament, yet escaped with only a light jail sentence.[48]

The king's intervention was generally "well received" at first. Even the liberal press ran the headline, "Only the Crown Can End the Crisis."[49] But here, as in so many cases, it is hard to determine the extent to which support for the intervention derived from frustration with disorder rather than democracy. We know that the supporters of terrorists "were few" in number and that these were overwhelmingly "university students and the bourgeoisie"—certainly not ordinary citizens in a nation of peasants.[50] We also know that the voting public supported democratically oriented groups when given the opportunity to do so. When a progressive and democratic bloc of parties formed an electoral coalition to challenge the corrupt and divided ruling elite in 1924, they won by three-hundred thousand votes.[51] This sort of evidence suggests that ordinary people were still betting on the future of democracy five years before its collapse. But when and whether they turned against democracy is difficult to determine.

The breakdown of democracy in the Kingdom of the Serbs, Croats, and Slovenes was the last of the six transitions that preceded the October 1929 stock market crash in New York. As we would expect, the economic depression that followed the crash contributed to the atmosphere in which anti-democratic parties of all sorts could build support. There should be no doubt that popular support for parliamentary government waned in all the regimes that broke down in the 1930s, but the effects that the Depression had on German politics were especially devastating.

GERMANY

The breakdown of democracy in interwar Germany was greatly affected by the activities of Germany's citizens. Ordinary Germans grouped themselves in antagonistic camps on opposite ends of a Left-

---

[47] The figure on the cabinet turnover and most of the facts presented here are from R. W. Seton-Watson and R.G.D. Laffan, "Yugoslavia between the Wars," in *A Short History of Yugoslavia*, ed. Stephen Clissold (Cambridge: Cambridge University Press, 1966), 174.

[48] Fred Singleton, *A Short History of the Yugoslav Peoples* (Cambridge: Cambridge University Press, 1985), 150.

[49] Seton-Watson and Laffan, "Yugoslavia between the Wars," 174–77.

[50] Ibid., 179.

[51] This was a coalition of Democratic Agrarians, Slovenes, and Moslems in the July 1924 election. Seton-Watson and Laffan, "Yugoslavia between the Wars," 172.

Right spectrum and did battle in a myriad of public spaces and at the polls as well. Polarization in Germany's Weimar Republic grew to such a height that its shadow darkened our visions of ordinary citizens everywhere. The popularity and eventual triumph of Germany's Nazi Party testified to the potential for anti-democratic movements elsewhere.

The political divisions in Weimar were especially visible because they involved such high levels of public violence. A "simmering threat of civil war" marred the regime from its very founding.[52] On 4 November 1918, leftists forcibly seized local governments and established workers' and soldiers' councils in Hamburg, Bremen, Hanover, Leipzig, Cologne, Dresden, and elsewhere. Within days, Munich was declared a Socialist republic, and by the first week of January 1919, a left-wing revolt had broken out in Berlin. The Right launched its first attack on the Weimar Republic with the Kapp Putsch in March 1919, and Hitler himself launched his first attack with the 1923 Beer Hall Putsch in Bavaria.[53] Each of these insurrections was reversed, but never without counterviolence and never by government forces acting alone. Privately organized citizen militias were always enlisted as allies of weakened state forces, and this set dangerous precedents, legitimating the private use of physical coercion and undermining state authority.[54]

Any new democracy would have been challenged by the boisterous street marches and loud public assemblies that became commonplace for burghers and workers alike,[55] but the violence that became endemic in taverns and gathering spaces of all sorts eventually became the regime's undoing.[56] A "private" Red Army of an estimated fifty-thousand men[57] and the white terror inflicted by right-wing militias of even greater size were facts of political life that ordinary Germans could not ignore.

The longing for order seems to have contributed mightily to defections from the bourgeois parties that occupied key spaces at the center of Germany's political spectrum. Middle-class voters defected from

[52] Eve Rosenhaft, *Beating the Fascists?: The German Communists and Political Violence, 1929–1933* (New York: Cambridge University Press, 1983), 1.

[53] Gordon Craig, *Europe since 1815* (New York: Holt, Rinehart and Winston 1971), 556–69.

[54] Juan Linz, "Political Space and Fascism as a Late-Comer," in Larsen et al., *Who Were the Fascists?*, 166.

[55] Peter Fritzsche, "Weimar Populism and National Socialism in Local Perspective," in *Elections, Mass Politics, and Social Change in Modern Germany: New Perspectives*, ed. Larry Eugene Jones and James Retallack (New York: Cambridge University Press, 1992), 302.

[56] Rosenhaft, *Beating the Fascists*, 1.

[57] Craig, *Europe since 1815*, 564.

traditional liberal elites in a reaction to a shared "hatred and fear of protests in the streets" and in response to the perception that the centrist parties could not restore order.[58]

The economic insecurity heightened by the onset of the Great Depression in 1929 also drove middle classes away from the political Center and toward the Nazis. People who had hitherto disdained the Nazis in favor of traditional conservative groups were driven to extremes by the specter of downward mobility.[59] Lepsius estimates that around 10 percent of the German population, "which otherwise would have stayed within the realm of moderate traditional or splintered party system," turned to the Nazis instead.[60]

Just as the defections from middle-class parties on the Center-Right benefited the Nazis, defections from the Center-Left SPD worked to the benefit of the Communists. Worker defections helped bring the vote for the KPD from 10.6 percent in 1928 to 14.6 percent in July of 1932.[61] The percentage of the vote garnered by the Nazis in the same period jumped from 18.3 percent to 37.3 percent. These figures alone suggest a polarization at the polls that mirrored the public polarization in taverns, streets, and meeting halls.

Yet, even in the German case we must not conclude that democracy died solely at the hands of ordinary people. Though the growth of extremism was, without question, the result of ordinary citizens' choices, the actual triumph of extremism was the fruit of profound and multiple errors on the part of Germany's political elite. A closer look at the dynamics of the Nazi movement and the chronology of elite decision-making shows that defections from the center of the political spectrum accounted for only a part of the German tragedy.

As A. J. Nicholls put it, the "*real* German problem lay in the political structure of Weimar and the decisions of its political leadership."[62] The flaws in Weimar's political structures are now well known. Proportional representation with no minimum threshold encouraged an overly fragmented party system.[63] A presidency with too much un-

[58] Detlev Peukert, *The Weimar Republic: The Crisis of Classical Modernity* (New York: Hill and Wang, 1989), 231.

[59] Roger Chickering, "Political Mobilization and Associational Life: Some Thoughts on the National Socialist German Workers' Club," in Jones and Retallack, *Elections, Mass Politics, and Social Change*, 327; and Peukert, *The Weimar Republic*, 238.

[60] Lepsius, "From Fragmented Party Democracy," 61.

[61] David Abraham, *The Collapse of the Weimar Republic: Political Economy and Crisis*, (Princeton, Princeton University Press, 1981), 266.

[62] A. J. Nicholls, *Weimar and the Rise of Hitler* (New York: St. Martin's Press, 1991), 158.

[63] It took only 6,000 votes in an electorate of 35 million to obtain a seat in Parliament. In the fateful election of 1930, a full nineteen parties polling fewer than 100,000 votes occupied seats in Parliament. For a detailed and sobering analysis of what unrestricted

checked power encouraged personalism and a weak parliament. The constitution allowed the president to name a government without the active participation of parliament, to issue decrees in states of emergency with only the chancellor's support, and to dissolve Parliament altogether without its consent.[64] This last power led to an excessive number of national elections. Six national ballots were held between May 1928 and November 1932 alone.[65]

The elite that occupied Germany's political institutions on the eve of the Great Depression was deeply flawed in judgment. Parliamentary representatives "virtually abdicated responsibility for the nation's affairs"[66] and dramatically decreased both their time in the legislature and the amount of legislation they produced. Parliament met for ninety-four days in 1930 and passed ninety-eight laws. In 1932, they met for only thirteen days and passed only five pieces of legislation.[67] As power slipped from Parliament to the executive, rule by decree became commonplace and the personalities of the president and the chancellor became decisive. The Social Democratic leader Friederich Ebert had been elected president in 1919 and had led the country through the political chaos and hyperinflation of the period immediately following the First World War. Ebert's commitment to parliamentary democracy was unambiguous and unwavering, but after his death in 1925, he was succeeded by Field Marshal Paul von Hindenburg, a man with dramatically different beliefs.

Hindenburg was the personal embodiment of the three social groups who were most fearful of the Republic. As an aristocrat, he was on the losing side of the Republican struggle and in constant contact with monarchists. As a landowner, he was linked to the most traditional sector of the propertied classes—a group with a longstanding fear of the Left, even the Center-Left of the Social Democrats. As a general, he was closely linked to the German officer corps, where parliamentary

---

proportional representation meant for Weimar's parliament, see Ferdinand Hermens, *Democracy or Anarchy?* (South Bend, Ind.: University of Notre Dame Press, 1941).

[64] M. Rainer Lepsius has a good summary of these powers and their implications. He notes that governments could be named by the executive alone as long as the Parliament did not organize a vote of no-confidence and that decree powers would be maintained unless Parliament actively went through a complicated procedure to revoke them. "Taken together, the presidential prerogatives allowed for government without active participation of the Parliament." "From Fragmented Party Democracy," 47.

[65] These included the two rounds of the presidential election in the spring of 1932.

[66] A. J. Nicholls, *Weimar and the Rise of Hitler*, 143.

[67] The corresponding figures for 1931 were forty-one days and thirty-four laws, suggesting that the drop in activity was independent of the fact that there were two parliamentary elections in 1932. Lepsius, "From Fragmented Party Democracy," 49.

government and the interests of the military as an institution were widely thought to be incompatible. The personal associations that derived from Hindenburg's social roots were to prove highly consequential as parliament weakened and "personal access to Hindenburg . . . defined political events." Relying on "a very small and publicly irresponsible group of people,"[68] Hindenburg made several egregious errors that eventually led to Hitler's triumph.

His gravest mistakes lay in his choices for the chancellorship. None of the three men he chose to govern the country in the last two years of the Republic had a commitment to parliamentary or even Republican rule. His first appointee, Heinrich Bruning, was an open proponent of presidential rather than parliamentary government and even sought the restoration of the Hohenzollern monarchy. Hindenburg appointed Bruning and his cabinet "on the explicit understanding" that they "would govern without parliament and would combat social democracy."[69] The man Hindenburg chose as Bruning's successor was Franz von Papen, an aristocrat whose antipathy to democracy was even deeper than Bruning's. Papen was an open advocate of a form of corporatism modeled loosely on Mussolini's new state.[70] He was in many ways an even worse choice than Bruning, for he lacked both "political experience and parliamentary support,"[71] was notoriously wanting in intellect,[72] and had come to the attention of the president mostly through an association with the latter's son.[73] Yet, Hindenburg named him chancellor on 1 June 1932 and vice-chancellor on 30 January 1933.

General Kurt von Schleicher was Hindenburg's third chancellor. His association with party government and Parliament was even more distant than those of his two predecessors. Bruning and Papen had served in Parliament, but Schleicher had spent his career entirely in the military and the defense ministry.[74] Passionately concerned that parliamen-

---

[68] Ibid., 49

[69] Peukert, *The Weimar Republic*, 258.

[70] Nicholls, *Weimar and the Rise of Hitler*, 134.

[71] Ibid., 133.

[72] Prompted by widespread rumors about Papen's dull-wittedness, an associate asked General von Schleicher, one of Papen's champions, whether the new chancellor had "much of a brain." Though the general had convinced Hindenburg to appoint Papen, the general replied, "He doesn't need one. He is a hat," meaning that he would just be a front for the men who were really running Germany. Gordon Craig, *Germany, 1866–1945* (New York: Oxford University Press, 1978), 561.

[73] Martin Kitchen, *The Cambridge Illustrated History of Germany* (New York: Cambridge University Press, 1996), 249. Papen was soon so reviled by the Centrist Party that he had to resign before he was expelled.

[74] Kitchen, *Cambridge Illustrated History*, 244.

tary government was hampering the modernization and expansion of Germany's armed forces, Schleicher sought strong presidential rule and a constitution that would favor "greater authoritarianism and militarism."[75] Hindenburg knew his views well, for he was one of the president's three closest advisors.

There can be no doubt that Hindenburg's choices for the chancellorship had negative consequences for the future of German democracy, but his responsibility did not end with these choices alone. On several, decisive occasions, Hindenburg refused to support policies that would have held the Nazis in check. When Bruning asked that the SA and SS be banned nationwide, Hindenburg forced him to resign.[76] When Schleicher asked for a ban on both the Nazi and the Communist Parties, Hindenburg refused again and began secret talks with Papen to plan a new government.[77] The argument in favor of bannings was strong, because they had worked well in the past; where governments instituted and enforced bans on Nazi activity, recruitment fared relatively badly.[78] Hindenburg was steadfast in his refusal to exert direct controls on the Nazi Party, despite the fact that he and his coterie had contempt for Hitler.

On other occasions, Hindenburg went beyond refusing to suppress the Nazis and endorsed policies that actively helped them. He backed Bruning's request for a dissolution of Parliament in 1930, despite warnings that calling elections during an economic crisis would only benefit extremists. He then remained "almost completely passive during the campaign," while Hitler's vote support jumped from 2.6 to 18.3 percent.[79] Hindenburg also allowed Papen to overturn a local ban on the SS in the state of Prussia. He was warned that this would provide a "license for murder," and in fact hundreds of people were killed by Nazi thugs as soon as the ban was lifted.[80] Yet, Hindenburg compounded his error by allowing Papen to expel Prussia's freely elected Social Democratic and Centrist rulers by decree in July of 1932 on the pretext that they seemed unable to maintain order.

[75] Peukert, *The Weimar Republic*, 227.

[76] Craig, *Germany, 1866–1945*, 559. Bruning did this at the insistence of state governments who were under constant assault from paramilitaries.

[77] Ibid., 567.

[78] William Brustein, *The Logic of Evil: The Social Origins of the Nazi Party* (New Haven, Yale University Press, 1996), 168.

[79] Craig, *Germany, 1866–1945*, 541.

[80] Official records list 99 people murdered in political violence in only five weeks. Craig, *Germany, 1866–1945*, 561. Rosenhaft points out that "105 of the 155 victims of political violence in Prussia in 1932 fell in June and July alone." *Beating the Fascists*, 8.

The forcible ouster of the Prussian government was a direct attack on a last bastion of German democracy and a portent of two other choices that proved fatal to the future of the free republic. In January of 1933, Hindenburg allowed Hitler to be named chancellor of Germany in a foolish attempt to buy Nazi support in the legislature. He soon allowed the new chancellor to dissolve the Reichstag and call new elections for March of 1933. With these two acts, the slow death of German democracy came to a tragic end.

Ordinary Germans are only partially implicated in this tragedy. Those who voted for the Nazi and the Communist Parties are certainly implicated: Hitler would have been ignored by Hindenburg and his chancellors if he had not had strong vote support, and his vote support would not have been as strong if the Communists were not perceived to be a threat. The smaller subgroup of Nazis and Communists who engaged in violence are implicated in this tragedy too, and to a much greater extent: the specter of civil war fanned the military's fear of their own ill-preparedness and provided a ready rationale for curbing freedoms and supporting authoritarianism. The democratic regime could never have collapsed if the armed forces had rallied to its defense.

This said, we must not conclude that the conservative, traditionalist clique that brought Hitler to power did so as representatives of the popular will—or of ordinary Germans. Quite the contrary, by decreasing the role of Parliament and political parties, Hindenburg and his clique lessened the role that ordinary Germans played in shaping government policy. If these leaders had been properly mindful of popular opinion, they would never have offered Hitler the chancellorship. In the last election before Hitler was named chancellor, the Nazis garnered only 33 percent of the vote. The Nazis "lacked sufficient electoral power to assume power on their own."[81] Indeed, the nation had shown, through its votes, that "it rejected dictatorship from the Left or the Right."[82] Even in 1932, democracy "still had not lost a chance for a majority."[83] The naming of Hitler to the chancellory had something to do with the wishes of ordinary Germans; but it had much more to do with the decisions of a small, reactionary elite who mistakenly saw the Nazis as both a positive counterweight to the Left and a force that they could co-opt.[84]

---

[81] Peukert, *The Weimar Republic*, 265.

[82] Nicholls, *Weimar and the Rise of Hitler*, 132.

[83] Lepsius, "From Fragmented Party Democracy," 38.

[84] A fear of even the center-left Social Democrats blinded the clique around Hindenburg. Schleicher confessed in a letter to Defense Minister Groener in March of 1932 that he was "really glad" that the Nazis were serving as a "counterweight" to the Left. He

AUSTRIA

The breakdown of democracy in Austria in March 1933 resembled the German case in that anti-democratic forces were widely popular and intensely active before the transition to dictatorship. Austria was, after all, the birthplace of Germanic National Socialism in the early part of the century.[85] When the Depression hit, its deep roots gave rise to several fascist movements. Historians report that the Fascists' call for "a new society found an enthusiastic echo among people at large . . . especially those whose position seemed hopeless."[86] There were plenty of hopeless citizens, for, by some measures, Austria's economic depression was the worst in Europe.[87] Thus, the Austrian case is not wildly out of line with the "madness" argument with which we began. But even here it is difficult to attribute responsibility for the collapse of Austrian democracy to the Austrian people themselves.

To begin with, the 1933 dictatorship was not established by the leader of a fascist party but by Engelbert Dollfuss, the leader of the Christian Social Party, which had governed the First Republic almost continuously since it was established. The Christian Socials were a diverse group with a large pro-democratic wing. They normally governed with a Pan German Party, but when the Pan Germans refused to form a coalition government in 1932, Dollfuss invited the Fascist Heimwehr to rule in coalition instead.[88] Here, as in all our other cases, Fascists were simply invited to share power. They did not come to power on the crest of a popular mandate. Non-Fascists simply handed them power in order to build an electoral coalition. The Heimwehr deputies "had next to no following among the voters." But this "mattered little" for "they held the balance of power in Parliament."[89] The Heimwehr also had control of a great many weapons. Many of its 150,000 members used their own arms, but the organization had at least 40,000 additional rifles, 15 howitzers and 170 machine guns.[90] Dollfüss sought to use these weapons and the paramilitary units behind them to battle the Socialists on his left *and* the Nazis on his right.

---

went on to say, "If the Nazis did not exist, we would have to invent them." Nicholls, *Weimar and the Rise of Hitler*, 133.

[85] Stanley Payne, *A History of Fascism* (Madison, Wisc.: University of Wisconsin Press, 1995), 246.

[86] Martin Kitchen, *The Coming of Austrian Fascism* (London: Croom Helm, 1980), 182.

[87] Craig, *Europe since 1815*, 597.

[88] Payne, *A History of Fascism*, 248.

[89] Walter Simon, "Democracy in the Shadow of Imposed Sovereignty," in Linz and Stepan, *Europe*, 112.

[90] Earl Edmondson, *The Heimwehr and Austrian Politics, 1918–1936* (Athens, Ga.: University of Georgia Press, 1978), 60.

The Austrian dictatorship thus became the first of several regimes that rationalized itself as a preemptive move against a more virulent form of right-wing authoritarianism.

The threat from the Austrian Nazi Party looked increasingly menacing in 1933. Local elections suggested that the Nazis had become Austria's third largest party. But close electoral analysis leads one to question whether the increase in Nazi support was the result of citizens turning to the extreme Right as a result of the Depression, or whether it was the result, instead, of the Nazis' ability to amalgamate the votes of nationalists and fascists whose support had been diffused among several different groups. Walter Simon's work has shown conclusively that most of the 1932 increase in Nazi votes in Vienna came from German Nationalists who had previously voted for Schober's fusion ticket and for the Heimatblock (a far-right coalition that ran in 1930 but not in 1932).[91] The overall picture is one of vote switching within a previously existing set of far-right groups rather than a crisis-induced change in mentality.

The lack of a crisis-induced transformation of the electorate is further suggested by the fact that "Hitler's party was losing votes in established strongholds" at the very time that the party seemed to be gaining ground in new places.[92] In any case, none of the anti-democratic groups on the Right "succeeded in winning the heartfelt support of anything like the majority of the Austrian population."[93] Dollfuss dismantled Austrian democracy less because of popular pressures than because he had personally come to embrace a kind of clerico-corporatist authoritarianism as a solution to Austria's problems. This was still a minority position in 1933. As late as February 1934, "indications abounded that the majority of conservative supporters were in favor of reconciliation with the Socialists."[94] This sounds little like polarization.

Estonia

Estonian and Latvian democracies collapsed almost simultaneously in 1934. The breakdown of democracy in Estonia was precipitated by the rapid rise of an anti-democratic movement called the Veterans' League, which formed just as the Depression began and built its support on

---

[91] Simon, "Democracy in the Shadow," 109.

[92] Ibid., 110.

[93] Bruce Pauley, "Nazis and Heimwehr Fascists: The Struggle for Supremacy in Austria, 1918–1938," in Larsen et al., *Who Were the Fascists?*, 235.

[94] Simon, "Democracy in the Shadow," 116.

the status anxieties of the urban middle class.[95] The immediate catalyst for the coup was a crisis over the national constitution. The document, written by a freely elected Constitutional Assembly in the early 1920s, had two unique features: it provided for no independent executive branch of government, and it allowed citizens to introduce legislation through referenda. The Veterans' League used the latter to introduce a major alteration of the constitution that provided for a strong, independently elected executive with substantial emergency powers. Much to the dismay of the parliamentary parties, the Veterans' referendum on the revised constitution was endorsed by 56 percent of the electorate.[96] When the movement won an absolute majority in key municipal elections in 1934, Konstantin Päts, the leader of the ruling Farmers' Party, engineered a coup. He quickly declared the Veterans' movement illegal, imprisoned its leaders, and, shortly afterward, suspended party politics altogether. The Päts coup was precipitated by the fear that the Veterans' movement would follow the same trajectory that the Nazi movement had taken in Germany.[97]

Given the movement's rapid growth and early electoral success, it is reasonable to conclude that the breakdown of democracy in Estonia was at least the indirect result of popular pressure. But this conclusion needs to be qualified in two essential respects. First, the mild authoritarian regime that replaced Estonia's democracy was the fruit of an effort to stop, rather than endorse, a more oppressive form of government.[98] Second, the Veterans' movement itself was very different from the right-wing anti-system parties that had mobilized elsewhere. Its leaders maintained a public commitment to working within legality.[99] Its rise "was not triggered by a perceived internal communist threat,"[100] and its goals were neither grand nor "far-reaching." Its main

[95] Tönu Parming, *The Collapse of Liberal Democracy and the Rise of Authoritarianism in Estonia* (London: Sage Publications, 1975).

[96] Parming, *The Collapse of Liberal Democracy,* 44.

[97] Andres Kasekamp, "The Estonian Veterans' League: A Fascist Movement?" *Journal of Baltic Studies* 24 (1993): 266, argues that the movement was the "largest mass political organization" in the nation when the coup took place.

[98] The Päts regime was much less oppressive than the better known dictatorships in Italy, Germany, and Spain. Päts was so secure in his ability to survive without extraordinary coercion that he granted amnesty to all but a few Communist and Veterans' movement leaders by 1938. Rein Taagepera, *Estonia: Return to Independence* (Boulder: Westview Press, 1993), 58.

[99] Kasekamp, "The Estonian Veterans' League," 266, argues persuasively that the Veterans' movement was not fascist.

[100] Kasekamp records that there were only 150 members of the Communist Party at liberty when the Veterans' movement arose. Andres Kasekamp, *The Radical Right in Interwar Estonia* (New York: St. Martin's Press, 2000), 67.

objective was "to amend the constitution,"[101] and when the Veterans succeeded in building a strong presidency and putting a "master in the house" (as they described it), their support seemed to wane. A Veterans' movement putsch against Päts in November of 1934 failed miserably.[102]

We do not have an accurate measure of how many people endorsed the movement's fascist goals and how many simply endorsed the emphasis on public order and a strong executive that the constitutional referendum provided. What we know is that, at the time of the coup, the Estonian people chose a national assembly that was overwhelmingly democratic in its composition and that they made these choices long after the depression had begun to be felt.[103] In this case, as in so many others, when ordinary people were given the option of choosing democratic versus anti-democratic leaders, most eschewed the latter. Most made the democratic choice even during an economic crisis.

LATVIA

Latvia's regime change was similar to Estonia's. There, too, the Depression increased the size of extremist groups on the Right, and the leader of the freely elected government engineered what he claimed to be a preemptive coup.[104] The coup was backed by Prime Minister M. Ulmanis, "a handful of like-minded individuals" from his Peasant Union Party, and the Latvian armed forces.[105] Latvia's constitution had been modeled on the Weimar constitution, and Ulmanis was concerned that his own parliament (with twenty-seven parties represented) might provide an opening for extremists on the far Right.[106] When he failed to shore up his executive power through standard legislative channels, he simply declared a state of siege. Though he eventually disbanded political parties of all sorts, his *first* move was to ban all organizations of the extreme Right (rather than the Left).

[101] Kasekamp, "The Estonian Veterans' League," 263–64. Parming, *The Collapse of Liberal Democracy*, 400, writes that the Estonian Communist Party had only three hundred members in 1929—including those in prison.

[102] Taagepera, *Estonia: Return to Independence*, 55.

[103] Parming, *The Collapse of Liberal Democracy*, 17.

[104] Alfred Bilmanis, *A History of Latvia* (Princeton: Princeton University Press, 1951), 358.

[105] Andrejs Plakans, *The Latvians: A Short History* (Stanford: Hoover Institution Press, 1995), 133.

[106] Rauch, *The Baltic States*, 146, reports that twelve of these parties had only one representative and only two had more than ten! It is significant that Ulmanis made an effort

The largest extreme Right group in Latvia in 1934 was the Thunder Cross. It provided a catalyst for the coup, but it was far from a mass movement. Its supporters were almost exclusively university students and urban intellectuals with little or no support from rural people—in a largely agrarian state. With a peak membership of some six-thousand (.03 percent of the population), its power to shape events derived not from its popularity or from its direct action, but from the international context of the time.[107] Ulmanis took preemptive action because he feared that the Thunder Cross might follow the trajectory of the Nazis if he did not. Ordinary Latvians played a peripheral role.

Spain

The breakdown of democracy in Spain in July 1936 was profoundly affected by its international context. But there can be little doubt that domestic support for anti-democratic movements was being widely expressed at the time that the transition to dictatorship began. The fact that the transition took the form of a civil war shows that the dynamic of this case is unique, for it was in Spain—and only Spain—that so many were willing to take up arms against anti-democratic forces. How did this highly contested regime change come about?

The fall of Spanish democracy probably began with the election of the Popular Front government in February 1936. The Front's victory meant that the Right/Center-Right coalition, which had ruled Spain for two years, would have to cede control of the government to the Left. As hordes of jubilant Popular Front supporters filled Spain's streets in celebration of the leftist victory, actors on the Right (including CEDA leader Gil Robles and Francisco Franco) began to lobby for the declaration of a state of siege and the nullification of the election's outcome. Much to their credit, the Center-Right prime minister and a number of generals refused to violate the constitution. Power was duly devolved upon a government of Left Republicans.

Two years of "aggressive" right-wing government had left Spain's working masses "in a far from conciliatory mood." Anxious to compensate for lost time, industrial and rural workers became increasingly engaged in strikes and property seizures while political violence in-

---

to reform the executive shortly after his visit to Hitler's Germany in the late Spring of 1933 (p. 154).

[107] Royal Institute, *The Baltic States*, 54–55, gives a brief description of the other fringe groups, including a small pro-Nazi group among German speakers and an officers' group on the Polish model. The restricted nature of all these groups is discussed in Rauch, *The Baltic States*, esp. 153.

creased dramatically.[108] The Socialist youth organization grew increasingly militant and eventually joined the Communist youth organization, while extreme-right student groups grew accordingly.[109] The struggle for power "shifted from the Chamber of the Cortes to the street, the club, and the officers mess."[110]

It was a small group of officers who finally moved against the regime in what was initially known as the Generals' Revolt. They acted in tandem with Gil Robles, who had been working surreptitiously to organize civilian support for a military coup for many months. Thousands of Spaniards took up arms on the side of the Nationalists, but an equal number took up arms in defense of the Republic. Thus the battle raged on for three devastating years.[111]

Ordinary people played a central role in the breakdown of Spanish democracy; but here, too, there are ambiguities and caveats that deserve emphasis. The most damaging public provocations—such as church burnings—were not the work of masses of people at all but of very small groups.[112] Statistics furnished by the Right itself imply that leftist mobilization might have actually been decreasing as the July coup approached; the high point of popular disorder was "the period right after the election rather than the late Spring."[113] The youth wings of the far-right parties were generally "not involved in street fighting and terror," as their counterparts in Germany or Italy had been.[114] Finally, the divisive issues that really did have broad popular support, such as Catalan nationalism, were not a source of destabilization at the time the regime broke down. Catalonia was surprisingly quiet in 1936.[115] Though it mustered a great deal of popular support, after the fact, the move against the Republic in Spain was still the work of a small sector of the Spanish Right. The numerical weakness of the original coup coalition is illustrated by the fact that only four out of sixteen generals with national commands supported the Nationalist cause.[116] The highest officers in the Spanish Navy and Air Force opposed the coup as well.

---

[108] Juan Linz, "From Great Hopes to Civil War," 189; Paul Preston, *The Coming of the Spanish Civil War* (New York: Routledge, 1994), 239, 268–69.

[109] Linz, "From Great Hopes to Civil War," 162; Raymond Carr, *Spain: 1808–1975* (Oxford: Oxford University Press, 1982), 642.

[110] Carr, *Spain: 1808–1975*, 640.

[111] Carr writes that "enthusiasm was the characteristic of life on both sides in the early days of the civil war." Ibid., 652.

[112] Ibid., 607.

[113] Linz, "From Great Hopes to Civil War," 192.

[114] Ibid., 192.

[115] Carr, *Spain: 1808–1975*, 641.

[116] Linz, "From Great Hopes to Civil War," 195.

GREECE

The breakdown of parliamentary government in Greece took place in the month after the Spanish Civil War began. It was not a transition in which popular forces played a major role. The trigger for this change—as for so many others—was an electoral outcome that frightened the Right. The pivotal election, held in January 1936, left the Royalists with only a two-seat parliamentary lead over the Republicans. For the first time in Greek parliamentary history, the balance of power was held by the Communist Party, with fifteen seats.[117] When the Communist Party mobilized an industrial strike campaign with clear political overtones, elite actors on the political Right began to panic. The key decision-maker in Greece (as in Italy and Bulgaria) was the monarch. The king simply invited General Metaxas, an open advocate of dictatorship, to assume the role of prime minister.[118] The king acted "without hesitation or consultation."[119] In a lamentable display of either naivete or irresponsibility, the Greek parliament gave Metaxas an overwhelming vote of confidence in April and left for a five-month summer recess.[120] Using rumors of a general strike as a pretext for their actions, Metaxas and the king established what came to be known as the Twin Dictatorship in August 1936.[121]

The citizens of Greece were not silent in the months leading up to Metaxas's seizure of power.[122] Strikes increased in number and social unrest led to a revolt in Thessaloniki in May. The army had to be called out after citizens rose up to protest the killing of twelve striking workers, but order was quickly restored. Overall, the threat decried so often by Metaxas was exaggerated. The vast majority of labor action was taken by Communist workers in the tobacco industry, and this was heavily concentrated in Macedonia. The party was "practically insignificant among other workers," and in the countryside the traditional, clientelist parties prevailed.[123]

[117] This was the outcome despite widespread intimidation of Republican voters. George Mavrogordatos, *Stillborn Republic: Social Coalitions and Party Strategies in Greece, 1922–1936* (Berkeley: University of California Press, 1983), 52–53; John Campbell and Philip Sherrard, *Modern Greece* (London: Ernest Benn, 1968), 157.

[118] Metaxas had participated in a failed assault on the Venizelist state in October 1923, so his inclinations were well known. See Mavrogordatos, *Stillborn Republic*, 30.

[119] Campbell and Sherrard, *Modern Greece*, 159.

[120] Ibid., 158–59.

[121] Mavrogordatos, *Stillborn Republic*, 54.

[122] For a carefully detailed history of labor mobilization before and during these years, see Seraphim Sepheriades, "Working-Class Movements (1780s-1930s) A European Macro-Historical Analytic Framework and a Greek Case Study" (Ph.D. dissertation, Columbia University, 1997).

[123] Mavrogordatos, *Stillborn Republic*, 148.

On the Right, Metaxas was hardly the charismatic leader of a mass movement. Before he was handed power in 1936, he had "no personal following," even in the army,[124] and his political party attracted only 3.9 percent of the vote. This was clearly a case of dictatorship by invitation and not by popular demand.

ROMANIA

Romania's electoral democracy was the last to fall in the interwar period. By 1938, its pivotal actors had nearly two decades of interwar history to learn from, so it is not surprising that this case would parallel others in several ways. Overall, though, it was an amalgam of various scenarios with no real duplicate. Romanian democracy differed from most of its contemporaries in that it was a two-party dominant system until the 1930s. The Liberal and Peasant Parties alternated in office in a system based heavily on clientelism but with relatively little of the policy paralysis that racked the proportional representation systems of other European states.

Between 1928 and 1930, three factors intervened to change the balance of forces. First, the National Peasant Party came to power in the 1928 elections, and though it made a concerted effort to strengthen democratic institutions throughout the country, it was unable to make the practical policy changes that the onset of the 1929 depression required.[125] Second, the world depression caused an erosion of Peasant Party support and a fragmentation of the party system which worked to the advantage of the nascent far-Right. Third, the situation was altered further when Carol II ascended the throne following the death of his father in 1930. King Carol "made no secret of his disdain for parliamentary institutions" nor his contempt for the Peasant Party leader Maniu.[126] Since the Romanian Constitution of 1923 accorded the monarch the power to choose and dismiss cabinet members, the king's preferences were of great importance.[127]

These preferences became painfully apparent in the mid-1930s as a ferociously anti-Semitic, fascist organization called the Iron Guard began to attract a broad base of support. King Carol opposed the organization and even backed its official dissolution in 1933, but allowed it to operate under another name, hoping that it would destabilize

---

[124] Campbell and Sherrard, *Modern Greece*, 162.

[125] Keith Hitchens, *Rumania: 1866–1947* (Oxford: Clarendon, 1994), 414–15.

[126] Ibid., 378.

[127] The monarch's powers were so great that one could question whether Romania was democratic at all. I describe it as a democracy here because it held competitive elections and maintained freedom of association.

what was left of Romanian democracy and thereby legitimize a royal dictatorship. The popularity of the Guardist organization exceeded King Carol's expectations and became a direct threat to his plans. In the 1937 elections, it attracted over 15 percent of the vote and became the third largest party in parliament. In so doing, it deprived the Liberal Party, the king's favorite, of the votes it needed to command a majority of seats in the legislature. In "what was unquestionably an immediate reaction to the Guardist [electoral] successes,"[128] the king established a preventive dictatorship. Fearing the Iron Guard's links to both the German and the Italian Fascists, he appointed a right-wing nationalist named Octavian Goga prime minister. Goga sought the establishment of a corporatist authoritarian state; but when National Peasant Party ministers opposed him, he quickly turned to Fascists for support. Fearing the establishment of a Fascist dictatorship along German or Italian lines, King Carol dismissed Goga's cabinet and swept away the institutions of the parliamentary system. He arrested all the major figures in the Iron Guard and charged its head with high treason.

The breakdown of Romanian democracy was very much the responsibility of the king himself, but there is no doubt that ordinary Romanians were attracted to anti-democratic groups as well. The authoritarian Christian League of National Defense eventually attracted around 9 percent of the vote, and the Iron Guard increased its share of the popular vote from 1 percent to over 15 percent between 1931 and 1935.[129] Support for the early Fascist movement was "substantial in academic circles,"[130] and party propagandists often found "responsive" and even "enthusiastic" receptions on their visits to rural villages.[131] Yet in this case, as in all our others, there are still open questions about the nature and extent of anti-democratic feeling. The Iron Guard seems to have had extremely efficient means of intimidating village voters,[132] and the fact that the Peasant Party was willing to join the Guard in an electoral alliance to defeat the Liberals in 1937 probably led to a great deal of confusion about the extremist party's real beliefs. The fact that King

---

[128] Stephen Fischer-Galati, "Fascism in Romania," in *Eastern European Nationalism in the Twentieth Century*, ed. Peter Sugar (Lanham, Md.: American University Press, 1995), 118.

[129] Communists and antidemocratic parties on the Left had little direct influence on political life even after the Depression. Hitchens, *Rumania: 1866–1947*, 397–98.

[130] Irina Livezeanu, *Cultural Politics in Greater Romania* (Ithaca: Cornell University Press, 1995), 273–74.

[131] Fischer-Galati, "Fascism in Romania," 116.

[132] Mattei Dogan, "Romania," in *Competitive Elections in Developing Countries*, ed. Myron Weiner and Ergun Ozbudun (Washington, D.C.: American Enterprise Institute, 1987), 384.

TABLE 2.3
How Dictators Got Control of Democracies in Interwar Europe

An Invitation to Rule	An Executive or Military Coup
Italy	Austria
Germany	Bulgaria
Greece	Estonia
Romania	Latvia
Yugoslavia	Lithuania
	Poland
	Portugal
	Spain

Carol failed in his own attempt to rally mass support for a royal dictatorship,[133] suggests that it was anti-Semitism and not anti-parliamentarism per se that the Guard supporters found most appealing. If they simply sought an end to parliamentary government, the king's alternative would have been more appealing. These caveats aside, Romania was clearly a case in which the level of anti-democratic popular mobilization was relatively high.

Looking at the entire set of ill-fated democracies gives us a more accurate picture of the role that ordinary people played in the destruction of democratic regimes. The thirteen cases that have been discussed illustrate that popular support for the interwar transitions to dictatorship varied greatly. Some transitions were similar to Germany's in that they were accompanied by supportive mass movements, but in other cases the regime change was almost wholly an elite affair. In virtually all our cases, anti-democratic leaders gained control of the state either because they were invited to rule by a king or president or because they seized power through military action. Table 2.3 reminds us that even where significant sectors of civil society backed the demise of democracy, elites always delivered the final blows.

In Italy, Germany, Greece, Romania, and the Kingdom of the Serbs, Croats, and Slovenes, anti-democratic leaders were simply handed power by an individual decision-maker who had the option of granting power to someone else. In all our other cases, democracies fell be-

---

[133] Hitchens, *Rumania: 1866–1947*, 424.

cause of military assaults or executive coups. Despite the many glaring inadequacies of democratic government in the interwar years, Europe's citizens were usually loath to take direct action against it. Looking at the continent as a whole, we can conclude that ordinary Europeans had only a peripheral role in the demise of interwar democracies.

Polarization in Interwar Europe

Did elites dismantle interwar democracies because ordinary people polarized? Looking at the realities of mass behavior in the whole set of interwar democracies enables us to appreciate both the strengths and the limitations of the polarization metaphor. If we conceive of polarization as Sartori does, the metaphor is only partially appropriate. Drawing on our discussion in chapter 1, we would expect a classic case of polarization to have the following core components. First, it would contain "relevant, antisystem parties" situated "two poles apart" on the Left-Right political spectrum. Second, it would involve mutually exclusive, bilateral oppositions flanking the democratic governments that fail. Third and most importantly, it would involve the "enfeeblement" of the political Center and "the prevalence of centrifugal drives over centripetal ones." Ordinary people, as voters, would embody these drives, deserting centrist parties and transferring their allegiance to the extremes of the Left-Right spectrum instead.

Only the second of these generalizations holds in nearly all our cases: ruling parties usually were flanked by mutually exclusive oppositions before democracies broke down. But mutually exclusive oppositions existed in most if not all of the survivor cases as well, so this system attribute does not seem to be decisive.

The other core components of the model seem even less appropriate to the realities of interwar Europe. At least two factors disturb the fit. First, determining which parties are "anti-system" and which are not is extremely difficult. According to Sartori, anti-system parties are those which "pursue and obtain a delegitimizing impact" on the regime they oppose. Unfortunately, a party's capacity to do this can only be known after the fact. If we adopt his alternative definition of anti-system parties as those that would change not "the government but the very system of government,"[134] we are still left wondering which aspects of the governmental system are decisive in the categorization. Though political scientists routinely use the term "system" in the singular, political systems are never all of a piece. By definition, all democratic political

---

[134] Sartori, *Parties and Party Systems*, 132–33.

systems involve some form of competitive elections, but many other important system characteristics are not shared. Electoral democracies can be republics or monarchies; unitary systems or federal systems; egalitarian or inegalitarian. They can be based on a broad suffrage or a narrow one, and they can grant great or little autonomy to subnational groups. Each of these variable but fundamental system attributes can be the wellspring of a political party. Indeed, Europe's interwar political landscape was filled with parties which were organized primarily to challenge or defend one or more of these system attributes. Which of these many parties qualify as "anti-system" parties is highly problematic, especially since almost none of them opposed their political systems in their entirety.

The second factor that detracts from the utility of the polarization metaphor is the multipolar nature of interwar European society. Our classic conception of polarization is bipolar and unidimensional. Parties and voters are supposed to array themselves along a singular Left-Right spectrum. Yet, in much of interwar Europe, party systems were decidedly multipolar. The Left-Right spectrum marked only one of several dimensions precisely because so many of the system attributes described above were publicly contested.

The importance and the implications of multipolarity are well exemplified by the case of Poland, where the salience of the Left-Right spectrum was often overshadowed by the salience of ethnic identity. Interwar Poland was a multinational state in which only 69 percent of the population actually described themselves as Polish. Ukrainians, Russians and Germans were the largest "nationality" groups, but nearly 8 percent of the Polish population described their nationality as "Jewish."[135] The multidimensional nature of the Polish party system is best illustrated by the fact that the parliament was routinely described as having the predictable Left, Center, and Right party groupings, plus a group known simply as the National Minorities that occupied a full 20 percent of the seats.[136]

Just as the importance of national minorities made the party system multidimensional in Poland, personalist, regionalist, and populist parties made systems multidimensional elsewhere. The importance of multidimensionality complicated the utility of the polarization metaphor throughout interwar Europe.

There were cases in which the Left-Right spectrum did represent the dominant division on the political landscape, but even in these cases, voters did not behave as polarization theory would predict. Pre-Fascist

---

[135] Ibid., 35–40.
[136] Ibid., 101.

Italy provides a clear example. A cursory look at Italian parliamentary history reveals that the "Center" of the Italian political system did not hold between 1919 and 1922. The polarization metaphor is apt in this sense, but we must clarify exactly which actors in the political system actually got polarized if the breakdown of democracy is to be properly understood. The enfeeblement of the Center was not due to the choices of ordinary people; the Center weakened because of the defection of party elites, not ordinary voters. It is risky to discuss "trends" at all with only two national elections, but what seems striking as one looks at voting data in historical context is not the electorate's defection and polarization but its consistency and continuity instead. This conclusion derives from two different sets of evidence.

First, two historical facts, related to extremist parties of the Left and Right, make it difficult to prove that the electorate defected to anti-system parties at all. The only unambiguously anti-system party on the Left was the Communist Party. It was formed in 1921, as the institutional expression of a long-existing faction of the Socialist Party.[137] It competed in the parliamentary elections of 1921, and attracted 4.6 percent of the vote, yet, because the party had no previous electoral experience, its support cannot be properly contextualized. Defection and polarization involve attitudinal change, but without some measure of people's affinity for Communism before 1921, we cannot know whether the party's votes were a reflection of a change in ideas or simply a change in institutions. Had Communist voters been radicalized and polarized by a frustrating experience with the centrist democracy? Or had the ideational positions of Communist voters been stable over time—and simply subsumed within the Socialist Party? With only one measure of party support, the case for polarization to the Left cannot be made. In any case, fewer than five out of every one hundred voters chose the PCI in the first place.

The case for polarization to the Right cannot be made either. Italy's interwar democracy had only two fairly competitive national elections (in 1919 and 1921). Though the Fascists (unlike the Communists) competed in both of these contests, it is difficult to track party support. The Fascists started their organizational transition from movement to party only a short time before the 1919 elections began and managed to run officially and alone only in the city of Milan. We know that they won

---

[137] The faction was led by Amadeo Bordiga, António Gramsci, Angelo Tasca, and Palmiro Togliatti. It was closely associated with the journal *Ordine Nuovo* and harshly critical of the majority of the party leadership who were openly reformist. For an overview of the parties of the period, see Massimo Salvadori, *Storia dell'età Contemporanea* (Turin: Loescher, 1976), 556–98.

under five-thousand votes there, but the baseline for their national con-stituency is nonexistent.[138] Men who identified themselves as Fascists ran for office on the lists of the Combattenti, but counting one party's votes as the baseline for another is always questionable. In this context, it would be especially misleading because, as Adrian Lyttleton re-minds us, the official ex-combatant movement "remained firmly dem-ocratic, opposed to the extreme bellicose and nationalist tendency of the *fasci* and suspicious of their dubious alliances."[139]

In the election of 1921, the Fascists were invited to join the Nationalist Block—a broad coalition of political notables from several parties in-cluding Liberals, Nationalists, Democrats, and Social Reformists. Since the Block was organized by a number of personalities who were closely identified with constitutional government, it lent a certain ambiguity to the Fascists' anti-system identity. If, as Farneti and others have argued, the Block made the Fascists "'respectable' in the eyes of moderate public opinion,"[140] interpreting support for the Block as support for anti-sys-tem parties is highly problematic.[141] The fact that two-thirds of the seats that were won by the Block were won by *non*-Fascists, shows conclu-sively that even Block voters preferred non-Fascists to Fascists by a large margin.[142] In any case, it seems that the non-Fascist parties in the Na-tional Block reaped no obvious rewards from joining forces with Musso-lini's party. The coalition garnered far fewer votes in 1921 than its indi-vidual member parties had in 1919.[143]

A second set of evidence showing the strength and resilience of mod-erate opinion comes from studying the electoral trajectory of non-ex-tremist parties. As table 2.4 indicates, the National Block failed to win even a plurality of the popular vote. The Block was beaten in the 1921

[138] Ibid., 591.

[139] Lyttelton, *The Seizure of Power*, 48.

[140] Paolo Farneti, "Social Conflict, Parliamentary Fragmentation, Instutional Shift, and the Rise of Fascism: Italy," in Linz and Stepan, *Europe*, 23.

[141] The extent to which the constitutionalists' invitation to the Fascists should be seen as an indication of elite defection to the anti-system Right might also be questionable. Giolitti and others insisted that they included the Fascists only because they hoped to control them and make the anti-system group more moderate. Salvadori, *Storia dell'età Contemporanea*, 579–603.

[142] Italy had proportional representation with preference voting—meaning that voters could choose from a list of Block candidates (some Fascists and some not) in each dis-trict.

[143] In the 1919 election, the Liberals, the Democrats, the Reform Socialists, and the Vet-erans garnered 1.4 million votes, or 25 percent of the total poll. The Block (with the Na-tionalists and the Fascists) won only 1.26 million votes—and dropped to only 19 percent of the poll.

TABLE 2.4
Votes for Major Parties in National Elections: Interwar Italy, 1919–1921

	1919		1921	
Parties and Lists	Number of Votes	Percent of Total	Number of Votes	Percent of Total
Italian Socialist Party (official)	1,834,792	32.3	1,631,435	24.7
Reformist and Unionist Socialists	82,172	1.5	—	—
Independent Socialists	33,938	0.6	37,892	0.6
Communist Party	—	—	304,719	4.6
Popular Party	1,167,354	20.5	1,347,305	20.4
Dissident Popolare	—	—	29,703	0.4
Liberal/Radical Democrats/Block	904,195	15.9	—	—
Democrats	622,310	10.9	—	—
Liberals	490,381	8.6	470,605	7.1
Veterans	232,923	4.1	113,839	1.7
Radicals	110,697	2.0	—	—
Economic Party[a]	87,450	1.5	53,382	0.8
Radicals, Republicans and Socialists	65,421	1.2	—	—
Republican Party	53,197	0.9	124,924	1.9
Fascist Party	—	—	29,549	0.5
Liberal-Democrats	—	—	684,855	10.4
Social-Democrats	—	—	309,191	4.7
Reformist-Democrats	—	—	122,087	1.8
National Block[b]	—	—	1,260,007	19.1
Slavic and German Parties	—	—	88,648	1.3
Total	5,684,833	100	6,608,141	100

Source: Ugo Giusti, *Dai Plebisciti alla Costituente* (Rome: Editrice Faro, 1945), 71 and 81.
[a] Agrarians, Laborists, and Syndicalists.
[b] Liberals, Nationalists, Democrats, Fascists, Reformist Socialists, and Veterans.

polls by two other parties, the Socialists and the Popular Party, or Popolare. Despite years of political turmoil, most Italian voters eschewed the new option embodied in the National Block and voted instead for the same parties that had won the previous national elections. A closer look at the nation's largest nonextremist parties confirms that continuity outweighed defection.

The Socialists had been burdened with an ambiguous identity in previous elections because they provided an institutional home for an anti-system Communist grouping. Yet, after the party split in 1921, the now more moderate PSI lost only two-hundred thousand votes. The PSI remained the most popular party in Italy with 24.7 percent of the vote, while the new Communist Party—the left-most pole in the polarizing system—garnered the support of only 4.6 percent of the electorate. If ordinary Italians were defecting from the Center and polarizing in opinion, the Communist Party would have proved much more popular. There is evidence to suggest that the Left was growing more rather than less moderate on the eve of Mussolini's appointment, because, by 1921, labor mobilization of all sorts had dropped off dramatically. Ivanoe Bonomi, a centrist and former prime minister, wrote at the time that strikes had dropped off to prewar levels and that "the country . . . was settling down again to normal life (PP1)."[144] As late as 1922, he saw the Italian masses as "sobered" and "exasperated by futile violence."[145] This is hardly a description of polarization.

The strongest evidence of the durability of centrist opinion among the Italian public comes from tracing the support for Italy's largest Center party, the Partito Popolare Italiano (PPI).[146] The PPI was formed only shortly before the 1919 elections but grew very quickly, tripling its membership during the electoral campaign to an impressive 100,000.[147] Though its founder, Don Luigi Sturzo, expected the new party to win 60 seats in the national assembly, the group won 100 seats instead.[148] In the second and last electoral contest in 1921, the centrist party in-

[144] Ivanoe Bonomi, *From Socialism to Fascism*, trans. John Murray (London: Martin Hopkinson, 1924), 84.

[145] Ibid., 201.

[146] The centrist position of the Partito Populare Italiano is discussed in John Molony, *The Emergence of Political Catholicism in Italy* (London: Croom Helm, 1977), 12–13; and in Bonomi, *From Socialism to Fascism*, 71. The party was a Catholic party in that it sought to infuse Italian political life with Chrisitian values, but it was distrusted by the Vatican, in part because (in the words of the liberal Bonomi) it had "abandoned the old clerical hostility to the secular state" (p. 71). The party was progressive in seeking land reform, the vote for women, and more social and economic equality.

[147] Luigi Salvatorelli and Giovanni Mira, *Storia d'Italia nel Periodo Fascista* (Turin: Einaudi, 1957), 105.

[148] Molony, *The Emergence of Political Catholicism*, 66

creased its vote and won 108 seats. If the voting public were defecting from the Center and moving to the extremes of the political spectrum, Italy's major centrist party would have withered away. Instead, the party attracted more supporters than ever, despite the fact that non-Fascists of all sorts were threatened, beaten, and even murdered throughout the electoral campaign.[149] Even in the face of physical danger, more and more Italians persisted in choosing a centrist leadership for their troubled nation.

The fact that these choices were made in Italy is especially significant. With the exception of Germany there is probably no nation in Europe for which the breakdown of democracy is thought to be more closely associated with the popular will. This is the sort of case where we should see the polarized behavior of ordinary people in stark relief. Yet, a careful look at the contours of polarization shows that most ordinary people are blameless. Our image of the Italian popular will has heretofore been crafted from two sources: those related to the political elites who defected from the Center and joined forces with the Fascists in 1921 and 1922, and those related to the expanding and highly visible anti-system movement around Mussolini himself. Polarization certainly occurred among elites in Parliament and in the streets. But we must not mistake the actions of some for the will of many. The broadest measure we have of the popular will is the popular vote, and despite substantial incentives to polarize, ordinary people actually attempted to reinforce the Italian Center.

Voters in Germany behaved differently from their counterparts in Italy in that they did polarize at the polls. Yet even in Germany a close analysis of the dynamics of the voting process suggests at least four important caveats about the connection between polarization and regime change. Taken together, these caveats reinforce our conclusions about elite rather than popular culpability.

The first caveat concerns the pace of polarization and the need to distinguish between defection from the Center and support for the extremes. The defection from the parties on the bourgeois Center and Right took place well before the rise of the Nazis. Voters were not lured from the Center to the extremes in one simple seduction. Party squabbling in the mid-1920s led to a "breakdown of voter identification with the established parties of the bourgeois Center and Right,"[150] but the

---

[149] Renzo De Felice calculates that 105 people were killed and another 431 injured during the five-week campaign. See *Mussolini il Fascista*, 87.

[150] Michael Bessel, "The Formation and Dissolution of a German National Electorate from Kaiserreich to Thrid Reich," in Jones and Retallack, *Elections, Mass Politics, and Social Change*, 403–4.

TABLE 2.5

Reichstag Election Results, 1919–1932

Party[a]	January 1919	June 1920	May 1924	December 1924	September 1928	May 1930	July 1932	November 1932
KPD	—	2.1	12.6	9.0	10.6	13.1	14.3	16.9
USPD	7.6	17.9	0.8	—	—	—	—	—
SPD	37.9	21.7	20.5	26.0	29.8	24.5	21.6	20.4
Center Party	19.7	13.6	13.4	13.6	12.1	11.8	12.5	11.9
DDP	18.6	8.3	5.7	6.3	4.9	3.8	1.0	0.9
DVP	4.4	13.9	9.2	10.1	8.7	4.5	1.2	1.9
DNVP	10.3	15.1	19.5	20.5	14.2	7.0	5.9	8.3
NSDAP	—	—	6.5	3.0	2.6	18.3	37.3	33.1
Particularistic Parties	1.6	7.4	11.8	11.5	17.1	17.0	6.2	6.5
Electoral Participation	82.7	79.2	77.4	78.8	75.5	82.0	84.0	80.6

Source: Richard F. Hamilton, *Who Voted for Hitler?* (Princeton: Princeton University Press, 1982), 476.
[a] I follow Lepsius, ("From Fragmented Party Democracy," 43) in my categorization of these parties. Beginning with the KPD (the Communist Party) and ending with the NSDAP (the Nazi Party), they are arranged from extreme left to extreme right. Particularistic parties are organized around a different political dimension involving region, ethnicity, or a single policy issue. USPD = Independent Social Democrats, SPD = Social Democrats, DDP = German Democratic Party, DVP = German People's Party, DNVP = German Nationalist People's Party.

majority of the citizens who shed their former identities either voted for nonextremist, single-issue parties or abstained from voting altogether. These facts are clear from table 2.5 above.

Though the erosion of support for traditional parties took place gradually, over several elections, 1928 marked a turning point. The centrist German Democratic Party (DDP) dropped to only 4.9 percent of the vote, after attracting as much as 18.6 percent of the vote in 1919. The conservative German Peoples' Party (DVP) dropped to 8.7 percent of the vote from a high of 13.9 percent in 1920. Yet, the Nazi Party was not advantaged by the new fluidity. Single-issue parties rose in support, abstentions hit an all time high of nearly 25 percent, and the vote for the Nazis actually declined.[151] Defecting voters eschewed the Nazis,

[151] For more on the dynamics of the 1928 election, see Larry Eugene Jones, "Generational Conflict and Political Mobilization," in Jones and Retallack, *Elections, Mass Politics, and Social Change*, 358.

at least initially. This means that if another, less heinous party had mounted the mobilization effort that Hitler did, German democracy might have endured. We cannot assume that the instincts and values that caused voters to defect from the parties run by traditional elites were fundamentally anti-democratic. On the contrary, defections seem to have been driven by demands for "inclusion" and for "the construction of a more accessible, less deferential social order."[152] These demands were fully compatible with a democratic movement, but none materialized. The Nazis were definitely not "the only endpoint of long-term aspirations for political enfranchisement." They were, instead, "a final, desperate alternative after seasons of economic dislocation and parliamentary disarray."[153] The Nazi Party did benefit from defections, but these came slowly, and only took off in 1930, after the effects of the depression were being felt.

The second important caveat about Germany's polarization concerns the source of extremist defections. Defections did not come from all the parties in the center of the spectrum. In a fully polarized polity the political Center would have collapsed entirely, but sectors of the German Center held together. The Catholic Center Party on the Center-Right was fairly successful in retaining its voters. The Protestant middle-class parties proved less able to maintain support, and thus the defectors that did gravitate to the Nazi extreme Right came from these groups.[154] As table 2.5 shows, the Social Democratic Party lost many voters to its left when Communist factions broke off after 1919, but the share of the vote it garnered in November 1932 was not very different from the share it garnered in 1920, over twelve years and six elections earlier. The Catholic Center was even more consistent in maintaining its base. The proportion of the vote gained by the Center Party fluctuated less than two percentage points across seven elections, beginning in 1920. The stability of support for both the Catholic Center and the

---

[152] Fritzsche, "Weimar Populism," 301.

[153] Ibid., 304.

[154] The continuities in voting compelled Michael Bessel to conclude, "The aggregate support for the various parties in the early 1920s appears not to have differed radically from their prewar predecessors and ... did not alter fundamentally until the NSDAP became a mass party." "The Formation and Dissolution," 402–3. For more on continuities in voting, see Lepsius, "From Fragmented Party Democracy," 60; and Rudy Koshar, "Cult of Associations? The Lower Middle Classes in Weimar Germany," in *Splintered Classes: Politics and the Lower Middle Classes in Interwar Europe*, ed. Rudy Koshar (New York: Holmes & Meier, 1990), 41. It should be underscored that the Center Party was much more successful than the Social Democrats in maintaining its base. Jürgen Falter has shown that many SPD voters switched to the Nazis after 1928. See "The Social Bases of Political Clevages in the Weimar Republic, 1919–1933," in Jones and Retallack, *Elections, Mass Politics, and Social Change*, 382.

TABLE 2.6
Percentage of Total Electorate Switching to NSDAP from
Various Sources, 1928–1932

	1928–30	1930–32[a]	1928–32[a] Total	July–Nov. 1932
SPD/KPD	2.18	3.10	5.28	−0.92
Center/BVP	0.90	0.70	1.60	−0.40
DDP/DVP	2.50	2.37	4.87	−0.25
DNVP	3.35	1.23	4.58	−0.93
Other	0.96	5.40	6.36	0.02
Nonvoters	3.42	3.36	6.78	−1.52

Source: Falter, "The Social Bases of Political Cleavages," 381.

Note: Numbers indicate the net percentage of the total electorate switching from the party in the left column to the NSDAP between the elections listed.

[a] July 1932 election.

Social Democratic Party is especially remarkable given that both parties were subject to severe and even deadly harassment from Nazi gangs at meetings and rallies.[155]

The third caveat we must note regarding German polarization regards the weight of defections in the overall support for the Nazis. Although defections from other parties were a source of Nazi growth, Jürgen Falter discovered that "nonvoters" contributed *"by far the largest share* of votes flowing to the Hilter movement."[156] As table 2.6 illustrates, nonvoters made up a larger percentage of the Nazi gain in votes between 1928 and 1932 than did defectors from any single party. Furthermore, newly mobilized voters were more likely to vote for the Nazi party than for any other.[157]

The Nazis lured defectors, as the polarization metaphor would predict, but their greatest strength seems to have been in attracting the support of outsiders. The movement attracted those who stood outside the preexisting party system and those who stood outside (or only precariously inside) associational networks of other sorts. In many areas throughout the country, the Nazi Party became "a focus for a

---

[155] Nazis seem to have physically attacked their opponents even in areas where they were relatively unpopular and did not have the force of numbers on their side. See, for example, a discussion of Nazi attacks on the Center majority in Upper Silesia in Richard Bessel, *Political Violence and the Rise of Nazism: The Storm Troopers in Eastern Germany: 1925–1934* (New Haven: Yale University Press, 1984), 1.

[156] "The Social Bases of Political Cleavages," 382, emphasis added.

[157] Jürgen W. Falter and Reinhard Zintl, "The Economic Crisis of the 1930s and the Nazi Vote," *Journal of Interdisciplinary History* 19, no. 1 (Summer 1988), 79.

milieu not otherwise tightly bound by associational ties of class or confession." The Nazis attracted the "village nobodies" and those unable to join more prestigious clubs.[158] The Nazis also attracted a disproportionate share of younger people. In 1930, around one-third of movement members were under thirty. Another 27 percent were between thirty and forty. Men in these cohorts were outsiders in the sense that their "life and career patterns had not been set." They were also "outsiders" in an economic sense, for these were the cohorts hit hardest by unemployment.[159]

A heavy reliance on new voters with precarious ties to both the economy and to other groups meant that the Nazi base of support was relatively unstable. Thus, the fourth caveat we must bear in mind regarding German polarization is that support for the Nazis was broad based but not deeply rooted. The party would benefit from defections, but it would suffer from defections as well. Support "was often short-term and conditional,"[160] and petit-bourgeois involvement in the movement was typically "provisional and fluid."[161] As table 2.6 shows, in the November 1932 election the Nazis, on net, lost votes to all of the other major parties. In the fall of 1932, the party entered into crisis. With the drop in support at the polls, the movement's decline became a palpable possibility.[162] The drop in dues became "catastrophic."[163] Membership in local groups fell rapidly and morale among those who stayed behind "plummeted."[164] Most ironically, part of the decline was the result of public revulsion toward Nazi violence. In the summer of 1932, storm-trooper violence began to detract from the party's electoral popularity and exacerbate internal tensions. As a Nazi propaganda chief lamented at the time, "Acts of terror . . . have repelled the population from us."[165] The sad truth is that German elites appointed Hitler chancellor just as ordinary Germans may have been turning against the Nazis.

The German case provides us with the best example of polarization in interwar European history. But in so doing, it also enables us to refine our thinking about the limits of the polarization model. Even in this,

---

[158] Chickering, "Political Mobilization and Associational Life," 314–15.

[159] Peukert, *The Weimar Republic*, 239.

[160] Bessel, *Political Violence*, 151.

[161] Rudy Koshar, "On the Politics of the Splintered Classes: An Introductory Essay," in Koshar, *Splintered Classes*, 17.

[162] Fritzsche, "Weimar Populism," 305.

[163] Bessel, *Political Violence*, 94.

[164] Ibid., 26. Peukert writes similarly that the party had sound "reason to fear a hemorrhage of its own supporters." *The Weimar Republic*, 270.

[165] Bessel, *Political Violence*, 93–96. The individual quoted is Joachim Paltzo.

our paradigmatic case, the largest extremist party gathered votes only gradually and only after a second economic trauma; a sizeable part of the political Center held; the growth of the triumphant extremist party derived from new voters as well as from switch voters; and finally, the fluidity that made polarization possible in the first place proved multi-directional. Voter support for the Nazis was eroding when Hitler was named chancellor.

Conclusion

My review of the role of ordinary people in the collapse of democracy in the interwar years suggests that citizens were less culpable than the common wisdom has led us to believe. Though the argument uses evidence from the whole set of interwar cases, it has left open at least two important sets of questions. First, are the conclusions drawn here somehow time-bound? The First World War and its aftermath left exceptional scars on Europe's many polities, transforming borders, dividing interventionists from noninterventionists, and forming new states from old peoples who had no previous sense of commonality. Was interwar political behavior therefore an artifact of an extraordinary period never likely to be even partially duplicated? This leads to the second set of questions: If my conclusions are not time-bound, are they place-bound, instead? Are they applicable in Europe but not in other regions? Did uniquely European divisions such as those between republicans and monarchists or Protestant and Catholics make polarization less likely in these cases than elsewhere?

In order to further examine these questions and to test the boundaries of the picture that seems to be emerging, I turn next to the role of ordinary people in the breakdown of democracy in South America.

PART II
SOUTH AMERICA AND OUR
LITERATURE REVISED

THE COLLAPSE OF NEW DEMOCRACIES in the decades after the Second World War reinforced the fear and cynicism associated with the rise of interwar fascism. Decolonization in Africa and Asia and the expansion of democratic institutions in Latin America initially produced hope in many quarters. The number of people enjoying democratic freedoms had, once again, expanded to an unprecedented level. Expectations for the successful defense of these freedoms were probably highest in South America, where the process of decolonization had already taken place. In 1959,Tad Szulc expressed the views of many when he announced the "twilight" of Latin American dictatorship.[1]

Yet cynicism and skepticism would soon win the day. Though seven out of ten South American states were polyarchies in 1960, by 1976 only two polyarchies remained intact. Analyzing the role of ordinary people in the breakdown of these regimes enables us to put the conclusions we drew from interwar Europe in comparative perspective and ask: Did the culpability of the citizenry vary across time and region?

To ensure that my answers derived from a sufficiently broad range of cases, I decided to study the twenty-year period between 1959 and 1979. I began with 1959 because I reasoned that the Cuban Revolution would play the same inspirational role in the sixties and seventies that the Russian Revolution played in the interwar years. I ended with 1979 because this is when the "third wave" of democratization began its slow sweep over South America. Within this twenty-year period I studied every democracy that gave way to a right-wing dictatorship. This meant a total of four cases in four different countries: Brazil, Uruguay, Chile, and Argentina. The table below lists each of my cases and the dates that dictatorships replaced democracies.

To what extent did ordinary people behave as predicted and respond to economic crisis in ways that destabilized the existing democracy? Was polarization in fact growing greater as these competitive political systems neared collapse? Did ordinary people relate to national party systems in any systematically different ways as the breakdown of democracy approached? These questions are the focus of the case studies that follow. Read in their entirety and in the context of what we now know about interwar Europe, they illustrate that political wisdom is much more common than the common wisdom of the social sciences has led us to believe.

[1] Tad Szulc, *Twilight of the Tyrants* (New York: Henry Holt and Company, 1959), 3.

Electoral Democracies Replaced by Right-Wing Dictatorships in South America, 1959–1979

Country	Date of Last Competitive Election		Winning Party/Ruler		Date of Coup and Regime Change
	Presidential	Congressional	Presidential	Congressional	
Argentina	September 1973	September 1973	Juan D. Perón (FJL)	FJL	March 1976
Brazil	October 1960	October 1962	J. da Silva Quadros (UDN/PDC)	PSD	March 1964
Chile	September 1970	March 1973	S. Allende (PSC)	CODE	September 1973
Uruguay	November 1971	November 1971	PC	PC	June 1973

Source: Dieter Nohlen, ed. *Enciclopedia Electoral Latinoamericana y del Caribe* (San José: Instituto Interamericano de Derechos Humanos, 1993).

The Left-Right polarization model is useful in that it captures the Communist vs. anti-Communist mentality that dominated world politics in the decades that concern us. It is also useful in that it captures an unmistakably powerful tension between certain political actors in each of our nations. But there are two reasons why we must not take the polarization metaphor too seriously.

First, the metaphor muffles the voices of ordinary people in these regimes. It gives us a distorted view of what ordinary people were actually doing, both with their votes and with their political voice more generally, as these democracies collapsed. The second reason we should be wary of the linear, polarization model is that it leads us away from another spatial metaphor that better captures the realities of most of our cases. I describe this alternative metaphor in the last chapter of the book. Our cases begin—as the 1960s did—with the breakdown of democracy in Brazil.

3

THE RELUCTANT COUP IN BRAZIL

IN THE SPRING OF 1964, when a group of high-ranking Brazilian military officers organized a coup against the democratically elected government of João Goulart, the civilian president vowed that he would defend his post with "popular forces" at his side.[1] The regime's best-known orator, Leonel Brizola, made an impassioned balcony speech calling for armed resistance,[2] and the minister of justice broadcast frantic radio pleas for popular opposition to fill the streets. Brazilians did flood the streets as the military took control, but only to learn more about the coup itself. They listened to radios and to one another in cafes, bars, and parks, but did little or nothing to defend the elected regime.[3] Democracy seemed to die undefended.

The ease with which Brazilian democracy collapsed emboldened coup-makers elsewhere to conclude that democracies in crisis could be toppled with minimal resistance and cost. Thus the Brazilian transition, like the Italian transition in 1922, marked the first of a new series of breakdowns in their respective regions.

The civilian government that was ousted by the Brazilian military fit the classic vision of a doomed democracy. Its chief executive was associated with the Left, and, as a consequence, the government began with powerful enemies in the military and the civilian elite. It struggled continuously with an unruly Congress and was blamed for policy failures related to inflation, investment, and agrarian reform. It was beset by highly visible strikes and land seizures and ruled in a context of what might be called "pendular" mobilization; demonstrations from one quarter were quickly followed by counter-demonstrations from another.

The salience of mobilization before Goulart's ouster and the absence of resistance to the coup itself make it easy to attribute the collapse of Brazilian democracy to popular defections and polarization. But a close look at the historical record proves that Brazilians were not fickle friends of democracy. What it proves specifically is that a surprising

---

[1] John W. F. Dulles, *Unrest in Brazil* (Austin: University of Texas Press, 1970), 337.

[2] Thomas Skidmore, *Politics in Brazil 1930–1964* (Oxford: Oxford University Press, 1967), 301.

[3] Ibid., 302.

number of ordinary Brazilians remained loyal to democracy and even to centrist politics even in the last months of the Goulart government. If we look carefully at which actors were polarized (as we did in the Italian case), we see that polarization reached different levels of intensity in different arenas. Consequently, it is dangerous to draw conclusions about one arena from looking at another. In the highly public arenas of the streets and the legislature, Brazilians who wanted rapid and broad-based change battled those who wanted to conserve what existed in a long series of highly publicized confrontational dramas. These dramas contributed mightily to the demise of democracy, and they were certainly a manifestation of polarization. They were not, however, a manifestation of what most ordinary Brazilians saw as politically desirable.

Behind the two-sided struggle that was played out so vividly in public spaces was a much less polarized Brazil of ordinary people. It was less visible than the world that was depicted in much of the media, but it was no less real and much better suited for some sort of lasting (albeit flawed) electoral democracy. The complex and contrasting arenas of Brazilian politics are described below.

Polarization in Public Spaces

Political behavior cannot be fully understood unless it is contextualized. We cannot understand the breakdown of democracy in Brazil unless we recall that João Goulart assumed the presidency less than two years after Fidel Castro took power in Cuba. The triumph of Communism in Cuba, like the triumph of Bolshevism in Russia, had profound effects on friends and foes abroad. As a leading Brazilian radical put it in the late 1980s, "It is impossible to speak of that period without understanding what the Cuban revolution meant to my generation. The young people who didn't celebrate it were considered unpardonable imbeciles. It was a fascinating thing."[4]

No one knew exactly how many Brazilians found Cuba's armed revolution inspirational, but politicians of many sorts scurried to associate themselves with Castro and his comrades. Jânio Quadros, the president who preceded Goulart, visited Cuba in an effort to win votes back home, despite the fact that he was running on a right-wing

[4] Carlos Vereza, as quoted in Dênis de Morães, *A Esquerda e o Golpe de 1964* (Rio de Janeiro: Espaço e Tempo, 1989), 22.

Populist ticket.[5] He then awarded Che Guevara the most prestigious medal awarded to foreigners during the latter's visit to Brazil in August 1961.[6]

The heroic status accorded to Che and Fidel, and the openings extended to Communist countries more generally, were a source of serious concern for moderate and conservative forces in Brazil because they coincided with what many viewed as a resurgence of Brazilian Communism. The Brazilian Communist Party had been banned from participating in elections since 1947 (when courts declared it an agency of a foreign power). But the party continued to maintain visible positions in trade unions and even in Congress by running candidates with other party labels. The fact that the party had once secured over 8 percent of the vote in national elections and an impressive 20 percent of the vote in the state of São Paulo was not forgotten.[7]

No one could know how much support the Communist Party maintained when Goulart assumed the presidency in September 1964, but the fact that the new president had cooperated with known Communists in the past was taken by many as an ominous sign. Goulart had worked closely with party militants when he was minister of labor in 1953 and had openly fostered electoral alliances between the Communist Party and his own Brazilian Labor Party, the PTB, as well.[8] There was no evidence that Goulart was a Communist himself (indeed he was profoundly distrusted in many Marxist circles), but his previous actions were a serious source of contention and a serious liability even before he assumed office. Public polarization began early.

The conditions under which Goulart assumed office made the potential for polarization even greater, for he was installed in the presidency only because the elected president resigned. Jânio Quadros had won the 1960 elections with a 44.8 percent plurality, but he left office suddenly in August of 1961.[9] The Brazilian constitution mandated that the vice president assume the presidency, and though Goulart had been freely elected to the vice presidential post, his real and imagined asso-

---

[5] Ronald H. Chilcote, *The Brazilian Communist Party* (New York: Oxford University Press: 1963), 74. He visited Cuba with Francisco Julião, the Marxist organizer of peasant leagues in northeast Brazil.

[6] Ibid., 74–75.

[7] Simón Schwartzman, "Veinte Años de Democracia Representativa en Brasil, 1945–62," *Revista Latinoamericana de Ciência Política* 11, no. 1 (April 1971): 42. The vote for the Communist Party peaked in 1945. The figures cited are for congressional elections.

[8] Chilcote, *The Brazilian Communist Party*, 61.

[9] Quadros's reasons for leaving were and remain mysterious. He cited "dark" forces that made it impossible for him to do what he needed to do for the people of Brazil. Outsiders thought his resignation was a ploy to get more power from Congress. He expected to be called back to office but was not.

ciation with the radical Left provoked a panic on the Right.[10] A group of right-wing generals threatened to seize power if Goulart were allowed to take office. While the possibility of civil war loomed large, the Brazilian Congress resolved the succession crisis with a compromise: Goulart would be allowed to assume office, but his powers would be diluted. He would rule in a parliamentary system until a permanent constitutional change was put to a referendum. The fact that the Brazilian Congress was able to hammer out a compromise and avoid armed confrontation meant that polarization in the legislature had not reached fatal levels in 1961.

Polarization in other arenas suggested that the succession crisis would be only the first of many for Goulart. Political society might prove able to compromise, but civil society seemed less so. Brazilian trade unions became increasingly visible and, for many, increasingly threatening. Brazil's corporatist labor system had allowed unions little autonomy from the state but had always accorded state-approved union bureaucrats control of substantial resources, including funds for pensions and administration. With a sympathetic figure in the presidency, union leaders enjoyed increased opportunities to use these resources for their own political agenda. The image of an expanding and increasingly radicalized workforce loomed larger than ever on Brazil's political landscape. An increasing number of Brazilians began to fear the eventual creation of a *República Sindicalista,* a state dominated by left-wing trade unions.

Strikes were the primary means through which this image was constructed and these increased rapidly under Goulart. Figure 3.1 shows the trend.

The increase in strikes was an indicator of polarization, for it meant that workers and employers were unable to resolve their differences in less conflictual ways. But the increase in strikes was also a stimulant for further polarization. As trade unions appeared to grow stronger and more assertive, employers and their allies had greater incentives for mobilization themselves.

In São Paulo in 1962, for example, businessmen organized a Fund for Social Action to combat what they saw as the "demagoguery and ignorance" that threatened to destroy the business community itself.[11] Funds such as these (with likely supplements from the U.S. Central Intelligence Agency) stimulated the growth of a highly visible network of civic associations and opposition groups. These included, among

---

[10] Brazil's constitution had separate but simultaneous elections for president and vice president.

[11] Dulles, *Unrest in Brazil,* 189.

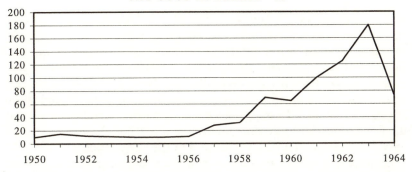

3.1. Strike activity in Brazil, 1950–1964. (*Source*: Salvador A. M. Sandoval, *Social Change and Labor Unrest in Brazil since 1945* [Boulder: Westview Press, 1993], 67.)

others, the Democratic Women's Campaign (CAMDE), the Democratic Youth Front (FJD), Democratic Parliamentary Action, and the Institute for Research and Social Studies (IPES). Attempts to resist the hegemony of Marxists in trade union leadership were embodied in new workers' associations in Rio, São Paulo, and other major cities.[12]

A process of pendular mobilization set in, giving politicians and citizens alike the sense that Brazil was separating into two camps. Left-wing and, later, right-wing activists worked to mobilize citizens in virtually all the major realms of Brazilian civil society. The vast Brazilian peasantry was a target of special concern. The peasantry had been excluded from the franchise in years past through the literacy requirement. By the early 1960s, the advance of literacy and the increasing talk of a change in the franchise laws gave peasant political preferences greater salience. Young people associated with Marxist or left-wing Catholic groups flooded into the countryside to teach reading and (not surprisingly) politics. The political content of their instructional materials became a source of nationwide controversy, especially since many were supplied at public expense by Goulart's Ministry of Education.[13] More controversial still were the efforts to mobilize rural trade unions

[12] These included groups such as REDESTRAL, the Democratic Resistance of Free Workers in Rio, and MSD, the Democratic Labor Movement in São Paulo. L. A. Moniz Bandeira, *O Governo João Goulart: As Lutas Sociais no Brasil* (Rio de Janeiro: Editora Civilização Brasileira, 1978), 69.

[13] The best known of these campaigns included the Movimento de Cultura Popular (MCP), sponsored by the government of Recife, the Centro Populares de Cultura (CPC), sponsored by the UNE in Rio, and the Movimento de Educação de Base (MEB), sponsored by the National Conference of Brazilian Bishops. For more details on the politics of the literacy campaigns, see Justina Iva de A. Silva, *Estudantes e Política: Estudo de um Movimento* (São Paulo: Cortez Editora, 1989), chap. 3.

and peasant leagues. A law passed on March 2, 1963 gave rural workers the same associational rights as industrial workers, and farmworkers' unions began to proliferate. The number of unions grew quickly,
from about 200 in January 1963 to about 1,800 by the time Goulart was
ousted. Most of them were controlled by the Communist União dos
Lavradores e Trabalhadores Agrícolas do Brasil (ULTAB).[14] Non-wage
laborers often joined peasant leagues. Those organized by Francisco
Julião became known internationally. Some 100,000 sharecroppers and
tenant farmers joined peasant leagues in the early 1960s.[15]

Landowners whose hegemony had been unquestioned for centuries thus found themselves facing a triple threat: left-wing peasant
voters, left-wing peasant unions, and peasant land-invasions that government forces either could not or would not reverse. They quickly
organized a series of counteroffensives that added to the sense of
growing polarities.[16]

In urban civil society, the mobilization of university students contributed to the sense of polarization as well. Brazilian students were mobilized before 1961, of course, but the level and scope of their activity
increased markedly in the Goulart years.[17] The National Students Union
(the UNE) took to the streets in Goulart's defense when right-wing
forces sought to deny him the presidency in 1961. The groups then took
Goulart's position on a number of controversial policy issues including
the Basic Reform. The UNE's links with left-wing workers' organizations expanded quickly, and new links with the rural poor were forged
through a series of literacy and theater programs funded through the
Ministry of Education.[18] The political content of the UNE programs, its
vocal opposition to foreign investment, its hostility to the United States,
and its new organizational ties to student groups from the Communist
Bloc led outsiders to conclude that the Marxist Left had gained hege-

[14] Dulles, *Unrest in Brazil*, 220–21.

[15] Philippe Schmitter, *Interest, Conflict and Political Change in Brazil* (Stanford: Stanford
University Press, 1971), 210.

[16] Some landowners felt so threatened that they hired small private armies equipped
with machine guns. For detailed coverage of the violence in the countryside from the
perspective of the Ligas and for a better understanding of the Ligas and their leaders,
see the compilation of Liga articles in *Ligas Camponesas*, ed. Francisco Julião (Cuernavaca:
CIDOC, 1969).

[17] The number of university students increased markedly as well. In 1960 there were
95,700 students in the country; by 1964 this number had grown to 121,000. For a detailed
history of the student movement from 1945–1966, see Robert Owen Myhr, *The Political
Role of University Students in Brazil* (Ann Arbor: University of Michigan Press, 1969). Figures on students are from p. 53.

[18] Government-UNE ties were especially strong during Paulo do Tirso's term as minister of education.

mony in the student community. The conservative press called the UNE a "province of the Soviet Union."[19] Divisions within the student community widened during a two-month long university strike and after violence broke out at a UNE national congress. In keeping with the patterns of pendular mobilization emerging elsewhere, centrist and right-wing groups organized a counteroffensive on this terrain as well. UNE headquarters were even machine-gunned by right-wing students associated with the Movimento Anti-Communista (the MAC).[20]

The image of a polarized citizenry grew increasingly vivid in March of 1964, when two major demonstrations took place. The first, on March 13 in Rio, was organized on behalf of Goulart by the General Confederation of Workers, the CGT. Its purpose was to provide physical evidence that the support for Goulart's most controversial reform proposals was strong and organized. Goulart had failed to secure congressional support for a number of projects, including the expansion of the suffrage to illiterates and a moderate agrarian reform. Frustrated and urged on by civic organizations to his left, the president decided to go over the heads of the political class and obtain what he hoped would be an irresistible popular mandate.[21] A herculean effort was coordinated with trade unions, student groups, and workers from rural areas. Literally thousands of individuals were bused into Rio at government expense. Some 150,000 people appeared in the Praça da República to cheer a long list of left-wing speakers, including Leonel Brizola and, finally, Goulart himself. Televised all over Brazil, the rally seemed to be (quite literally) a spectacular success. Goulart made plans for other similar rallies, in other locales, but the Rio rally was to be his last.

The coup began just eighteen days later, shortly after a vast counter-demonstration took place in São Paulo. The demonstration, called the Family March with God for Liberty, was organized in direct response to Goulart's rally six days before. Lore has it that a nun named Ana de Lurdes conceived of the rally on the night of the thirteenth while watching the Rio demonstration on television. On the fourteenth, fifty leaders of São Paulo civic associations met to plan the events. Five days later, with the assistance of over thirty different civic groups, half a

---

[19] This term appeared in the newspaper *O Estado do São Paulo.*

[20] Myhr lists the conservative opposition groups as the Democratic Youth Front, the University Solidarity Movement, and the Democratic University Vanguard, among others. He also gives some details on how more conservative groups began to win elections within the university community. For more details on the student movement in Brazil, see Silva, *Estudantes e Política.*

[21] For an insightful analysis of how and why Goulart took this action, see Skidmore, *Politics in Brazil,* 298.

million people flooded the streets of São Paulo to march from the Praça da República to the Praça da Se.[22] The marchers included predictable groups and figures from the extreme Right, but they also included "re-form-minded but moderate Catholics" and other centrists who simply "feared that Goulart was endangering economic growth."[23] The march-ers' placards were directed largely to the president himself. Some de-manded that he be impeached, others demanded that he be jailed. The turnout was even greater than expected, and plans were made to mobi-lize similar marches in cities throughout Brazil. A March 25 rally at-tracted thirty-thousand people in the port city of Santos, despite the fact that the CGT was especially strong there.[24] These demonstrations gave Goulart's opposition new confidence and additional incentives for further organization. Polarization in public spaces had reached a new high. It showed no signs of diminishing as the military coup began on March 31.[25]

The Meaning and Depth of Public Polarization

Our inquiry began by asking whether polarization was growing greater as South American democracies collapsed. The brief historical sketch given above illustrates that there was an increase in public po-larization in Brazil. Public spaces were filled with hordes of people whose behavior destabilized democracy. But what was the depth of public polarization? Was the polarization played out on Brazil's streets and TV screens a microcosm of Brazil as a whole? There is a great deal of evidence suggesting that the actors who were most visible in the drama of political polarization were not representative of ordinary Bra-zilians. Though radicals on both the Left and the Right may have be-lieved that they commanded intense popular support, they were suf-fering from a number of mutually reinforcing delusions.

The Left was much weaker than many actors across the political spectrum believed. Part of its weakness derived from serious internal

[22] The groups are listed in *O Estado de São Paulo*, 17 March 1964, 17. For a vivid descrip-tion of both the mobilizing capacities and the politics of women's civic associations, see Schmitter, *Interest, Conflict and Political Change*, 280.

[23] Skidmore, *Politics in Brazil*, 298–99.

[24] Dulles gives a vivid, English-language description of the march based on interviews with participants in Dulles, *Unrest in Brazil*, 274–78.

[25] For more details on mass mobilization in the last months of the Goulart regime, see Alberto Dinis et al., *Os Idos de Março e a Queda en Abril* (Rio de Janeiro: J. Alvaro, 1964); and Mario Victor, *Cinco Anos que Abalaram o Brasil: de Jânio Quadros ao Marechal Castelo Branco* (Rio de Janeiro: Editôra Civilização Brasileira, 1965).

divisions. The leaders of the Brazilian Communist Party and the less experienced members of the "Fidelista," or "Jacobin" Left, battled constantly over policies and tactics. Their differences were so dramatic that Brazilians often spoke of "the *Lefts*" rather than simply "the Left," but few observers recognized how frequently internecine struggles distracted leaders from forging the strong links to ordinary people that lasting loyalty required.

The Lefts' links to workers, peasants, and students were not nearly as strong as the dramas in public spaces made them seem. Outside observers seemed to view the situation as the television cameras did: both used wide-angle lenses that captured images of breadth rather than depth. A clearer focus on the microlevel would have given everyone a more realistic and more modest assessment of how much support leftist leaders actually had.

Brazil's working class was not nearly as radical as leftists hoped and rightists feared. Radicals had captured the leadership of nearly all the nation's union federations, and this strengthened interunion leadership networks. It also strengthened the ability to mount mass strikes. But those who analyzed people in their workplace recognized that "working class organizations rested on weak grassroots structures. Unions had little penetration in the factories."[26] A detailed study of automotive workers in São Paulo found that most people were not members of their workplace union at all and that 90 percent of those who were members virtually never went to their union hall.[27] The individuals who chose to join unions did so overwhelmingly for the medical, dental, and legal services that the unions provided and not for ideological reasons.[28]

A broad range of survey research suggests that the beliefs of working-class Brazilians differed from the beliefs of union leaders in dramatic ways. Workers attributed their low standard of living to "the government and politicians" rather than to "owners and employers."[29]

[26] Sandoval, *Social Change and Labor Unrest*, 91. For a similar conclusion, see John Humphrey, *Capitalist Control and Workers' Struggle in the Brazilian Auto Industry* (Princeton: Princeton University Press, 1982), 128.

[27] Leôncio Martins Rodrigues, *Industrialização e Atitudes Operárias* (São Paulo: Editôra Brasiliense, 1970), 107. When asked why they did not join the union, 32 percent said they saw no advantage in it. Fourteen percent said that unions did not assist workers, and 12 percent said they were simply not interested.

[28] Ibid., 108. Only 19 percent of the respondents said they joined unions because unions defend the workers' interests. Sixty-four percent of the respondents said they joined unions for medical, dental, or legal services.

[29] Ibid., 137.

Studies of job actions illustrated that workers struck for economic rather than political reasons[30] and that even some of the more publicized strikes derived from "non-revolutionary " motives devoid of "any ideological passions."[31] Studies of party preferences suggested that workers were not concentrated in the parties on the Left. In Belo Horizonte, workers were not likely to have a party preference at all, but those who did were more likely to prefer the moderate PSD over the PTB.[32] In Rio de Janeiro, workers' support for the PTB equaled but did not exceed support for other more conservative parties.[33] Manual workers' beliefs about policy issues were more left-leaning than those of other urban Brazilians, but statistically significant differences were "very tenuous." Only 19 percent of the workers interviewed favored a "profound agrarian reform," only 22 percent believed that U.S. companies hurt Brazil, and only 38 percent were in favor of extending voting rights to illiterates.[34] A study of trade union activists conducted just before Goulart came to power found that even workers who identified themselves as Communists or Socialists preferred "conciliation" to "conflicts with factory owners."[35] Even workers in the "labor aristocracy" (i.e., workers who had the most resources to resist class domination) were found to be "accomodationist" and "resistant to politicization."[36] Relatively moderate political beliefs seem to have been

[30] Youssef Cohen, *The Manipulation of Consent: The State and Working-Class Consciousness in Brazil* (Pittsburgh: University of Pittsburgh: 1989), 41 no. 28, citing Kenneth Paul Erickson, *The Brazilian Corporative State and Working-Class Politics* (Berkeley: University of California Press, 1977).

[31] Tocary Assis Bastos and Nilza da Silva Rocha, "Anotações Sobre a Greve dos Bancários em Minas," *Revista Brasileira de Estudos Políticos* 14 (January 1962): 128. The authors studied the 1961 bank strike in Minas.

[32] Of the 247 manual workers surveyed, 59 percent expressed no party preference, 15 percent preferred the PTB, 18 percent preferred the PSD, and 6 percent preferred the UDN. Antônio Octávio Cintra, "Partidos Políticos em Belo Horizonte Um Estudo do Eleitorado," *Dados* 5 (1968) 103.

[33] Ibid., 105.

[34] Ibid., 106.

[35] Michael Lowy and Sarah Chucid, "Opiniões e Atitudes de Líderes Sindicais Metalúrgicos," *Revista Brasileira de Estudos Políticos* 13 (January 1962): 150. The study was conducted in 1959 and directed toward leaders of the metalworkers' unions in São Paulo and Rio. A few years after the study was done, these unions were in the vanguard of the Left. It is thus particularly interesting to note the following responses to the question "What kind of person makes the best trade union leader?" Of the leaders 40.04 percent said "Communists and Socialists," 28 percent said nonpartisans and independents, and 32 percent said moderates. Lowy and Chucid, "Opiniões e Atitudes," 155. Even in a vanguard union, some 60 percent of activists preferred the leadership of noncommunists and nonsocialists.

[36] Carlos Estevam Martíns, "Integración Social y Movilización Política de la Clase Baja Urbana del Brasil," *Revista Latinoamericana de Ciência Política* 2, no. 1 (April 1971): 72.

TABLE 3.1
Lower-Class Residents' Party Preferences: Rio de Janeiro, 1960

Parties	Percent	N
Democratic Union (UDN)	29.2	182
Social Democratic Party (PSD)	8.0	50
Brazilian Workers Party (PTB)	52.3	326
Socialist Party (PSB)	1.8	11
Christian Democratic Party (PDC)	0.6	4
Social Progressive Party (PSP)	4.8	30
Republican Workers Party (PTR)	1.3	8
Popular Representation party (PRP)	0.5	3
Others	1.4	9
Total Respondents	74.1	623
Don't know/No answer	25.9	218
Total Sample	100	841

Source: G.A. Dillon Soares, principal investigator, *Voting Attitudes in Rio de Janeiro, Brazil*, ICPSR Edition, Inter-University Consortium for Political and Social Research, Ann Arbor, Michigan, 1976.

particularly prevalent among workers in private firms. As a result, strike calls were uniformly less effective in the private sector.[37]

Moderate beliefs may have had a strong foothold in lower-class urban communities in general. The study of party preferences summarized in table 3.1 illustrates that nearly one-third of those who expressed a party preference preferred the UDN over the PTB.

Analysts emphasized different factors in explaining the workers' moderation. Some argued that radical leaders had simply not tried "to change workers' beliefs and values."[38] Others argued that the same patronage networks that hampered radical politics in the countryside hampered politics in the city as well,[39] but whatever the cause, Brazil's working class was not nearly as mobilized and radical as the polarization in public spaces led people to believe.[40]

[37] Humphrey, *Capitalist Control and Workers' Struggle*, 21.

[38] Cohen, *The Manipulation of Consent*, 103.

[39] Fabio Wanderley Reis, "Participación, Movilización e Influencia Política: 'Neo-Coronelismo' en Brasil," *Revista Latinoamericana de Ciência Política* 11, no. 1 (April 1971): 75.

[40] Schmitter's extensive research on Brazilian associational life led him to conclude that people "vastly overestimated the ideological coherence of the radical populists and the degree of mass availability." He also wrote that "Brazil's vast number of less formal

The polarization of public space in the Brazilian countryside gave people an exaggerated image of peasant radicalization too. The expansion of farmworkers' unions and peasant leagues led many to believe that a revolution was brewing in the countryside. Yet, while government leaders warned of bloody violence and "unpreventable revolutions,"[41] sympathetic outsiders observed that peasant organizations "were less formidable than portrayed," that they involved "relatively little participation and still less leadership on the part of the peasantry themselves,"[42] and that their "revolutionary nature" and "class consciousness" were overrated and overpublicized.[43] Scholars who studied the peasantry and the rural proletariat in detail concluded that the rural labor movement was hampered by "competition between various [urban] leaders groups,"[44] that *camponeses* were not acting autonomously,[45] and that "the Peasant Leagues were in decline even before the military coup of 1964."[46]

Though some of the more experienced leftist leaders were fully aware of the moderate and conservative elements in working-class and peasant culture,[47] many others were deluded. Success in mobilizing

---

intermediary bodies" gave ordinary people other sets of loyalties that would not be so easily broken. *Interest, Conflict and Political Change in Brazil*, 390. Stepan also noted this in "Political Leadership and Regime Breakdown: Brazil," in *Latin America*, ed. J. Linz and A. Stepan (Baltimore: Johns Hopkins University Press, 1978), 124.

[41] These are the words of the governor of Rio Grande do Norte. See Manuel Correia de Andrade, *The Land and People of Northeast Brazil* (Albuquerque: University of New Mexico Press, 1980), 206.

[42] Peter Flynn, *Brazil: A Political Analysis* (Boulder: Westview Press, 1979), 263. Philippe Schmitter noted that peasant leagues were not only led from cities but actually based there. Anthony Leeds studied the region of the ligas in the early 1960s and found "no instance in which a leader of a peasant league or even a syndicate has arisen from the masses themselves." See Anthony Leeds, "Brazil and the Myth of Francisco Julião," in *Politics of Change in Latin America*, ed. Joseph Maier and Richard Weatherhead (New York: Frederick Praeger, 1964).

[43] Stepan, "Political Leadership and Regime Breakdown: Brazil," 112.

[44] Anthony W. Pereira, *The End of the Peasantry: The Rural Labor Movement in Northeast Brazil, 1961–1988* (Pittsburgh: University of Pittsburgh Press, 1997), 33. Pereira's study focuses on Pernambuco, where the rural movement was most developed. See pp. 29–35. For more on internal divisions, see Elide Rugai Bastos, *As Ligas Camponesas* (Petrópolis: Vozes, 1984), 100–117. For a detailed history of how Communist-led unions conflicted with the peasant leagues, see Fernando Antônio Azevêdo, *As Ligas Camponesas* (Rio de Janeiro: Paz e Terra, 1982), 85–112.

[45] Marta Cehelsky, *Land Reform in Brazil: The Management of Social Change* (Boulder: Westview Press, 1979), 45. She even goes as far as to say that the peasantry was "manipulated."

[46] Pereira, *End of the Peasantry*, 35.

[47] See, for example, Dênis de Morães and Francisco Viana, *Prestes: Lutas e Autocríticas* (Rio de Janeiro: Vozes, 1982), 171–72, where Prestes writes of the need for "the most basic struggles to elevate the consciousness of [Brazilian] workers."

TABLE 3.2
University Students' Party Preferences, 1964

Parties	Percent	N
Social Democratic Party (PSD)	12.9	132
Democratic Union (UDN)	41.1	421
Communist Party (PCB)	1.9	19
Christian Democratic Party (PDC)	19.6	201
Brazilian Workers Party (PTB)	8.4	86
National Workers Party (PTN)	2.4	25
Social Progressive Party (PSP)	5.8	59
Socialist Party (PSB)	5.2	53
Others	2.8	29
Total Respondents	77.5	1025
Don't know/No answer	22.5	297
Total Sample	100	1322

Source: S. M. Lipset, principal investigator, *University Students' Values, Vocations, and Political Orientations: Brazil*, ICPSR Edition, Inter-University Consortium for Political and Social Research, Ann Arbor, Michigan, 1964.

mass strikes and mass demonstrations "deceived left-wing leaders as to the extent of their strength."[48]

The highly publicized mobilizations of university students proved deceptive as well. An extensive study of student opinion concluded that though the "radical left" was "outstanding in providing a large share of demonstrators," its visibility was "entirely out of proportion with its actual support in the whole student body."[49] Even in the philosophy faculty (i.e., a group which was thought to be especially radical), moderate and centrist opinions were majoritarian. Only 32 percent of those interviewed even favored the legalization of the Communist Party.[50]

The survey of Brazilian university students summarized in tables 3.2 and 3.3 suggests the diversity of student opinion. Well over a third of those who expressed a party preference identified with the centrist PSD and PDC. Surprisingly, over 40 percent of the respondents preferred the conservative UDN.

[48] Sandoval, *Social Change and Labor Unrest*, 102.
[49] Glaucio A. D. Soares, "The Active Few," in *Student Politics*, ed. Seymour Martin Lipset (New York: Basic Books, 1967), 134.
[50] Ibid., 135.

TABLE 3.3
University Students' Political Orientations, 1964

Selected Items	Percent of Respondents	N
Approval or strong approval of the ideas and political actions of Francisco Julião	13.2	175
Approval or strong approval of the ideas and political actions of Fidel Castro	16.4	217
Favorable toward a completely command economy	5.6	74

Source: S. M. Lipset, principal investigator, *University Students' Values, Vocations, and Political Orientations: Brazil.*

Note: For the first, second, and third items the percent of the sample (N = 1322) not responding is 31.5, 6.6, and 12.7, respectively.

The rejection of radicalism is confirmed in table 3.3. Well under one-fifth of the students responding expressed agreement with the actions of Fidel Castro or with the actions of radical peasant leader Francisco Julião. Support for a fully command economy was even weaker.

Given the ideological differences outlined above, it is not surprising that well-informed leftist analysts would observe the "political limitations" of Brazil's student movement, underscoring that the growth of movement activity was "restricted to only the most politicized sectors" of the student body.[51]

Polarization's Limits

The polarization metaphor fits the Brazilian case only partially. The leaders of civil society were often polarized, and they often inspired their followers to confront their polar opposites in public spaces. These dramatic confrontations were certainly a form of polarization, but the evidence presented above suggests that ordinary people were not nearly as polarized as their leaders. Electoral data confirm this impression and further undermine the utility of the polarization metaphor. Sartori's classic conception of polarization focuses on the act of voting: due to the choices of ordinary voters, anti-system parties grow pro-

[51] Francisco Weffort, "Política de Massas," in *Política e Revolução Social no Brasil*, ed. Octavo Ianni (Rio de Janeiro: Editôra Civilização Brasileira: 1965), 166.

gressively stronger, and centrist parties grow progressively weaker. Neither of these trends is evident in Brazil.

There is no hard evidence that anti-system parties were growing more popular as Brazilian democracy approached its collapse. Anti-system groups were certainly more visible, but visibility and popularity are conceptually distinct. How much vote support did anti-system parties attract? The most obvious candidate for the "anti-system" label on the Left was the Brazilian Communist Party, but the party's identity was so ambiguous that the label might be inappropriate. The PCB's official documents contained statements of an anti-system nature (including warnings about "violent confrontations with reactionary forces"),[52] but in the real world of Brazilian politics, the party was "a voice for caution."[53] Luis Carlos Prestes, the PCB's leader, was a centripetal rather than a centrifugal force in the months leading up to the coup. He constantly warned against actions that would drive the bourgeoisie away from the reform coalition and against any "premature attempt to radicalize the country."[54] He joined forces with moderates in the PTB, the PSD, and the UDN for the formation of a Broad Front to promote cooperation in the Congress and to ensure that the 1965 elections would indeed be held.[55] Finally, he tried to ameliorate the fears brought on by the tone of the March 13 demonstration in Rio. In a highly publicized speech three days after the rally, he reassured listeners that "the structural reforms that are being demanded" are still possible "under the present system." He insisted that "the patriotic and democratic forces in ... the country be unified," that they were "very wide-ranging [reaching] even into the urban middle classes and into the national bourgeoisie," and that "the peaceful pathway" was "in the best interests of the workers."[56] Prestes sought to stem rather than stimulate polarization and was therefore the opposite of the classic "anti-system" leader.

Regardless of whether the PCB was anti-system or not, its popularity could not accurately be measured because the party was restricted from electoral competition. Ironically, the PCB's electoral exclusion enabled people on both the Left and the Right to construct mutually reinforcing fantasies about the party's increasing support. The best evidence available suggests that the popularity of the PCB was not

---

[52] Chilcote, *The Brazilian Communist Party*, 81.

[53] Skidmore, *Politics in Brazil*, 278.

[54] Stepan, "Political Leadership and Regime Breakdown," 124.

[55] For more on Prestes and his conciliatory attitudes, see Skidmore, *Politics in Brazil*, 282–83.

[56] Ibid., 293.

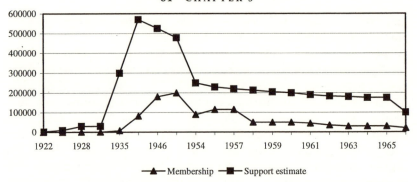

3.2. Membership and support: Brazilian Communist Party, 1922–1966. (*Source*: Chilcote, *The Brazilian Communist Party,* 117.)

increasing at all in the years prior to Goulart's ouster. Ronald Chilcote makes the point clearly with the evidence presented in figure 3.2.

Even when it ran candidates using other party labels, the PCB's support was surprisingly weak. The Partido Socialista Brasileiro was a favorite Communist refuge and completely legal, but its electoral returns were surprisingly meager. Running alone or in coalition, it obtained only 5 of the 409 seats in the 1962 Congress. Contradicting what we would expect in a situation of polarization, this represented a dramatic *loss* of seats from a high of 9 in 1958. All told, Communist Party members (running on various slates) won only 4 percent of the contested seats in 1962.[57] For better or worse, the parties that situated themselves on the far left of the political spectrum received the electoral support of only a tiny minority of ordinary Brazilians.[58]

On the far right of the party spectrum we see the same meager vote support. The nation's largest (and possibly only) right-wing extremist party was the Partido de Representação Popular, the PRP. Advocating a corporatist form of government modeled loosely on the Salazar regime in Portugal, the party offered a clear authoritarian alternative, yet voters rejected this option overwhelmingly. Despite the turmoil of the early Goulart years, the PRP gained a paltry 1.2 percent of the seats in the 1962 congressional races. This meant a slight increase over past

---

[57] This figure comes from PCB Party leader Luis Carlos Prestes, as quoted in Dulles, *Unrest in Brazil,* 184.

[58] Nélson Sampaio de Sousa wrote that "the communists were a highly active but small minority and the socialists were simply a club of intellectuals without an electorate." "As Eleições Bahianas de 1962," *Revista Brasileira de Estudos Poíticos* 16 (Janeiro de 1964): 172.

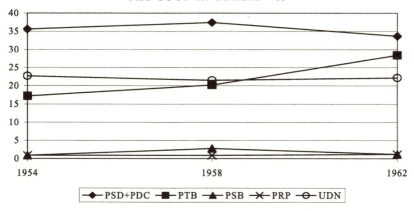

3.3. Voters' party choices in the Brazilian Congressional Elections, 1954–1962: Percent of seats won by selected parties. (*Source*: Nohlen, *Enciclopedia Electoral*, 110.)

trends but can hardly be considered a groundswell of support. [59] The very small percentage of the vote garnered by parties who situated themselves on the extremes of the political spectrum make it impossible to argue that ordinary people were turning to anti-system parties as Brazilian democracy collapsed.

A look at the evidence summarized in figures 3.3 and 3.4 shows that the other hallmark of polarization is not evident in the Brazilian case either. Ordinary people were not defecting from centrist parties en masse in October of 1962. Brazil had two parties that were widely identified as centrist in the years before Goulart's fall: the Social Democratic Party (PSD) and the Christian Democratic Party (PDC). Though the PSD's share of congressional seats dropped six percentage points between 1954 and 1962, the loss was nearly offset by the increase in the proportion of seats won by the centrist Christian Democratic Party. Figure 3.3 shows the trend.

The Center parties actually increased the absolute number of seats they won between 1954 and 1962, from 116 to 138. Figure 3.4 shows this pattern. In terms of both seats and votes, centrist parties held their own in the 1962 elections. Voters simply did not polarize as predicted.

[59] The votes attracted by coalitions that had the PRP as a member dropped from 9.4 percent of the vote in 1958 to 5.2 percent of the vote in 1962 (1,087,125 voters vs. 633,859 voters). See Dieter Nohlen, ed., *Enciclopedia Electoral Latinoamericana y del Caribe* (San José: Instituto Interamericano de Derechos Humanos, 1993), 110–11, for figures.

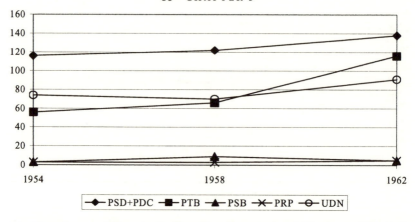

3.4. Voters' party choices in the Brazilian Congressional Elections, 1954–1962: Number of seats won by selected parties. (*Source*: Nohlen, *Enciclopedia Electoral*, 121.)

The highly politicized media often failed to emphasize the resilience of the Center and emphasized changes in support for other parties instead. This was not hard to do because changes in the size of congressional party delegations were easily misread as dramatic changes in voter preference. The UDN, for example, was Brazil's major conservative party. Though its composition was heterogeneous, it was the party home of some of the most ultraconservative figures in the country. When the 1962 elections added an impressive twenty-seven deputies to the UDN's congressional delegation, left-wing newspapers wrote of an ominous swing to the Right, but the change in seats was largely the result of an increase in the size of Congress. As figure 3.3 shows, the *percentage* of congressional seats held by the UDN was constant from 1954 through 1962.

The pattern of support for the PTB was different. The percentage of the electorate voting for PTB candidates rose significantly from 1958 to 1962. But this change was also subject to misinterpretation.[60] When the PTB increased its 1962 congressional delegation by fifty seats, newspapers on the Right wrote that Brazilian voters were making ominous moves leftward.[61]

---

[60] The seat figures come from Scott Mainwaring, "Brazil: Weak Parties, Feckless Democracy," in Mainwaring and Scully, *Building Democratic Institutions*, 360; and Nohlen, *Enciclopedia Electoral*, 121.

[61] Despite its highly heterogeneous following, the party was often seen simply as a party of the Left. The party was formed by Getulio Vargas to attract the votes of Brazil's growing urban working class, but its voting base was much more diverse.

Yet the dramatic increase in the number of seats was not the result of a radical change in the preferences of ordinary people. Three facts enable us to understand the increase in context. First, at least a dozen of the deputies in the PTB delegation were not elected on the PTB slate at all. They joined the party delegation after the elections, just as congress convened.[62] Second, the vast majority of the thirty-eight seats that the party actually did win were won in a diverse range of coalitions. In the constituencies where the PTB ran alone, its absolute number of votes actually *decreased* by more than 100,000.[63] Third, the heterogeneity of the PTB and its candidates made it problematic to read its vote support as a straightforward endorsement of the Left anyway. As scholars from the United States emphasized, "Despite its association with urban labor, the PTB has also been the party of numerous wealthy individuals and interests, particularly in areas where there is little or no urban working class."[64] The PTB still had a complicated identity and a mixed electorate in 1962. Fourth, and most importantly, the Brazilian electorate itself had expanded dramatically during the years in which the PTB expanded its support. Some 2,788,522 new voters joined the electorate in 1958. A further 2,068,224 voters were enfranchised by 1962. This means that 16.3 percent of those who voted in 1962 had probably never voted before. This change in the electorate should not be confused with a change in voter preferences. Indeed, given the massive growth of the voting population, it is remarkable that there was not much more change in patterns of party support. It is not surprising that so many of the newly enfranchised voters would be attracted to the PTB. Most of the new voters were either young people who had just reached voting age or adults who had previously been unable to pass the voting literacy test. Both of these groups, but especially the latter, were the "natural constituency" of a labor party. Put in this context, the continuities in party seat shares seem more remarkable than the changes.

Despite the dramatic mobilization of civic groups in public spaces, analysts of the 1962 elections noted the absence of a "clear-cut trend either to the Left or to the Right on the national level."[65] They noted the presence of "the same faces in Congress as for many years past"[66] and the "marked tendency for those already holding office to be re-

---

[62] *Brazil Election Factbook* (Washington, D.C.: Institute for the Comparative Study of Political Systems, 1965), 67.

[63] Nohlen, *Enciclopedia Electoral*, 110.

[64] *Brazil Election Factbook*, 44.

[65] Skidmore, *Politics in Brazil*, 231.

[66] Flynn, *Brazil: A Political Analysis*, 241.

elected."[67] Thomas Skidmore's conclusion is especially relevant: "The congressional elections of October 1962 . . . confirmed the strength of the Center. The Congress retained its relatively non-ideological character and the middle positions in most parties continued to hold the balance of power within the two chambers."[68]

The endorsement of continuity that was reflected in the 1962 congressional elections was reflected in the gubernatorial elections as well. Eleven governorships were being contested in October 1962. In a highly decentralized federal system, these races were of substantial political importance. But like the congressional races, the vast majority were conducted with surprising "calm."[69] Those that were hotly contested were often the subject of exaggerated fears. The race for the governorship of Pernambuco, for example, was constructed by some as a choice between Communist dictatorship and freedom. When the Socialist candidate, Miguel Arraes, won the popular mandate, right-wing forces throughout the country read it as an ominous sign. In fact, Arraes's personal commitment to democracy was unassailable,[70] and he owed his electoral victory less to a massive groundswell of revolutionary fervor than to his plodding success at gaining the votes of newly enfranchised sugarcane workers. Exemplifying the ambiguity of so many political identities in Brazil, Arraes also owed his victory to the financial backing of a wealthy São Paulo industrialist.[71]

Overall, the 1962 gubernatorial elections "confirmed the strength of the Center."[72] Rather than being torn asunder by centripetal forces, the Brazilian party system was finally becoming consolidated.[73] Instead of aligning themselves in intransigent blocs, parties showed themselves to be increasingly willing to cooperate and form coalitions. As table 3.4 illustrates, the proportion of governors elected by coalitions was rising as democracy collapsed.

The number of governors elected with *mixed* coalitions—that is, the number of governors who attracted votes from the Center, Right, and Left—went up dramatically in 1962. This is the opposite of what we

[67] Ibid., 240.

[68] Skidmore, *Politics in Brazil*, 223.

[69] Flynn, describes them as "calm and relatively insignificant." *Brazil: A Political Analysis*, 240.

[70] Skidmore, *Politics in Brazil*, 282.

[71] The support came from José Ermirio de Morais, who ran for the federal Senate on the PTB ticket and won (with Arraes's endorsement). See Skidmore, *Politics in Brazil*, 231. For more on how Arraes differed from anti-system actors such as Brizola, see Skidmore, pp. 281–83.

[72] Ibid., 223.

[73] Antônio Lavareda, *A Democracia nas Urnas: O Processo Partidario Eleitoral Brasileiro* (Rio de Janeiro: Rio Fundo Editoria, 1991), 121.

TABLE 3.4
Brazilian State Governors by Party, 1960–1962

Party	1960	1962
PTB	—	Acre
UDN	Alagoas, Guanabara, Mato Grosso	—
PSD	Goiás, Rio Grande do Norte	Sergipe
PST	—	Pernambuco
Center-Left Coalitions	—	—
Center-Populist Coalitions	Pará	Rio de Janeiro, São Paulo
Center Coalitions	Santa Catarina	
Center-Right Coalitions	Paraná	Piauí, Rio Grande do Sul
Mixed Coalitions with Center Parties	Maranhão	Amazonas, Espírito Santo, Ceará
Mixed Coalitions without Center Parties	Paraíba	Bahia
Right Coalitions	Minas Gerais	—

Source: *Brazilian Election Factbook*, 59.
Note: Coalitions were classified according to the following scheme: Left: PCB and PSB; Populist: PTB, PTN, PSP, PST, and MTR; Center: PSD and PDC; Right: UDN, PL, PR, PRP, PPS, and PRT. These categorizations are based on those of Mainwaring, "Brazil: Weak Parties, Feckless Democracy," 356.

would expect in a polarized system. The fact that the candidates backed by centrist parties triumphed in ten out of eleven gubernatorial races argues against the polarization metaphor, too.

The final set of evidence weighing against the idea that ordinary people were polarizing at the polls comes from the referendum of 6 January 1963. This poll gave voters two choices. They could vote to continue the semiparliamentary regime that had been imposed to placate the opposition to Goulart's assumption of the presidency, or they could vote to restore the full powers of the presidency embodied in the 1946 constitution. Despite all the turmoil in the streets and the economy and despite widespread criticism of Goulart as a leader, Brazilians gave overwhelming support to a restoration of the constitution. Seventy-seven percent of those who went to the polls voted to restore presidentialism and increase Goulart's powers. The fact that the support for presidentialism reached as high as 71 percent in states where the PTB was weak (such as Minas Gerais) suggests that voters were not behaving in a rigidly partisan way.[74] This level of consensus is out of keeping with the image of a polarized polity. It bolsters the evidence that Brazilians wanted some continuity with the past rather than radical change. The fact that such consensus was still possible just fourteen months before the March 31 coup is remarkable.[75]

It is clear that polls and public spaces sent out radically different political signals. Which were more representative of ordinary Brazilians? The signals sent at the polls coincided with those tapped by public opinion surveys. Public opinion data provide a final set of arguments against the polarization metaphor.

Overall, Brazilians were still embracing moderate positions even in March of 1964. Polls administered just weeks before the coup suggested that Brazilians were neither radical nor reactionary but reformist instead. This image was confirmed in various types of questions, including those about specific policies, specific candidates, and general policy orientations. Table 3.5 presents public opinion on three concrete policy issues.

The first subtable shows that a broad proportion of Brazilians was supportive of an agrarian reform. Only a small sector of society refused to recognize the need for redistribution. The second subtable shows that the specific land-reform policy advocated by Goulart attracted the support of an overwhelming 60 percent of those polled. Despite the frenzy in the conservative press when Goulart announced his plan, most Brazilians supported his project. The third subtable shows the limits of the reformist mentality. A solid 76 percent of those polled rejected the idea of legalizing the Brazilian Communist Party. This reform was advocated by Goulart too, but was extremely unpopular. Brazilians were willing to back change, even a change in property relations, but they feared giving free rein to what they thought to be an anti-system party.

That ordinary Brazilians were still overwhelmingly "pro-system" is illustrated by their projected choices for a future president. Table 3.6 shows the popularity of a wide range of presidential hopefuls. Miguel Arraes, the governor of Prenambuco, represents the option farthest to the Left. Carlos Lacerda, the governor of Guanabara, represents the option farthest to the Right. The centrist position is dominated by Jus-

---

[74] These figures are taken from the *Brazilian Election Factbook*, 81.

[75] The fact that turnout would reach over 66 percent was remarkable, too, since political machines were not working especially hard to get out the vote. See Bonifacio Furteo, "Democracia de Poucos," *Revista Brasileira de Estudos Políticos* 16 (Janeiro 1964): 57.

TABLE 3.5
Public Opinion on Three Divisive Policy Questions

A. Percent of Citizens Favorable to an Agrarian Reform

Selected States	Favorable	Unfavorable	Don't Know
São Paulo	66	13	21
Rio de Janeiro	82	9	9
Belo Horizonte	67	16	17
Porto Alegre	70	17	13
Recife	70	7	23
Salvador	74	9	17
Fortaleza	68	13	19
Curitiba	61	11	28
Total	72	11	16

B. Percent of Citizens Favorable to Goulart's Agrarian Reform Proposed on March 1964

Selected States	Favorable	Unfavorable	Don't Know
São Paulo	56	21	23
Rio de Janeiro	66	19	15
Belo Horizonte	54	22	24
Porto Alegre	63	22	15
Recife	59	13	28
Salvador	55	1	34
Fortaleza	55	17	28
Curitiba	60	14	26
Total	60	19	21

C. Percent of Citizens Favorable to the Legalization of the Brazilian Communist Party

Selected States	Favorable	Unfavorable	Don't Know
São Paulo	13	77	10
Rio de Janeiro	16	75	9
Belo Horizonte	10	84	6
Porto Alegre	18	77	5
Recife	20	65	15
Salvador	12	75	13
Fortaleza	19	69	12
Curitiba	7	83	10
Total	14	76	9

Source: Antônio Lavareda, *A Democracia nas Urnas: O Processo Partidario Eleitoral Brasileiro* (Rio de Janeiro: Rio Fundo Editoria, 1991), 157–59.

TABLE 3.6
Voters' Projected Choices for President in Selected Brazilian States, 1964

State	Juscelino Kubitschek	Carlos Lacerda	Carvalho Pinto	Miguel Arraes	Ademar De Barros	Magalhães Pinto	Alziro Zarur	DK/ DA
São Paulo	22	16	24	3	9	3	1	21
Rio de Janeiro	27	33	4	10	7	2	5	11
Belo Horizonte	52	17	1	5	6	6	2	9
Porto Alegre	18	19	11	10	12	4	1	24
Recife	24	17	4	34	3	0	1	17
Salvador	40	17	3	6	9	3	2	18
Fortaleza	32	19	5	2	9	0	3	29
Curitiba	52	16	2	13	4	0	0	12
Total	28	22	12	8	8	2	2	17

Source: Lavareda, *A Democracia nas Urnas*, 154.
Note: Values are in percent

celino Kubitschek and Carlos Carvalho Pinto. Though there were no unambiguously anti-system options available to chose from, the extremes of the questionnaire's spectrum were not especially popular. A full 40 percent of the people polled chose one of the moderates as their top candidate. Juscelino Kubitschek alone polled a plurality of 28 percent in a field of seven. In a follow-up question that narrowed the choices to only four candidates, 37 percent said they would vote for Kubitschek. Carlos Lacerda was second with 25 percent support.[76] An absolute majority of Brazilians chose a moderate candidate.

Brazilians' choices for president were in line with their general policy orientations. When asked if their national government should follow a rightist, centrist, or leftist policy line, Brazilians gave the responses described in table 3.7.

The centrist position was most popular in the nation as a whole, attracting 45 percent of the population. In six out of ten regions, at least 49 percent of the population sought a government with a centrist orientation. This is remarkable in a nation in the depths of economic and mobilizational crises.

[76] Lavareda, *A Democracia nas Urnas*, 155. Respondents were asked to choose between Ademar de Barros, Kubitschek, Lacerda, and a moderate from the UDN named Magalhães Pinto.

TABLE 3.7

Voters' Policy Orientation in Selected Brazilian States: Left, Right,
or Center? (June–July 1963)

State	Right	Center	Left	Don't Know
São Paulo	21	51	16	12
Guanabara	33	38	17	12
Belo Horizonte	17	62	11	10
Porto Alegre	13	21	46	20
Recife	14	36	39	11
Salvador	12	49	24	15
Fortaleza	11	59	15	15
Curitiba	15	49	14	22
Belém	19	54	10	17
Niterói	37	30	13	20
Total	23	45	19	13

Source: Relatorio IBOPE as presented in Lavareda, *A Democracia nas Urnas*, 156.
Note: Values are in percent.

More remarkable still is the tenacity with which people held to the centrist position. Table 3.8 summarizes the results of a poll taken a year after the one summarized above. The poll asked voters which presidential candidate they would chose if they had to choose among four men. The centrist options, Magalhães Pinto and Juscelino Kubitschek, got a total of 44 percent support. Thus is just one percentage point below the support for Center policies recorded in June and July the year before. Rising strike rates, rising inflation, and even the March 13 rally in Rio failed to enfeeble the Center in the manner that the polarization hypothesis would predict.

The evidence presented above suggests that most ordinary Brazilians were centrist in their political orientation when the military dictatorship began in 1964. They did not polarize as predicted, and they were not guilty of actively petitioning for a dictatorial solution to Brazil's many performance crises.[77]

[77] My perceptions jibe with those of Bolivar Lamounier, who has long argued that Brazil has an "underappreciated tradition of political pluralism" and that it was strong enough inside the military and out to soften military rule. A cogent summary of his position appears in Frances Hagopian, *Traditional Politics and Regime Change in Brazil* (New York: Cambridge University Press, 1996), 12.

TABLE 3.8

Voters' Projected Choices for Major Presidential Candidates, March 1964

State	Ademar de Barros	Juscelino Kubitschek	Carlos Lacerda	Magalhaes Pinto	DK/DA
São Paulo	10	32	22	8	28
Rio de Janeiro	8	36	34	6	16
Belo Horizonte	6	54	19	9	12
Porto Alegre	16	25	24	13	21
Recife	6	45	19	4	25
Salvador	9	45	18	6	21
Curitiba	11	36	19	1	33
Fortaleza	5	60	16	3	15
Total	9	37	25	7	23

Source: Relatorio IBOPE, as presented in Lavareda, *A Democracia nas Urnas*, 155.
Note: Values are in percent.

Ordinary people were guilty of passivity when the military moved against the constitutional government, which seems discordant with the facts presented thus far. If a large sector of the politically active population were still in favor of democracy, why was the coup carried out so easily? Fear and the disorientation brought on by mass arrests are powerful explanations. They are not sufficient explanations though, for both are sometimes overcome, as the defense of the Spanish Republic illustrates. An additional explanation derives from the fact that civilians were simply unaware that the Brazilian military was going to establish a longstanding dictatorship. Their misperceptions were based on both historical and contemporary experience.

Prior to 1964, the Brazilian military had always played a moderator role, occasionally stepping in to remove civilian governments but never assuming governmental power itself. Military and civilian elites made distinctions between military intervention and military rule, and the latter had long been deemed illegitimate by both groups.[78] There is little evidence that civilians expected the military to behave differently in 1964. Historical experience had led people to expect a brief intervention, followed by new elections.

Contemporary experience reinforced this erroneous expectation because even Goulart's most strident right-wing civilian opponents

[78] Alfred Stepan, *The Military in Politics: Changing Patterns in Brazil* (Princeton: Princeton University Press, 1971), 85–121.

seemed wedded to the discourse of democracy and constitutionalism. The Family March for Liberty began with a speech declaring "faith in the armed forces" and "faith in democracy."[79] It ended with a cathedral mass dedicated to democracy's "salvation."[80] A content analysis of newspapers in the weeks immediately preceding the coup found *no* editorials that explicitly asked the military to assume power. Yet dozens of editorials called for the military to intervene and remove Goulart so that democracy might be preserved.[81]

One of the main reasons that democratic discourse resonated with such a broad spectrum of the political class is that a good many politicians were optimistic about their own abilities to play the electoral game and win.[82] Under Brazil's constitution, presidents were not permitted consecutive terms and even presidents' relatives were unable to rule in their succession. This meant that the upcoming October 1965 presidential election was a wide-open race. Neither Goulart nor Brizola could run. A broad set of political leaders sought presidential nominations and thus had a vested interest in the continuation of electoral democracy. Right-wing figures who might have been the natural allies of the military coup-makers were restrained from joining a coup coalition by their own electoral ambitions. If they had a chance of winning or even benefiting from the upcoming race, the game should go on.[83]

The March 13 rally was thus a turning point, not simply because it posed a threat to property relations but because it posed a threat to the electoral game that so many sought to play. Brizola's strident calls to close down the Congress and rewrite the constitution were mistakenly attributed to Goulart as well.[84] These threats gave the strong impression that the president himself was about to change the rules of the game and that the elections that so many sought would never take place.[85] Elites who had been constrained only by electoral ambitions

[79] These are the words of Auro de Moura Andrade, as quoted in Dulles, *Unrest in Brazil*, 276.

[80] Ibid.

[81] Stepan, *The Military in Politics*, 115–16.

[82] See Stepan, "Political Leadership and Regime Breakdown," 121, and Skidmore, *Politics in Brazil*, 273–74, for more discussion of Brazil's many presidential hopefuls.

[83] The key example here is Carlos Lacerda, who was likely to get the nomination for presidency at the UDN congress scheduled for April. Another example is Ademar de Barros, who was also a serious presidential contender. Relying only on his personalist, São Paulo–based PSP for support, he needed the national exposure brought on by his battles with Goulart to improve his position.

[84] Goulart called for constitutional changes but took pains to emphasize that he would have them ratified by the existing Congress. Flynn, *Brazil: A Political Analysis*, 282.

[85] As Stepan writes, "When it appeared that Goulart was trying to restructure the political system, an attempt which might preclude their attempts at the presidency, [the

now found defection easier. Ordinary people who had been waiting patiently for new elections to produce a new set of national leaders now found military intervention much less unpalatable. The military coup became, for some, a bizarre guarantee that elections would indeed be held.[86] This tragic irony does much to explain why so many people were passive when the military finally took control.

What finally caused the coup? In Brazil, as in so many European states, the ouster of the elected government was ultimately the result of factors only peripherally related to the political actions of ordinary citizens. People's reactions to the government's "performance failures" certainly played a role in Brazilian democracy's collapse, but what seems most remarkable in retrospect is how little economic crisis contributes to explaining the nature and timing of regime defections. The coup coalition was built precariously and late—long after the onset of economic crisis. As Stepan reminds us, even "twelve days *after* the 13 March rally, no winning coalitions existed to overthrow Goulart." [87]

Ultimately the coup coalition was forged only when the president threatened the principle of military discipline. The catalyst for this coup (and many others) was a conflict between the chief executive and the military as an institution.

The conflict began when a small group of sailors, led by a university-trained conscript named José Anselmo, organized a sort of trade union for sailors called the AMFBN. Anselmo had been active in radical groups within the UNE and saw his conscription as an opportunity to radicalize enlisted men by forging stronger ties between working-class men within the military and trade unionists within the CGT. When he proposed that the organization demonstrate in support of the government and in solidarity with Petrobras workers, the minister of the navy, Admiral Silvio Mota, said no. Arguing that military units must remain "tranquil and apolitical," Silvio Mota warned that those participating would be punished. The demonstration took place anyway and when the admiral ordered the arrest of the twelve directors of the Associação, nearly two-thousand enlisted men defied orders and met in solidarity with Anselmo in the headquarters of the Metalworkers' Union. Some six hundred men stayed to occupy the building, in clear (and televised) defiance of their military superiors. Goulart made the fatal mistake of siding with the mutineers. He accepted Silvio Mota's

---

governors of São Paulo and Minas Gerais] began to plot actively against Goulart." "Political Leadership and Regime Breakdown," 128.

[86] Kubitschek, who was the most popular presidential hopeful, sought assurances on this score and backed Castelo Branco only when he had the general's assurances that the October elections would indeed take place. Dulles, *Unrest in Brazil*, 353.

[87] Stepan, "Political Leadership and Regime Breakdown," 129.

resignation and agreed to an amnesty for Anselmo and his supporters.[88] His willingness to side with civilians on the Left against even the most progressive and loyal elements of the military was devastating to executive–military relations. It was also fuel for reactionary forces who had argued that the nation was on the verge of a Bolshevik-style coup. The fact that, days before the occupation, Goulart's Ministry of Education had sent the Sailors' Association the classic film *Potemkin* fueled conspiracy theories even further.[89] The conflict reached the boiling point when Goulart made a televised speech on March 30 and accused those "speaking about discipline" of being "the eternal enemies of democracy."[90]

The president's actions threatened even his key military allies, most notably General Amaury Kruel, the commander of the Second Army. Kruel was a trusted friend and feared that Goulart's behavior was the result of Communist manipulation. He urged Goulart to make a public statement dissociating himself from a long series of "individuals and organizations most provocative to the armed forces." When Goulart refused to make the statement, General Kruel made a momentous statement of his own. He directed it toward the growing number of officers who were abandoning the legalist position. The Second Army, he announced, was now determined to "break the circle of Communism which now compromises the authority of the government of the Republic."[91] The defection of Goulart's most strategic ally meant the undoing of Brazilian democracy.[92]

To the extent that ordinary people played a significant role in this drama at all, it was a perverse one. They became semifictional characters accorded different attributes by different principal actors. For Goulart (near the end of his presidency if not before), the people of Brazil were the saviors of reform. Congress was his nemesis, but if he could appeal directly to the people themselves, the profound political and economic changes he sought might be realized. He believed that a critical mass of ordinary Brazilians was not only leftist but willing to fight for the preservation of his government. The emotional reception

---

[88] For more details of these complicated events, see Victor, *Cinco Anos que Abalaram o Brasil*. For a succinct and lucid English language analysis, see Stepan, "Political Leadership and Regime Breakdown," 130–31.

[89] Flynn, *Brazil: A Political Analysis*, 287–88.

[90] *Correio da Manha*, 31 March 1964.

[91] This interpretation draws heavily on Flynn, *Brazil: A Political Analysis*, 296. The words in the second quotation cited are those of Kruel himself.

[92] For more on the coup and the strategic role played by Kruel, see Jayme Portella de Mello, *A Revolução e o Governo Costa y Silva* (Rio de Janeiro: Guavira, 1979).

he got at the March 13 rally reinforced this vision and strengthened the arguments of his most radical advisers.

Many of Goulart's enemies constructed an image of ordinary Brazilians that overlapped in ironic ways with the president's own. Conservative and reactionary forces opposed the expansion of voting rights and the legalization of the Communist Party precisely because they feared that poor Brazilians really were as Goulart hoped: ready to back anti-system forces en masse.

The ultimate irony was that the voices of ordinary people were often drowned out by the cacophony of elite haranguing. Brazil's party system, the set of institutions that was supposed to carry the clearest messages about popular preferences, failed miserably. It did not fail because it was a vehicle for polarization. It failed, in a curious way, because it bore so *little* relation to the bipolar model that the polarization metaphor uses for a base. Brazil's party system was multipolar and opaque.[93] This is why the resilience of centrist opinion was obscured. This is also why the strength of anti-system parties and the Left in general were the subject of such delusion.

The strength and resilience of centrist opinion was obscured by the multipolarity of the Brazilian party system. Personalism, regionalism, and populism meant that many important political parties were not easily fitted on a Left-Right ideological spectrum. Each contained its own internal Left, Center, and Right divisions, and many attracted the support of centrist voters. Since centrist voters did not concentrate their support in a single party, they assumed a less salient presence in the system as a whole. Centrist parties existed and were still maintaining most of their vote support (as was shown above), but their resilience was often overshadowed by changes in support for parties with more complex identities, such as the populist PTB or the populist, personalist, and regionalist PSP. The diversity within Brazilian parties, and the importance of cleavages based on regionalism, religiosity, and personalism meant that the multipolar system could not be "read" as easily as a unilinear system might have been. Voter preferences of all sorts were obscured.

The Brazilian electoral system was highly exclusionary and this, coupled with multipolarity, made the party system partially opaque. The polarization metaphor requires that parties be arrayed on a singular

[93] Hagopian's carefully crafted research on traditional politics in Brazil illustrates the multipolarity and opacity of the political system beautifully. She writes: "Because regionalism, clientelism and personalism permeated the political parties and framed the way society was organized . . . society was deprived of opportunities for developing horizontal, national solidarities through parties." *Tradititional Politics*, 72.

Left-Right dimension, with visible anti-system parties anchoring both poles, yet because the Brazilian electoral system excluded the Communist Party, one of the poles was not fully visible.

The opacity created by the exclusion of the PCB was compounded by the exclusion of illiterate voters. Illiterate Brazilians, comprising approximately 50 percent of the adult population, were a source of great uncertainty for anyone trying to forecast party-system direction.[94] No one could be certain when, or even *if*, illiterates would be incorporated into the electorate, and no one could be certain how their incorporation might affect patterns of party support.

The extraordinary uncertainty generated by Brazil's multipolar and opaque party system affected President Goulart himself. Because he recognized both the exclusive and the corrupt nature of the party system around him, he looked elsewhere for the information he needed to make his key political calculations. It was natural that he turn to the public spaces of Brazil. These highly mobilized settings allowed him to see and hear the voices of the citizenry with a directness that the electoral process did not afford. But public spaces and the polarized camps within them were not a microcosm of the larger society. They led both reactionary and progressive forces to overstate the strength of the Left. They also led Goulart himself to make a series of fateful mistakes in March of 1964. We cannot know whether Brazilian democracy would have survived without those mistakes. We do know that ordinary people played only a peripheral role in its demise. The people had weathered severe economic crises and a whole range of performance failures without being driven to extremes.

---

[94] UNESCO, *Situaçao Social da América Latina* (Rio de Janeiro: Latin American Center for Social Science Research, 1961).

4

THE SLOW-MOTION COUP IN URUGUAY

JOÃO GOULART FLED TO URUGUAY when the Brazilian military drove him from power in 1964. His choice of destination was political as well as geographic, for Uruguay was still a functioning democracy when its northeastern neighbor fell to authoritarianism. Indeed, by certain criteria Uruguay was the strongest democracy in South America as the sixties began. Its elections were based on universal suffrage. Its political parties were among the oldest in the West,[1] and its political leaders prided themselves on having a military that was essentially "decorative." Uruguay had "the only real, enduring process of democratization in Latin America during the first quarter of the century,"[2] and even when Uruguayan democracy faltered in 1933, civilian politicians maintained control of the state.[3]

Uruguay's unique experience with democracy was linked to the unique features of its society. Peopled almost exclusively by European settlers,[4] Uruguay was a racially homogeneous, predominantly urban country in which most inhabitants identified themselves as middle class.[5] With the highest literacy rate in all of Latin America,[6] a welfare state that dated from 1916,[7] and a political system dominated by two

[1] Luis E. González, "Continuity and Change in the Uruguayan Party System," in Mainwaring and Scully, *Building Democratic Institutions*, 139.

[2] Luis E. González, *Political Structure and Democracy in Uruguay* (South Bend, Ind.: University of Notre Dame Press, 1991), 116.

[3] Ruth Berins Collier and David Collier write that "the military remained marginal" to the events of 1933, that the coup was the work of the civilian Colorado leader Terra, "that the scope of repressive control was limited," and that it "involved mainly the police." *Shaping the Political Arena* (Princeton: Princeton University Press, 1991), 444.

[4] Edy Kaufman, *Uruguay in Transition: From Civilian to Military Rule* (New Brunswick: Transaction Books, 1979), 8.

[5] Constanza Moreira, *Democracia y Desarrollo en Uruguay* (Montevideo: Ediciones Trilce, 1997), 69, 85.

[6] Martin Weinstein, *Uruguay: The Politics of Failure* (Westport, Conn.: Greenwood Press, 1975), 95.

[7] Uruguay's Colorado president, José Batlle y Ordoñez, pushed a broad range of progressive policies through the national legislature between 1911 and 1916, including pension systems, an eight-hour day, and guarantees of the right to vote, unionize, and strike. He rationalized his programs to his critics with the argument that "the nation can not be said to be really well off as long as the worker's economic situation is not good." Milton Vanger, *The Model Country: José Batlle y Ordoñez of Uruguay* (Waltham, Mass.: Brandeis University Press, 1980), 129.

decidedly cross-class parties, Uruguay had a "political system blessed with both high stability and a significant degree of popular legitimation."[8] Until at least the late fifties, the nation "satisfied most—if not all—of the conditions usually cited as prerequisites for a democratic political order."[9]

Uruguay was thus dramatically different from Brazil. Yet by June 1973, its democracy would also fall to military dictatorship. Even the most sympathetic analysts concluded that Uruguayans had either "acquiesced or participated in" the creation of authoritarian rule. Faced with two alternatives, they had "chosen dictatorship over democracy."[10]

Though the vast majority of Uruguayans did acquiesce to military rule, I shall argue below that very few actually chose dictatorship. In this case, as in our others, ordinary people showed a surprising commitment to democracy despite extraordinary levels of economic and political chaos. There was certainly a high degree of public polarization, but a close analysis of voting behavior and opinion data show that the Uruguayan Center held fast, that support for a far-right pole was almost nonexistent, and that assessments of support for the anti-system Left were exaggerated. I make this argument after giving an overview of the coup and its antecedents.

The Slow Erosion of Democracy

The term *coup* is probably a misnomer in the Uruguayan case. The word connotes a swift blow, but the regime change took place incrementally. Uruguayan democracy died a slow and painful death. Most analysts agree that the trouble started in the late fifties when the nation entered a period of economic decline that struck at the very heart of the system that sustained its cross-class, democratic parties. The parties that controlled the democratic state had long used public sector employment and spending to win elections, mitigate potential social tensions, and prevent the growth of strong left-wing parties. When the economy entered a period of obvious stagnation in the late 1950s, the system suffered severe strains. "Levels of education and urbanization exceeded available levels of employment and income," generating

[8] Gerónimo de la Sierra, "Introducción al Estudio de las Condiciones de Ascenso de las Dictaduras: el Caso Uruguayo," *Revista Mexicana de Sociología* 39, no. 2 (April–June 1977): 568.

[9] Luis E. González, "El Sistema de Partidos y las Perspectivas de la Democracia Uruguaya," *Revista Mexicana de Sociología* 47, no. 2 (April–June 1985): 67.

[10] Weinstein, *Uruguay,* 112, 138.

"high levels of structural tensions," political radicalization, and massive out-migration.[11]

Democratically elected governments seemed unable to restart the nation's economy. The decline started in the aftermath of the Korean War, when the nation's meat- and wool-based export sector fell behind its competitors in New Zealand and Australia.[12] The decline in the agricultural export sector spread to domestic industries, and overall investment dropped from approximately 20 percent of GDP in the 1950s to 10 percent in the 1960s.[13] GNP dropped a full 12 percent from 1956 through 1972.[14]

The 1958 elections signaled that the nation's economic downturn might have important political repercussions. Even before the formal founding of the state, Uruguayan politics had been dominated by two catch-all parties: the Blancos, or Nationalists, and the Colorados. The Colorados had managed to dominate elections for decades, but in 1958 the electorate turned to the Blanco Party instead, marking a "turning point from Colorado predominance to competitive bipartism."[15] In 1962 the Blanco Party won the elections again but still failed to reverse the downward spiral of the economy.

Frustrated with continued economic decline, the electorate endorsed a Colorado candidate named Oscar Gestido in the November 1966 elections. Significantly, he was a centrist figure, widely respected for his commitment to democracy. Tragically, he died only nine months after assuming office. His death proved fatal for democracy itself, for executive power fell to his little-known vice-president, Jorge Pacheco Areco, who immediately made a number of authoritarian policy changes. These included the banning of the Socialist Party, the closing of several leftist newspapers, and the imposition of "emergency security measures" to justify coercive action against political, labor, and student opposition. Pacheco's initiatives fell short of an outright regime change, but they included two challenges to basic policy-making institutions within the state: he abolished the wage councils that had mediated worker demands for a quarter of a century,[16] and he formed

[11] César Aguiar, *Uruguay: País de Emigración* (Montevideo: Ediciones de la Banda Oriental, 1982), 49.

[12] J. Kirby, "On the Viability of Small Countries: Uruguay and New Zealand Compared," *Journal of Inter-American Studies and World Affairs* 17 (August 1975): 263–67.

[13] Charles Gillespie, *Negotiating Democracy: Politicians and Generals in Uruguay* (Cambridge: Cambridge University Press, 1991), 36.

[14] Howard Handelman, "Labor-Industrial Conflict and the Collapse of Uruguayan Democracy," *Journal of International Studies and World Affairs* 23, no. 4 (November 1981): 375.

[15] González, "Continuity and Change," 151.

[16] Gillespie, *Negotiating Democracy,* 38.

the "gabinete empresarial"—the first cabinet in modern Uruguayan history to exclude the traditional political class.[17] The naming of the new cabinet was seen as "the rupture" of the political model that had governed the country for over half a century.[18]

Pacheco failed in his attempt to win a second term in the election of 1971, but the man who replaced him was his ally Juan Bordaberry. Uruguayan democracy eroded faster under the new administration. With Bordaberry's support, the military took stronger and stronger measures against the opposition in civil society. It also mounted a highly divisive campaign against "political corruption," aimed at both houses of the legislature. In a move replete with symbolic and real political ramifications, the campaign included the arrest and detention of Colorado senator Jorge Batlle—a direct descendant of one of the founders of Uruguayan democracy. By 1973, change became frenetic. In January, Bordaberry seized control of the university. In March, he established a Military Security Council, institutionalizing the role of the armed forces in government. Finally, on June 24, at the military's insistence, he closed down the Uruguayan legislature. The regime change had taken over five years.

Public Polarization

The erosion of democratic freedoms in Uruguay was rationalized from its very beginning as a means of controlling destabilizing forces in civil society. The downward economic trends summarized above had stimulated dramatic mobilizations of both new and previously less active groups. In Uruguay, as in Brazil, many of these groups were inspired by the Cuban revolution. Luís Cladera estimates that the Cuban revolution stimulated 90 percent of what the Left did.[19] The Blanco government (elected just before Castro's triumph) sparked a number of pro-Cuban mobilizations by taking defensive, anti-Cuban policy initiatives. In 1961, the government declared the Cuban ambassador persona non grata and ordered his expulsion from the country. In 1962, while hosting the Inter-American Foreign Ministers Meeting, the government openly

---

[17] Manuel Alcántara Sáez and Ismael Crespo Martínez, *Partidos Políticos y Procesos Electorales en Uruguay 1971–1990* (Madrid: Centro Español de Estudios de América Latina, 1992), 51–52. This took place in May and June 1968.

[18] Nelson Minello, "Uruguay: la Consolidación del Estado Militar," *Revista Mexicana de Sociología*, 39, no. 2 (April–June 1977): 588.

[19] From an interview with Luis Cladera (an ex-Maoist, now an historian), Ana María Araujo, and Horacio Tejera, *La Imaginación al Poder* (Montevideo: Fundación de Cultura Universitaria, 1988), 24.

endorsed Cuba's expulsion from the Organization of American States. In September of 1964, the Uruguayan government broke relations with Cuba altogether. Each of these events provoked protests and mass demonstrations. In so doing they provided publicity and legitimation for a whole series of new Cuban support groups, such as the Comité Coordinador de Apoyo a la Revolución Cubana. These committees and the protests that developed around Uruguay's relations with Cuba politicized and radicalized hordes of young Uruguayans who were searching for new political models.[20] The government's reactions to the pro-Cuban activities often involved police violence and consequently sparked even more opposition. A shooting during Che Guevara's visit to the University in Montevideo in 1961 and violent clashes during two large demonstrations for Cuban diplomats undercut the legitimacy of the elected government among many leftist groups.[21]

Four of these groups would eventually join together to form the Tupamaros (MLN-T)—the most notorious and polarizing of all the new associations to emerge in the 1960s. These founding groups included: a group from the cane-cutters' union founded by labor lawyer Raúl Sendic in 1961; a small group of young people from Montevideo calling themselves the Movement for Peasant Help, or MAC; a group composed of disaffected Communists calling itself MIR; and finally, a group of individuals from the official Socialist Party who had gotten frustrated with electoral politics and had been inspired by the Cuban example.[22]

The groups formally organized as the Tupamaros in 1964 at the seaside resort of Parque de la Plata. In January 1966 they held their first National Convention at the Coastal resort of El Pinar and made a formal commitment to armed struggle. This group, which would soon be known throughout the world, had, at its founding, approximately fifty members.[23]

The Tupamaros's contribution to public polarization was profound. It began even before the organization itself, for the small groups that eventually founded the Tupamaros engaged in a number of highly

[20] For personal testimonies on the causes and the effects of these mobilizations, see Eleuterio Fernández Huidobro, *Historia de los Tupamaros: los Orígenes* (Montevideo: Tupac Amaru Editores, 1986), 1:19, 52; and Marta Harnecker, *Frente Amplio: Los Desafíos de una Izquierda Legal*, (Montevideo: La República, 1991), 1:21.

[21] These occurred first when a large group assembled at the national airport to bid farewell to Cuban diplomats in 1961, and then in 1964 when riots broke out protesting the government's breaking of diplomatic relations.

[22] The most extensive and best documented study of the Tupamaros available in any language is Astrid Arrarás, "Armed Struggle, Political Learning and Participation in Democracy: The Case of the Tupamaros" (Ph.D. dissertation, Princeton University, 1998).

[23] Eleuterio Fernández Huidobro, *Historia de los Tupamaros: el MLN*, (Montevideo: TAE Editorial, 1988), 3:10–11.

publicized revolutionary acts before they were formally united into a single movement. These included: the theft of weapons for a land seizure on 31 July 1963, a weapons heist from a government customs office on 1 January 1964, and two failed bank robberies.[24] Even in its earliest stages, individuals and groups who sought affiliation with the movement had to undertake at least one "military action" before being allowed to join.[25]

Between its formal founding and 1968, the Tupamaros directed most of their actions toward the theft of arms, cash, and explosives. On occasion, they also set off bombs to kill particular police and military personnel whom they held personally responsible for specific acts of repression. By 1968–69 their armed operations increased and became the focus of more attention. They bombed or seized control of radio stations, bombed two sites on U.S. Embassy property, set fire to the General Motors plant, bombed the homes of several police officers and cabinet members, took control of the city of Pando, and kidnapped two heads of major companies—all in less than a year.[26] In an ironic affront to the existing regime, they even stole arms and munitions from the police, the navy, and the army.

In 1970–71, the Tupamaros's operations grew more daring and more violent. They killed police officers, kidnapped a well-known judge, abducted two men associated with the American embassy, and kidnapped a high-ranking diplomat from Brazil. After killing one of their American hostages—a man who had been training the Uruguayan security forces—they went on to abduct five members of the Uruguayan elite plus the British ambassador. The head of a meatpacking plant was also abducted.

Several spectacular initiatives gave the impression that the MLN-T was organizationally superior to the coercive forces of the Uruguayan state. The group orchestrated two dramatic jailbreaks, releasing 38 women on 30 July 1971 and 106 men on September 6.[27] They ended the year with a series of daring actions that struck at the very heart of the state's security system. With stolen explosives and munitions, they seized a radio station, took over police headquarters in the town of Constancia, and seized the military airport at Paysandú. On 1 January

[24] Arrarás, "Armed Struggle," 61.

[25] This rule applied originally to a group called the Coordinator, which included all the Tupamaros's founders plus other groups.

[26] These and many other actions are described in detail in Movimiento de Liberación Nacional, *Actas Tupamaras* (Montevideo: TAE Editorial, 1988).

[27] Both escapes took place through tunnels connected to sewer networks. The second was from the Punta Carretas Prison and cleverly coordinated with street rioting in a poorer neighborhood far from the prison, deliberately timed to distract the police.

TABLE 4.1
Number of Unions by Sector of the Workforce: Uruguay 1922–1963

Year	Wage Workers	Salaried Employees (SE)	Mixed	Others
1922	101	—	—	—
1946	80	21	61	9
1963	63	32	116	5

Source: Alfredo Errandonea and Daniel Costabile, *Sindicato y Sociedad en el Uruguay* (Montevideo: Biblioteca de Cultura Universitaria, 1968), 95.

1972, the Tupamaros issued the Proclamation of Paysandú, declaring civil war on the Uruguayan state.

The Tupamaros' war was soon to end in total defeat, but it began with all the violence promised. They killed a major prison official, bombed the homes of two police commissioners, abducted one member of a government death squad, and then killed four others. They seized control of two police stations (including one in the capital itself) and abducted the head of a major newspaper. Breaking with a policy of targeting only individuals whom they deemed personally responsible for political oppression, the MLN-T murdered four enlisted men who were simply guarding the house of an officer and then fatally poisoned a peasant who had unwittingly discovered one of their rural hideouts. This particular killing was a tragic irony because the MLN-T was on the verge of launching a rural offensive to complement their urban struggle. Their rural offensive would never come to fruition. Desperate to eradicate the MLN-T, the state had put the armed forces in charge of internal security. Under emergency provisions authorized by the executive and the legislature, the military moved against the Tupamaros with full force. According to its official records, the military charged and imprisoned 2,873 "subversives" in just seven months. By August 1972, nearly all of the top MLN-T leadership (including Raúl Sendic) were in military hands. By December 1972, the Tupamaros and a whole host of smaller revolutionary groups were essentially destroyed.

The mobilization of Uruguayan labor spanned a longer time period than the mobilization of the revolutionary Left. Labor militancy began a dramatic increase in the latter half of the 1950s as a predictable response to the precipitous drop in real income. Sectors of the labor force who had never been affiliated with unions got organized. As table 4.1 shows, the professional composition of the unionized workforce changed dramatically as the Uruguayan economy declined.

Strikes increased dramatically in nearly all work environments, sometimes in a general response to particular government policies, other times as a response to more narrow enterprise conflicts. The number of man-days lost to strikes doubled between 1957 and 1963.[28]

Public-sector workers were hardest hit by the drop in real earnings. Real wage and salary income dropped around 24 percent between 1957 and 1967 for the labor force as a whole. For workers in the public sector, the drop was a full 40 percent.[29] Though most of these employees held white-collar jobs, they swiftly became the most militant members of the labor union community. It is significant that only 86 percent of the man-hours lost to strikes and stoppages in 1963 were associated with exclusively blue-collar unions.[30] The role of white-collar workers in strike action indicates that nature of labor's vanguard was changing fast.

The increase in the number of strikes and the change in the composition of organized labor corresponded with a major structural change in Uruguayan labor federations. The socialist and anarchist federations that had existed since 1929 lost ground by the early sixties. By 1966, most of the nation's unions had joined forces with the CNT—the National Worker's Convention, led by the Uruguayan Communist Party.[31]

Workers who had never had national visibility gained key roles in the 1960s as more and more people took collective action. Sugarcane cutters from the distant region of Artigas had not been organized until 1961. They initially demanded only wage increases and the fair application of existing labor laws. However, when their relatively moderate demands met with harsh resistance, demands for land became a priority.[32]

Uruguay's employers and public sector managers were clearly facing a newly threatening labor force. They reacted with a level of repression that led to more and more mobilization. When the cane cutters marched across the country to Montevideo to publicize their demands, their leaders were arrested and their protests stopped with force. The march was met with the imposition of the highly controversial *medidas prontas de seguridad*—emergency security measures. These measures, which constituted key watersheds in the erosion of Uruguayan democracy, were invoked in reaction to every major labor disturbance. Their use against a strike of utility workers in 1963 and against bank workers in 1968 were among the most notorious. At least one analyst of Uru-

[28] Errandonea and Costabile, *Sindicato y Sociedad*, 136.

[29] Handelman, "Labor-Industrial Conflict," 375; and Weinstein, *Uruguay*, 119.

[30] Errandonea and Costabile, *Sindicato y Sociedad*, 98.

[31] For a detailed history written by a CNT activist, see Enrique Rodríguez, *Un Movimiento Obrero Maduro* (Montevideo: Ediciones Pueblos Unidos, 1988), esp. 141–56.

[32] Alberto Sendic, *Movimiento Obrero y Luchas Populares en la Historia Uruguaya* (Montevideo: Liberación Nacional, 1985), 79.

guayan labor has pointed out, "Almost every escalation of government repression prior to the coup was closely connected to labor unrest."[33] (The exception was the government's declaration of "internal war" after the Tupamaros declared a civil war in April 1972.)

The state's use of security measures restricting job actions was rationalized as essential to correcting Uruguay's economic crisis, but the measures had at least three ironic political results. First, by reinforcing the idea that the traditional channels for negotiation were no longer viable, the measures actually increased the amount of protest that took place outside of institutional channels.[34] Second, by providing a focal issue of high salience, the security measures provided a common enemy that helped to unite a previously divided set of labor groups. It is not coincidental that a left-wing labor front developed in 1966, five years before a left-wing party front.[35] Third, and most ironically, the measures increased mobilizations, at least in the short run. In 1968 alone over 700 strikes took place, "paralyzing the country's economic life."[36]

Uruguayan university students were sympathetic to the causes of striking workers and mobilized in solidarity with the labor movement. They also mobilized around foreign and university policy issues and thus constituted a third source of intense polarization. To at least one sympathetic observer, the "university represented the most active center of both the violent and non-violent extreme Left."[37]

The country's single university, the Universidad de la República, was a natural arena for opposition protest at the time that economic crisis set in. Its composition was overwhelmingly middle rather than upper-class, and many leading members of its administration and faculty were veterans of the opposition to the Terra dictatorship.[38] Its governing structure was substantially more open than those of its counterparts in other Latin American countries,[39] and by 1958 the university was legally granted complete "academic, political and administrative autonomy" from the Uruguayan state.[40]

---

[33] Handelman, "Labor-Industrial Conflict," 386.

[34] Juan Rial, *Partidos Políticos, Democracia y Autoritarismo* (Montevideo: Ediciones de la Banda Oriental, 1984), 2:24.

[35] Rial, *Partidos Políticos*, 1:55.

[36] María del Huerto Amarillo, *El Ascenso al Poder de las Fuerzas Armadas* (Montevideo: Cuadernos de Paz y Justicia, 1986), 13. She writes, "Far from putting the brakes on agitation, the MPS [emergency social measures] . . . multiplied the confrontations."

[37] Kaufman, *Uruguay in Transition*, 41. I say "sympathetic" because of the author's association with Amnesty International.

[38] Gonzalo Varela, *De la República Militar al Estado Militar* (Montevideo: Ediciones del Nuevo Mundo, 1988), 45.

[39] Ibid., 43.

[40] Ibid., 45.

University students were in a unique structural position as the sixties began. They had a long tradition of playing a role in university governance, having been granted a position on the institution's administrative board as early as 1908.[41] They also had a tactical alliance with sectors of the administration and faculty, for all three groups were dependent on state budget allocations and the latter two groups needed the former as a means of exerting pressure on the state.[42] A third factor that distinguished their structural position was the strength of their alliance with trade unionists. Institutionalized student-worker alliances dated back at least as far as 1918, after which the groups often drew on one another's resources in common cause. Unions joined students in mobilizing for the legal autonomy of the university in 1958. The Student Federation (FEUU) participated in the establishment of the Central Labor Federation in 1966. Student leaders were even accorded nonvoting membership in the CNT.[43]

Given the structural context (and the fact that the universities produced many more graduates than the economy could employ), student radicalization was predictable. Violent clashes between students and security forces were frequent in the years leading up to the coup. Many protests were directed toward symbols of U.S. imperialism. Students pelted visiting President Eisenhower with tin cans in 1960. They burned a huge cardboard rat in front of the U.S. embassy in solidarity with the cane cutters' union.[44] They were the backbone of several massive pro-Cuban demonstrations, and they protested Nelson Rockefeller's visit in June of 1969 with gunshots and rioting.[45]

The most widely publicized student mobilizations took place in 1968, when police clashed with students over domestic policy issues. In June, when students demonstrated for higher spending on education and transportation, 10 police were injured and 266 students were jailed. In August, when police raided the campus to search for the kidnapped head of the national utility company, ten days of fighting ensued and 4 students were killed. In September, more rioting broke out when police attempted to dismantle student-created barricades. Two

---

[41] Ibid., 43.

[42] As Varela saw it, the need for an activist student movement became more and more important as a means of both defending the autonomy of the university and of demanding increases in the university budget. Ibid., 44.

[43] Ibid., 39–40.

[44] Errandonea, in Araujo and Tejera, *La Imaginación al Poder*, 43.

[45] The international press estimated that the rioting caused one million dollars worth of damage. *El Nacional* (Mexico), 22 June 1969, p. 1. *The New York Times*, 20–23 June 1969, p. 1 each day.

more students were killed and the government closed the university altogether. Secondary schools were closed as well.

In 1969–70, student mobilizations focused more on labor struggles than on issues connected directly to the university. Strikes of government workers, utility workers, bank workers, and meatpackers all received highly publicized student support. University students even set up roadblocks to charge tolls and support union strike funds. As a former secretary general of the FEUU saw it in retrospect, "The FEUU was converted almost exclusively into an organization supporting other struggles,"[46] meaning struggles that involved actors who were not members of the university community.

Throughout the years preceding the coup, the politicization of university life was frenetic. As an activist put it in retrospect, "If you were not associated with some group—some acronym—you were thought to be useless—a stray bullet."[47] Clashes between politicized groups were a constant, and teaching activities were barely able to continue.[48]

Pacheco and many others believed that the university provided shelter and support for violent activities of the Tupamaros and other left-wing groups. The medical school was one of the three divisions that had been most politicized, and the university-run hospital was the target of police raids whenever a kidnapping took place.[49] Many sites within the university were thought suspect by government authorities. As early as 1968, long before the peak of Tupamaro activity, an official military report concluded that the offices of certain student organizations were "places of refuge" for "illegal activities" and storehouses for bombs, weapons, and other "material used for the disruption of public order."[50]

From 1971 until the coup itself, student activists continued protests in solidarity with strikers of all sorts but focused more often on defending students and the university from police assaults. Many students were killed during the last years of the regime. Some were tar-

[46] Landanelli, in Araujo and Tejera, *La Imaginación al Poder*, 56. Landanelli became secretary general of the FEUU in 1971.

[47] From an interview with María Gravina, in Araujo and Tejera, *La Imaginación al Poder*, 15.

[48] Alfonso Lessa, *Estado de Guerra* (Montevideo: Fin del Siglo, 1996).

[49] Weinstein, *Uruguay*, 120. The other suspect schools were Architecture and Fine Arts.

[50] For a vivid picture of how the military saw the Left, see its official publication, *Junta de Comandantes, Las Furezas Armadas al Pueblo Oriental*, esp. Tomo 1, *La Subversión* (Montevideo: Fuerzas Armadas, 1976). The collection begins with a quote from Sun Wu saying "Know your enemy and yourself and you can fight a hundred battles without risk of defeat." The quote in my text is from *Documentos*, 24 November 1973, Publicación Oficial Conjunta. Ministerio del Interior, Ministerio de Defensa Nacional, in Kaufman, *Uruguay in Transition*, 41.

gets of clandestine death squads. One was gunned down by a right-wing terrorist group while inside a school. Others were killed in violent confrontations with police during riots. On each occasion, students and unions organized massive funerals to honor the martyred dead and to denounce the government. Retributions in the form of bombings and attacks on police usually followed each attack on students and kept the pendulum of violence in constant motion. When Pacheco Areco proposed a massive educational reform to gain firmer government control of public education, faculty and students went to the streets again. The mobilization even reached the nation's grammar schools, but the bill was passed anyway, just a month before the coup.[51]

The Meaning of Public Polarization

The violence of the Tupamaros, the constancy of strikes, and the continuous chaos created by student-police confrontations gave many observers the impression that Uruguayan society was being wrenched in two. An increasingly powerful, revolutionary Left pulled politics and citizens in one direction, while an increasingly violent, reactive Right pulled them in another. Even the most careful and knowledgeable outsiders concluded that the Uruguayan "capitalist system quite literally appeared on the verge of disintegration."[52]

Behind the easily visible reality of paralyzing strikes and rampant violence were less obvious, alternative realities that were far less polarized and much more in keeping with the Uruguay of the past. In Uruguay as in Brazil, there were important political differences between highly visible activists and the ordinary people who shared their sociological space.

Uruguay's union rank and file was much more moderate than most of its official leadership wished. This moderation had historical roots in a relatively inclusive welfare state, in the fact that over 90 percent of Uruguayan firms employed twenty or fewer workers,[53] and in "a political culture with an aversion to extremes."[54] Links to traditional parties were longstanding. Many wage earners regularly voted for moderate political leaders during national and local elections and then

[51] Weinstein, *Uruguay,* 130.

[52] Robert Kaufman, "Industrial Change and Authoritarian Rule in Latin America: A Concrete Review of the Bureaucratic-Authoritarian Model," in *The New Authoritarianism in Latin America,* ed. David Collier (Princeton: Princeton University Press, 1979), 191.

[53] Handelman, "Labor-Industrial Conflict," 374.

[54] Alexandra Barahona de Brito, *Human Rights and Democratization in Latin America: Uruguay and Chile* (London: Oxford University Press, 1997), 36.

for militant labor leaders during union elections.[55] This pattern continued even after the economic crisis set it. Though many people believed
otherwise, "there is *no* evidence" that the chaos of the Uruguayan
economy "was paralleled by any dramatic rise in class voting."[56]

Moreover, the union leaders who won labor elections were often
very different from the leadership who led the most highly publicized
strikes. The majority of trade union leaders adhered to gradualist
rather than revolutionary positions.[57] Labor struggles were long lasting
and hard fought, but they were generally not about changes in property relations, as the cane workers struggles were. They were usually
about "the *maintenance* of what had already been won,"[58] and "much
less revolutionary than rights-based."[59]

The university community, like labor, was also much more divided
internally than its solidaristic public actions suggested. Though social
scientists (and government officials) were correct in deeming it "the
most active center of both the violent and non-violent extreme Left,"[60]
it was much more than this. There were, for example, important divisions between leftists who were associated with the Communist Party
and those who were not. In Uruguay, as in Brazil, the Communists did
not endorse armed struggle. On the contrary, as Che Guevara himself
implied when he visited Montevideo in 1961, the party recognized that
Batista's Cuba and democratic Uruguay were profoundly different. In
a highly publicized speech, Che urged Uruguayan students to eschew
armed struggle in their own country. Uruguayan Communist Party
leaders came directly to the Tupamaros and offered them passage to
Bolivia—in explicit recognition of the fact that their plans were inappropriate to the Uruguayan context.[61]

Divisions between different leftist groups coupled with divisions between militants and nonmilitants. What looked to outsiders like an
endless supply of young activists was really the fruit of arduous efforts
on the part of a highly mobilized vanguard. As a former secretary general of the FEUU recalled it years later, "It was very difficult to organize a truly mass mobilization. . . . Changes in the structure of the student movement created truly enormous organizational difficulties. In

[55] Gillespie, *Negotiating Democracy,* 25.

[56] Ibid., 26. Emphasis added.

[57] Varela, *De la República Militar,* 75.

[58] Rial, *Partidos Políticos,* 2:23. Emphasis added.

[59] Moreira, *Democracia y Desarrollo,* 97.

[60] Kaufman, *Uruguay in Transition,* 41.

[61] See Arrarás, "Armed Struggle"; and Huidrobro, *Historia de los Tupamaros.* For solid,
historical investigative reporting on the whole tenor of the period, see Nelson Caula and
Alberto Silva, *Alto el Fuego* (Montevideo: Rosebud Ediciones, 1993).

some of the departments the situation became pathetic. In the Medical School, for example, the official leadership was so atomized, that large sectors of the student body were merely spectators. . . . On one side stood the militants, on the other side stood the students, without the creation of any links between the militants and the base."[62]

The university community of the sixties and early seventies was certainly different from the community of the past. It embraced a much larger segment of Uruguayan society,[63] it produced many more graduates than the economy could absorb, and its students did not have as strong a connection to the traditional parties as their parents did.[64] The Left, with its many variations, was clearly hegemonic there, but in this, too, the community reflected only a small segment of the Uruguayan reality.

The segment of the Uruguayan reality represented by the Tupamaros was even smaller, for they were representative of only a small section of the Uruguayan Left. Though the Tupamaros and other violent groups often attracted sympathy as champions of egalitarianism and victims of human rights abuse, their own use of violence was unambiguously rejected by ordinary citizens of all sorts. Whether citizens identified themselves as sympathetic with the Left or with one of the two traditional parties, their commitment to lawful, orderly change was overwhelming. A full 88 percent of self-identified leftists believed that Uruguay's problems should be solved while preserving law and order. Ninety-seven percent of Colorados and 99 percent of Blancos believed the same.[65]

The images produced by the polarized struggles in public space were dramatically different from those produced by votes and public opinion polls. In Uruguay, as in the Brazilian case, there were pockets of polarization, but contrary to the image that certain figures on the Right sought to convey, polarization was not profound and the country was not on the verge of revolution. On the contrary, as I shall illustrate below, the traditional parties retained their hegemony despite economic crisis, the Left coalition was neither as strong nor as threatening as it appeared, and, finally, ordinary Uruguayans combined a remarkable tolerance for disorder with an undeniable reluctance to abandon democratic norms.

---

[62] These are the words of Jorge Landinelli, from an interview in Araujo and Tejera, *La Imaginación al Poder*, 56.

[63] Varela, *De la República Militar*, 44.

[64] Moreira, *Democracia y Desarrollo*, 96.

[65] Gillespie, *Negotiating Democracy*, 41.

Polarization's Limits: Continuities in Electoral Behavior

Uruguay's economic crisis did not produce a massive or even a moderate defection from the two traditional parties. As table 4.2 illustrates, the votes garnered by the two traditional parties fluctuated very little between 1958 and 1966. This was despite the fact that by 1966 inflation had reached record levels, unemployment was rising, and thousands of Uruguayans were emigrating annually to find work abroad.[66]

The Blancos (the alternative party) had won the last two elections but had been unable to reverse the economy's downward spiral. The context seemed appropriate for a swing to either the Right or the Left, but the voters gave a resounding endorsement to a centrist faction of the party that had ruled the country for most of the twentieth century.

The presidency was won by retired army general Gestido—a man who represented "the center of the Center"[67] but who was widely respected even "within the Left."[68] The parties on the Left gained only modestly, if at all. The Communist Party coalition (named FIDEL) gained 27,000 votes over its total in 1962, but the Socialists lost votes. Zelmar Michelini, who headed the largest leftist faction within the traditional parties in 1962, lost votes, too. Less than seven years before the Uruguayan democracy collapsed, ordinary people were still rejecting nontraditional parties and usually embracing the more centrist official factions within the traditional groups.

In 1971, voting choices seemed to change. This is the election which scholars and other observers cite as proof of polarization. Voters certainly did polarize in that an all-inclusive coalition of leftist parties (the Broad Front, or Frente Amplio) won an impressive 18 percent of the poll, but in this case (as in the Brazilian) the growth of the Left was easily misunderstood.

Following closely on the heels of the 1970 electoral victory of the Unidad Popular in Chile, the surge in popularity of the Uruguayan Left was seen by many as a portent of an Allende-style government in Uruguay. It was not. It was not even indicative of a lethal level of polarization. Four points need to be clarified for the 1971 election to be properly understood. First, Uruguayans were not abandoning the Center of the

---

[66] The number of Uruguayans emigrating annually rose by over 500 percent between 1963 and 1966. Between 1966 and 1972 an average of nearly ten thousand Uruguayans emigrated annually. Given the size of the population, this is a substantial drain. See Aguiar, *Uruguay: País de Emigración*, 59

[67] Solari, *Uruguay Partidos Políticos y Sistema Electoral* (Montevideo: El Libro Libre, 1988), 190.

[68] González, *Political Structure*, 111.

TABLE 4.2

Percentage of Vote Won by Centrist and Leftist Parties in Presidential Elections
in Uruguay, 1950–1971

	1950	1954	1958	1962	1966	1971
Centrist Traditional Parties						
Colorado Party[a]	52.6	50.6	40.3	44.5	49.4	40.9
Blanco Party	38.5	38.9	49.7	46.5	40.4	40.2
Subtotal	91.1	89.5	90.0	91.0	89.8	81.1
Left-Wing Parties[b]						
Civic Union/Christian Democrat[c]	4.4	5.0	3.7	3.1	3.0	—
Socialist Party (and allies)[d]	2.1	3.3	3.5	2.3	0.9	—
Communist Party (and allies)[e]	2.3	2.2	2.7	3.5	5.7	—
Subtotal	8.8	10.5	10.0	9.0	10.1	0.6
New Space Coalition	—	—	—	—	—	5.8
Broad Front Coalition[f]	—	—	—	—	—	12.5
Subtotal	—	—	—	—	—	18.3

Source: *Elecciones Uruguayas*, compiled by Julio T. Fabregat, as presented by Luis E González in
Mainwaring and Scully, *Building Democratic Institutions*, 150.

[a] In 1958, a small Colorado group voted outside its *lema* (obtaining 2 percent of the total vote) and
is included here in the Colorado share of the vote.

[b] Very minor parties are not listed separately.

[c] The Unión Cívica became the Partido Demócrata Cristiano in 1962. In 1966, a small splinter group
voted outside the Christian Democrats' *lema*.

[d] In 1968, former allies of the Socialists voted outside the SP *lema*.

[e] In 1958, 1962, and 1966 the subtotal of nonrelevant parties exceeds the sum of the parties listed
here because other unlisted parties won some votes.

[f] The New Space (the alliance of the Christian Democrats and the Partido por el Gobierno del Pueblo
and the former Lista-99 Colorado splinter group) voted with the Broad Front under the same *lema*
in 1971.

political spectrum in significant numbers. Second, the Left's increase in
popularity was not as great as a superficial look at the vote count suggested. Third, the votes the Left did attract were less the result of voter
defections than the result of changes in the composition of the electorate. Finally, the surge in support for the Left was not mirrored in a surge
of support for parties on the Right. Uruguay never produced an extreme-right party. I elaborate on each of these points below.

The resilience of the Uruguayan Center and the setting in which the
1971 elections took place can only be understood with a basic knowledge of the country's party system. Unlike the other South American

polyarchies that fell to dictatorship in the 1970s, Uruguay had maintained an essentially two-party system since nearly the beginning of the century. The Blanco and the Colorado Parties were loosely structured catch-all parties with nearly indistinguishable general policy orientations.[69] The parties' policy similarities were largely the result of similar structures and voting bases. Structurally, each party was a composite of official factions called *sublemas*. These factions were often not of a catch-all nature. They could often be classified as left, right, center, personalist, or regional. Since the mix of factions within each of the two parties was usually similar, their policy positions were, too.

This outcome was reinforced by similarities in voting bases. The Colorado Party was generally more urban and more secular than the Blanco group,[70] but both parties were decidedly cross-class, embracing "both the wealthiest and the poorest sectors of Uruguayan society."[71] This heterogeneity extended to the parties' sublemas, for these too were cross-class. If Uruguayan voters had sought to defect from their traditional, moderate, cross-class parties, there was no first-past-the-post system to stop them. The country's proportional representation system could be used to the advantage of new, third parties and indeed had helped to make the Broad Front's gain in votes possible.

As table 4.2 shows, however, the vote for the traditional parties in 1971 was not very different from the vote in 1966. The Blanco, or National, Party dropped only 0.2 percentage points in its share of the overall vote. The Colorado Party dropped 8.5 percentage points if we look only at the raw number of Colorado Party votes across two elections, yet this drop should not be interpreted as it might be in a standard two-party system. As explained above, the Colorado Party was an amalgam of sublemas, each with an identity of its own. For several elections preceding the 1971 poll, the Colorado leader Zelmar Michelini had led a faction named Lista-99, which was closely identified with the Left. Prior to the 1971 elections, Michelini severed his ties with the Colorado Party and formally joined the Broad Front. His voters went with him.

Technically, the Lista-99 voters defected from the Colorado Party and might therefore be counted as people who contributed to polarization. Yet their defection constituted a very different form of vote switching than that implied by the polarization model. The supporters of Lista-99 did not necessarily change their ideas or grow more radical. They voted, in fact, for the same ideas and the same leader over time. What looks at first like a change of voter opinion is, in fact, a change

---

[69] González, *Political Structure*, 16, and Rial, *Partidos Políticos*, 1:35.

[70] González, "Continuity and Change," 141.

[71] Rial, *Partidos Políticos*, 1:29; González, *Political Structure*, 113.

of *elite* identity. The drop in votes is less reflective of citizen polarization than of polarization among elites. There is thus an important distinction between what we might call *individual* polarization, in which voters defect from a party as individuals, and *factional* polarization, in which citizens vote for the same leaders over time but defect with a faction. If we make these distinctions and control for factional polarization in analyzing the 1971 elections, the drop in the Colorado vote is only 2.5 percentage points.[72]

If we ignore factional polarizations and focus only on how aggregate percentages change over time, we compute an 8.5 percentage-point vote loss. This is certainly a more impressive drop, but this figure and the corresponding increase in the vote amassed by the Broad Front have to be seen in the context of another fact not immediately obvious from the voting data: voting became mandatory in September 1970.[73] Thus the number of people voting in the 1971 election was 42 percent higher than the number voting in 1966. The fact that half a million new voters would have so *little* effect on the distribution of party support suggests that the existing Uruguayan party system had remarkable absorbency.

Despite all the public polarization described above, and a deeply troubled economy, new voters did not forge a dramatically new party system. Over 81 percent of the electorate voted for the same parties that had dominated Uruguayan government for over six decades. Even within the two traditional parties, all these seemingly destabilizing factors failed to alter the popularity of the leading sublemas. As Charles Gillespie concluded, "The 1971 election produced a *consolidation* of the *majority* sectors in both traditional parties."[74] In a classic case of polarization, factionalization is supposed to increase. In Uruguay we see arenas of consolidation instead.

The continuity in support for Uruguay's traditional parties shows how variables related to "performance" and "efficiency" are at best only partially helpful in predicting rates of defection. The strength of voters' party identification can have compelling explanatory power. Family socialization patterns had reinforced party identification for decades prior to 1971 and were not easily undone.[75] Even on the eve of democratic breakdown, party identification in Uruguay was stronger

---

[72] Juan Rial does not draw a distinction between individual and factional polarizations but follows the same logic as I do in his analysis of the 1971 poll. He too deducts the votes of the Lista-99 from the Colorado's 1966 voting total to compare changes over time. See his *Partidos Políticos*, 1:42.

[73] The change was authorized by Law 13.882 of 18 September 1970.

[74] Gillespie, *Negotiating Democracy*, 44.

[75] Moreira, *Democracia y Desarrollo*, 83; Aldo Solari, *El Desarrollo Social del Uruguay en la Postguerra* (Montevideo: Editorial Alfa, 1967), 167–72.

than in Chile (where the party system was deeply rooted), stronger than in North America, and about comparable to that of Norway.[76]

Though the traditional parties were clearly threatened by the highly mobilized new coalition of parties in the Broad Front, their internal organization maintained continuity. The eight-thousand campaign "clubs" established by the traditional parties in Montevideo in 1966 were established again in 1971.[77] Despite a profound sense of threat among certain traditional party elites, the traditional parties "survived unhurt."[78] At maximum (i.e., discounting the effects of factional polarization), the two traditional parties *combined* lost only 8.7 percentage points of the total vote in 1971. Put in comparative perspective, this seems a small loss rather than a great one.

The endurance of the Uruguayan Center is further exemplified by two other aspects of the 1971 polls: the voters' presidential choices and the results of a plebiscite on the 1967 constitution. The presidential candidate who attracted the most votes in 1971 was Wilson Ferreira Aldunate, a moderate leader of the Blanco Party whose dedication to democracy was unquestionable. Wilson, as he was known, beat his nearest competitor, Colorado leader J. M. Bordaberry, by over 60,000 votes. Wilson beat his main Blanco rival, the "strongly conservative" Mario Aguerrondo, by well over 200,000 votes.[79] The fact that Uruguayan voters shunned the more conservative candidate of the opposition party in a context of extraordinary social and political turmoil is highly significant.[80] Because Uruguayan electoral law allows parties to run more than one presidential candidate at a time (normally those representing the largest factions within the party), voters might have easily "polarized" *within* the traditional parties. They chose not to.

Uruguayan voters also chose not to endorse two constitutional amendments that would have weakened existing democratic structures. In keeping with a national tradition of rotation in power and collegial executive government, Uruguay's constitution prevented

[76] González, *Political Structure*, 116.

[77] These neighborhood "clubs" are a key part of the Uruguayan electoral system because the parties have no official membership lists and no permanent local branches. See González, *Political Structure*, 28; and Rial, *Partidos Políticos*, 2:31. For a detailed discussion of the clubs, see Gérman Rama, *El Club Político* (Montevideo: ARCA, 1971).

[78] César Aguiar, "Clivajes sociales, tiempos políticos y redemocratización," *Revista Mexicana de Sociología* 47, no. 2 (April-June 1985): 28.

[79] Manuel Alcántara Saez and Ismael Crespo Martínez, *Partidos Políticos y Procesos Electorales en Uruguay (1971–1990)* (Madrid: Fundación Centro Español de Estudios de América Latina, 1992), 62.

[80] The fact that the electorally most popular candidate did not actually become president was even more significant, but this will be explained in a discussion of the Bordaberry presidency.

presidents from succeeding themselves. Pacheco Areco, for obvious reasons, wanted this provision amended. The voters rejected the idea by an enormous margin: only 10 percent of all voters endorsed Pacheco's plan.[81] The voters also rejected the proposal that the president have the right to dissolve the legislature and call new elections. This initiative should, in theory, have been popular as a means of strengthening executive authority in the face of an increasingly unruly and leftist legislature. Yet, it received only 1,870 votes nationwide. Only .1 percent of the voters endorsed strengthening the power of the executive at the expense of the representational assembly.[82] An electorate that was ready to defect from democracy would have voted otherwise.

The Uruguayan Left

The members of the electorate who voted for the Broad Front were not as threatening as their more conservative opponents made them appear. The sheer scope of the coalitions' surge in popularity seemed impressive (especially in a political system accustomed to the stability of a two-party system), yet the nature of the victory suggested that the coalition would have limited horizons. First, the Front's voting base was limited almost exclusively to Montevideo. Of the eighteen seats the party won in 1971, thirteen were from the capital. The Broad Front attracted only 10 percent of the vote outside of Montevideo—the same percentage the Left attracted in the whole country in 1966.[83] "It was clear," to quote Luis González, "that the party had little popular appeal outside the capital."[84]

A second limitation on the Left's horizon derived from the sociological narrowness of its base. The Broad Front supporters were overwhelmingly young and often first-time voters.[85] The coalition's capacity to lure older voters away from the traditional parties was limited. Relying on younger voters was intrinsically problematic in a country such as Uruguay because out-migration had reached crisis proportions. The Broad Front's leadership realized this—one of their most memorable campaign slogans was "Don't Leave, Buddy, There's Some Hope"—yet party leaders had little influence over who would leave and who would not.

[81] Alcántara Saez and Crespo Martínez, *Partidos Políticos*, 57–58.

[82] Ibid., 57.

[83] Ibid., 6.

[84] *Political Structure*, 113.

[85] Aguiar, "Clivajes sociales," 31, and *Uruguay: País de Emigración*; and Gillespie, *Negotiating Democracy*, 26.

The party leadership also had limited capacity to alter what one observer called the "pre-Marxist political mentality" of the nation's working class.[86] Class cleavages were important between elections. This is why leftist parties had long been hegemonic in the nation's trade unions. But at election time, class identities were trumped by other identities.[87] The only setting in which class was a good predictor of the vote was for the Left coalition itself, but this was only because the Left received "relatively *more* support from the *upper* and *upper middle* classes than from other strata."[88] This ironic reality raised serious dilemmas about how the Left coalition should present itself to the voters. Could wage-workers who had been immune to the appeals of the Communist and Socialist Parties for decades be lured into supporting a Left coalition run by the young people of the middle and upper classes? If not, were there many more upper- and middle-class Uruguayans who might vote against their own material interests and endorse the Left?

These dilemmas were unique to the Uruguayan Broad Front. No other leftist group in Latin America faced a working class with such strong bonds to traditional centrist parties. As a result, the coalition was different from its counterparts elsewhere and probably less threatening.

Though the Front was often seen as the Uruguayan twin of the Unidad Popular, it embraced a much "broader section of the Left-Right continuum."[89] In terms of both its composition and its policy positions, the Front "was more Center-leaning" than the Chilean coalition.[90] At least one widely respected analyst argued that the Broad Front was adopting the tactics of a "catch-all" party because this is what the moderate political culture of the electorate required.[91] The fact that the Front chose a fairly moderate, nonaligned retired general named Líber Seregni as its presidential candidate suggests that this view was at least partially correct.[92]

The key to the Broad Front's appeal might have been based less on its ideological platform than on the nature of the political experience it offered its supporters. Unlike Brazil and many other countries, Uru-

---

[86] Solari, *Uruguay Partidos Políticos*, 106. Solari is using Duverger's phrase here.

[87] Aguiar, "Clivajes sociales," 23–24.

[88] Ulises Graceras, "Intergenerational Cleavages and Political Behavior: A Survey Study of the 1971 Presidential Elections in Uruguay" (Ph.D. dissertation, Michigan State University, 1977), 51.

[89] González, "Continuity and Change," 152.

[90] González, *Political Structure*, 39.

[91] Solari, *Uruguay Partidos Políticos*, 148.

[92] Weinstein, *Uruguay*, 124.

guay had had legal Socialist and Communist Parties for decades. The programs offered by the Left were thus not new, nor for the most part were the parties and personalities that offered them. The country's economic crisis was not new either and had not caused a surge in left-wing voting before. The element that distinguished the Left of 1971 from the Left of 1966 was the successful promotion of "participatory citizenship."[93] Uruguay's new Left offered an activist, hands-on, direct political experience that distinguished it from both the older Left on the one hand and the traditional parties on the other. The newborn "hope" that figured prominently in the Broad Front's slogans derived precisely from this. As one of the Front's intellectual leaders described it in retrospect, what the Front offered "was less a program than a state of being, an experience of something new. [The old forms of] living-out democratic norms were worn out. Many of the most dynamic sectors of society, including a great many young people and intellectuals looked . . . above all for new forms of direct, mass participation."[94]

The fact that the Left provided these opportunities and that a "great many young people and intellectuals" did in fact seize them is amply illustrated by the level of public polarization described above. Yet, the fact that the Left put so much emphasis on direct, visible action led insiders and outsiders to exaggerate its strength. Mobilization sent off so much smoke that no one could judge the size of the fire itself. Thus, within the Pachequista government rumors circulated that the Broad Front would take the election with 30 percent of the vote. Meanwhile, the Tupamaros forged plans for a countercoup "in case the Frente Amplio won and was prevented from taking power by a right-wing coup."[95]

Of course, the Left lost by a wide margin. Even in its stronghold of Montevideo it attracted less than half the votes of the victorious Colorados. The Left was unambiguously successful in that its representation in the Legislative Assembly jumped from ten seats in 1966 to twenty-three seats in 1971, but six of these—more than 25 percent—were the result of factional polarization based on elite defections from the Colorados and the Blancos.[96]

We cannot know how many votes the Left would have won without these defections. We do know that the main components of the Broad Front, meaning the Christian Democrats, the Socialists, the Popular

[93] For more on why this term (taken from Almond and Verba) aptly describes the Frente Amplio's activities, see Moreira, *Democracia y Desarrollo*, 98.

[94] Gerónimo de Sierra, "La Izquierda en la Transición" *Revista Mexicana de Sociología* 47, no. 2 (April-June 1985): 114.

[95] Arrarás, "Armed Struggle," 141.

[96] Alcántara and Crespo, *Partidos Políticos*, 60; see graphic illustration and copy.

Union, the Lista-99, and the leftist Liberation Party, won a total of 13.7 percent of the vote in 1966. In coalition, in 1971, they won 18.3 percent of the vote.[97] In the context of a 30 percent increase in the size of the electorate, a 4.6% increase is neither surprising nor alarming. Even on the Left there was more continuity in voting than was immediately apparent. The dramatic mobilizations that filled highly visible public spaces were not mirrored in equally dramatic mobilizations at the polls.

The Absence of a Party of the Far Right

The gulf that existed between what happened in the streets and what happened in the voting booth made Uruguay similar to pre-coup Brazil. Yet Uruguay was unique in never developing an independent party of the far Right. The far Left was extremely active, but the far Right never emerged as an identifiable component of the party spectrum. As Juan Rial put it, "Right-wing radicalization expressed itself within the traditional parties without being associated with a specific sector of the parties or even with identifiable sublemas."[98] The absence on an independent far Right was not the result of structural barriers. (Right-wing sublemas might have broken away from the traditional parties just as left-wing sublemas did.) The absence of a far Right was rooted more deeply in the fact that Uruguay's longstanding liberal and lay traditions made extreme Right and Fascist programs seem alien.[99] Liberal myths were so "sacred" that it was, according to Juan Rial, "almost inconceivable that a party would [even] call itself conservative," much less fascist.[100] The extreme Right certainly existed in Uruguay. It was embodied in youth groups such as *Juventud Uruguaya en Pie* and in the "counter-guerrilla" groups that attacked the Left throughout the Pachequista and Bordaberry administrations. It had its own small publications and even extended into secondary schools.[101] However, it simply never had much numerical support. Its activities "remained marginal," especially if compared with the activities of the far Left.[102] The Left was often involved in violence and often the target of attacks, but its adversaries were almost always police or soldiers and not politi-

---

[97] Ibid., 59–60. Gillespie, *Negotiating Democracy,* 26, also attributes the growth of the Broad Front to the defection of the Blanco faction led by Erro and the Colorado faction led by Zelmar Michelini.

[98] Rial, *Partidos Políticos,* 1:26.

[99] Moreira, *Democracia y Desarrollo,* 93.

[100] Rial, *Partidos Políticos,* 1:108.

[101] Weinstein, *Uruguay,* 125.

[102] Kaufman, *Uruguay in Transition,* 35.

TABLE 4.3
Citizens' Evaluation of the State of the Union

	1967	1968	1969
Good	6	7	6
Fair	39	41	36
Bad	34	33	35
Very Bad	20	17	20
Don't Know	1	2	3

Source: Gallup Uruguay, *Informe Gallup 1970: Futuro Inmediato y Previsible del Uruguay* (Montevideo: Gallup Uruguay, 1970), 12.

Note: Individual Gallup polls were published without a listed sample size, but front matter states that samples varied between 750 and 900 randomly chosen individuals. See *Informe Gallup 1970*, 5.

cized civilians. Ordinary people were not lured into the streets by the far Right, and the absence of a far-Right party helps explain why. The absence of a far-Right party also helps explain why the Uruguayan legislature behaved differently from its Chilean counterpart. As González explains it, the fact that "the Center and Right were partners . . . within the traditional parties" had a "conciliatory effect." Despite the new strength of the Left, the "logic of bipartisan politics" was still preserved and helped to "temper" polarities.[103]

Polarities were also tempered outside of the political elite among the public in general. A review of public opinion data in the years prior to the coup reveals that people were not panicked by the turmoil described above and that they adhered to norms of tolerance through even the most turbulent moments of the pre-coup period. Tolerance survived despite the fact that Uruguayans were painfully aware of the chaos around them. As table 4.3 indicates, people were quite consistent in assessing the state of the nation in mixed to negative terms.

This caution and pessimism were mirrored in the private sphere. As table 4.4 indicates, most citizens were not expecting their own situations to improve in the immediate future. Though pessimism in 1970 was slightly down from the previous year, less than 40 percent of those polled thought that their own lives would be better in the year to come.

On the eve of the 1971 elections, most Uruguayans expected unemployment to rise,[104] and a solid majority of citizens identified either

[103] González, "El Sistema de Partidos," 78.

[104] Gallup Uruguay, *Informe Gallup 1970* (Montevideo: Gallup, 1970), 25–26. Respondents were asked if they expected unemployment to rise or fall. 54 percent of those interviewed expected a rise, 33 percent expected a fall.

TABLE 4.4
Citizens' Expectations of Family's Future

	1969	1970
Will Get Better	24	39
Be the Same	36	34
Get Worse	29	23
Don't Know	11	4

Source: Gallup Uruguay, *Informe Gallup 1970*, 11.

general or specific economic problems as the most important issues facing their families.[105] Forty-seven percent of those interviewed saw the country as "gravely troubled," and an additional 37 percent saw it as "troubled."[106]

It is highly significant that these negative assessments were not reflected in a panicked move to the reactionary Right at the polls. They were not reflected in support for increased authoritarianism within the nation's existing democracy either. As table 4.5 illustrates, the majority of the Uruguayan citizenry rejected restrictions on civil liberties—even in a context of growing terrorist activity. A plurality had an unfavorable opinion of the ban on public meetings. Solid majorities rejected both the continuation of emergency security laws and the option of detention without trial, and a full 62 percent of those interviewed believed the Parliament should revoke the special security laws.

Most significant of all, the vast majority of Uruguayans rejected, without equivocation, the idea of a military government. As table 4.6 clearly indicates, Uruguayans did not defect from democracy even during the high points of urban terrorism. Just months before the coup, an impressive 79 percent of the citizenry preferred democracy with disorder to no democracy at all.

The moderation reflected in the responses summarized above was mirrored in a cautious optimism among experts from a broad range of

[105] Gallup Uruguay, *Informe Gallup 1971* (Montevideo: Gallup Uruguay, 1971), 8, asked, "What are the most important problems facing your family today?" 47 percent reported "economic problems in general," 6 percent reported "unemployment," and 5 percent reported "the cost of living." Significantly only 3 percent reported "a lack of social peace."

[106] Ibid., 26.

TABLE 4.5
Citizens' Support for Restrictions on Civil Liberties

Opinion on prohibition of public meetings	
Favorable	40%
Unfavorable	47%
DK/DA	13%

Opinion on security measures (emergency laws)	
Beneficial to the country	33%
Not beneficial	58%
DK/DA	9%

Opinion on detention without judge's approval	
Favorable	11%
Unfavorable	69%
DK/DA	20%

Opinion on whether parliament should revoke the special security laws	
Should revoke laws	62%
Should not revoke laws	29%
DK/DA	9%

Source: Instituto de Ciencias Sociales, as reported in Enrique Carpena, "Clase Social, Ideología y Opinión Pública," in *Uruguay: Poder, Ideología, y Clases Sociales,* ed. Instituto de Ciencias Sociales (Montevideo: Facultad de Derecho y Ciencias Sociales, Instituto de Ciencias Sociales, 1970), 64–72.

TABLE 4.6
Citizens' Preferences for Democracy vs. Military Government

	October '72	July '71	January '71	May '68
Democratic, even with disorder	79%	78%	73%	71%
Military, strong, ordered	13%	11%	16%	21%
No Opinion	8%	11%	11%	8%

Source: Juan Rial, *Partidos Políticos, Democracia y Autoritarismo* (Montevideo: Ediciones de la Banda Oriental, 1984), vol. 2:34, quoting Gallup polls.

TABLE 4.7
Experts' Expectations of Political Future

	Certain	Very Likely	Unlikely	Impossible	DK
Unity of trade unions with students	3%	14%	33%	44%	6%
Higher levels of public mobilization with successful general strikes	3%	3%	33%	55%	6%
Unleashing of a social revolution	—	—	14%	80%	6%

Source: Gallup Uruguay, *Informe Gallup 1970*, 25.
N = 69

TABLE 4.8
Experts' Expectations about Popular Political Preferences

How Will Popular Preferences Change in the Future?		
% of Respondents Expecting People to . . .	Middle Classes	Lower Classes
Turn to the Left	13%	19%
Turn to the Right	13%	16%
Stay the Same	74%	65%

Source: Gallup Uruguay, *Informe Gallup 1970*, 17.

professional categories.[107] Gallup surveys of expert opinion revealed an optimism about the future on a number of key dimensions. The panic that might be associated with reactionary behavior on the part of the privileged was absent. As table 4.7 illustrates, most experts did not expect the alliance between trade unions and students to grow stronger in the future. Only a small minority expected mobilization to increase or for general strikes to be effective. Most important, no one seemed to think a social revolution was in the making. Ninety-four percent of those sampled thought a social revolution was either unlikely or very unlikely.

As table 4.8 indicates, experts expected some of their fellow citizens to become more sympathetic to the Right or the Left in the future, but expectations of continuity were dominant.

[107] For every year covered here, the Gallup team chose a representative sample of individuals whom they deemed "experts" from economics, business, the academy, industry, agriculture, religion, politics, banking, and international affairs. See *Informe 1970*, 4–5, for a sample description.

TABLE 4.9
Experts' Forecasts on the Future of the Tupamaros

The Popularity and Prestige of the Tupamaros . . .

Will grow	—	
Will remain the same	56%	
Will decrease	38%	
Other responses	6%	

The Tupamaros . . .	*Yes*	*No*
Will cause the fall of the government	—	100%
Will continue its current attacks	95%	5%
Will be destroyed	1%	99%

Source: Gallup Uruguay, *Informe Gallup 1971* (Montevideo: Gallup Uruguay, 1971), 27.

Expert opinions on the future of the Tupamaros showed a similar level of confidence and little suggestion of panic. As table 4.9 shows, none of those interviewed thought the group would grow more popular, and nearly 40 percent thought its popularity would drop. Only 1 percent thought the Tupamaros would be "destroyed," but not a single respondent believed that the MLN-T would topple the government.[108]

Table 4.10 shows that knowledgeable Uruguayans were not panicked about the future. Experts' long-term projections about the economy were not pessimistic. None of the people polled expected the economy to be worse in either 1975 or 1980. Indeed, 67 percent expected it to be better in just a few years. Long-term expectations regarding civic order were also fairly positive. Though many experts were not willing to venture an opinion on this issue, those who did were surprisingly optimistic. It is important to note that this optimism was not borne of any expectation that the Uruguayan democracy would not exist in 1975. Not only did experts treat the 1976 elections as a given, one-third of them even predicted that the Broad Front would compete in the elections with "good results."[109]

As late as 1971, respondents did not even expect a tightening, much less an elimination, of the existing democratic system: 70 percent expected that the legislature would not approve stricter penalties for political crimes.[110] Only 6 percent expected the government to close the

[108] Gallup Uruguay, *Informe Gallup 1971*, 28.
[109] Ibid., 23.
[110] Ibid., 28.

TABLE 4.10

Experts' Forecasts on the Future of Uruguay's Economy and Society

How will the economy be in 1975? How will it be in 1980?

	1975	1980
Better	67%	56%
The same	—	—
Worse	—	—
Other opinions	5%	6%
No opinion	28%	38%

What will be the state of public order in 1975? What will it be in 1980?

	1975	1980
Conflictual	22%	11%
Pacified	56%	62%
No opinion	22%	27%

Source: Gallup Uruguay, *Informe Gallup 1971*, 65.

universities for long periods of time, and only 17 percent expected the government to place significant limits on university autonomy.[111] Put in this context, the overwhelming popularity of democracy evinced in table 4.6 is especially impressive. The lasting popularity of democracy is even more impressive if we consider that the 1971 elections were "accompanied by a level of violence unparalleled since the civil war."[112] Uruguayans demonstrated a remarkable level of tolerance in the years leading up to the coup.

Polarization among Elites

The tolerance displayed by the citizenry in general was a reflection of relatively low levels of polarization among legislative elites. In Brazil, Chile, and Argentina, legislative elites were severely polarized over a broad range of issues. In Uruguay, legislators were less divided and more steadfast in their endorsement of democratic government. There was certainly polarization at the top of the Uruguayan state, but it took the form of executive-congressional conflict. Parties that might have

[111] Ibid., 61.
[112] Weinstein, *Uruguay*, 125.

polarized united instead against what they viewed as an undemocratic executive.

The peculiarities of the Uruguayan case derived in part from its unique electoral system. As already explained, a moderate politician named Wilson Ferreira Adulnate of the Blanco Party won the most votes for the presidency in 1971. However, Uruguayan law dictates that the office is awarded not to the candidate with the most votes but to the party with the most votes. Since the Colorado Party beat the Blanco Party, the Colorados' front-runner, Juan Bordaberry, became president. He did so with only 22.8 percent of the vote. His weak mandate was partially a reflection of the ambivalence Uruguayans felt toward his stronger predecessor and patron, Pacheco Areco. It was also a reflection of the fact that Bordaberry himself had little personal prestige. He was a little-known member of a rural conservative faction of the Blanco Party as late as 1966 and had only joined the Colorado Party because of his friendship with Pacheco Areco.[113] Bordaberry's weak mandate forced him to cobble together a coalition of factions to gain a majority of seats in the Congress. Rejected by progressive groups within his own party, he had to enlist the support of a conservative Blanco faction to gain control of even a bare 51.1 percent of the seats.[114]

Bordaberry's relationship with Congress would soon prove his undoing. Though the legislature was not obstructionist at first,[115] conflicts broke out as soon as Bordaberry attempted to extend the authority of the executive and the armed forces at the expense of the legislature. There were three arenas of conflict. One involved a government campaign against corruption. Using documents secured by the extreme Left, the executive and the armed forces began to investigate allegations of corruption among politicians and entrepreneurs.[116] When Colorado senator Jorge Batlle publicly challenged the military's authority to conduct these investigations, he was immediately arrested and jailed. A broad range of representatives leapt to his defense.

A broader range of legislators battled the president in a second arena over the suspension of public liberties and the extension of states of

[113] This is why Luis E. González writes that Bordaberry "was not a truly Colorado politican" (*Political Structure*, 42) and why Wilson Ferreira Adulnate wrote that the president "reacted against the political parties because he did not really belong to either of them." "Introduction," in Kaufman, *Uruguay in Transition*, x.

[114] A more detailed discussion is presented in Alcántara Saez and Crespo Martínez, *Partidos Políticos*, 65.

[115] See Ferreira Adulnate's introduction to Kaufman's *Uruguay in Transition*, xi. Bordaberry's vice-president Sapelli saw the 1971 Parliament as an improvement on its predecessor. See Gillespie, *Negotiating Democracy*, 47.

[116] Minello, "Uruguay: la Consolidación," 589.

security. In several well-publicized episodes, Congress voted to lift security restrictions, only to have the president reimpose them.[117] As the defeat of the Tupamaros became obvious, more and more legislators saw these laws as unnecessary and an affront to the democratic order. The executive met with resistance "even among its own majority." Eventually, "Congress refused to vote any further measures" that threatened individual freedoms.[118]

The third and most telling conflict between the president and the Congress involved a battle over immunity for Broad Front leader Enrique Erro. The military (and the president) sought to prosecute Erro for aiding and abetting the MLN-T, but as a member of Congress he was protected from prosecution. When the executive demanded that his immunity be suspended, Congress refused to cooperate. Given the distribution of seats, Erro would have been sacrificed immediately in a more polarized legislature. Instead, a broad segment of Congress stood steadfast in his defense. On 27 June 1973 the military closed the National Assembly altogether,[119] but the legislature maintained its stature as a defender of elected government and rule of law. Despite widespread disillusion with the traditional political parties and with the legislature's inability to cure the country's many ailments, the Congress maintained its democratic credentials. Though "inefficiently and too late," Uruguayan parliamentary majorities "stood for democracy against [a] president who did not."[120]

A Curious Coup

The nature of citizen sentiment and the behavior of legislative elites make the breakdown of Uruguayan democracy unique and perplexing. Why was democracy replaced by dictatorship in 1973? Theories of bureaucratic authoritarianism lead us to seek our answers in the economic crises that emerge from the exhaustion of import substitution, in the hypermobilization that emerges as different groups battle over a shrinking pie, and in a coup-coalition that opts for authoritarianism to block an overload of political demands coming from a hyper-

[117] Rial, *Partidos Políticos*, 2:29; and Gillespie, *Negotiating Democracy*, 47.

[118] Ferreira Adulnate, "Introduction," xi.

[119] For a brief summary of what happened, see Gillespie, *Negotiating Democracy*, 49.

[120] González, *Political Structure*, 48. Wilson Ferreira Adulnate was convinced that despite all its shortcomings, the Uruguayan people "regarded the Parliament as the defender of public morality." "Introduction," xi.

mobilized society.[121] This line of reasoning is helpful in part. There can be little doubt that the regime change of 1973 was related to the economic crisis that manifested itself in the late fifties, and there is widespread agreement that the mobilization of labor and the emergence of disloyal and semiloyal oppositions were rooted in economic crisis as well.

Beyond these key connections, though, the model falls short. First, Uruguay's economic crisis was triggered by problems in the primary export sector, not by a crisis of import substitution, which was never a possibility in a tiny economy. Second, the coup came only after the trade union movement was showing signs of weakness and after the Tupamaros, the most serious disloyal opposition by far, had been decisively routed.[122] Third and most importantly, the coup coalition that emerged in Uruguay had neither the breadth nor the resources that the theory would lead us to expect. Uruguayan capital as a whole did not support the institution of a military regime. Industrialists, who were exhausted and threatened by a level of labor mobilization they had never seen before, did support the coup. Coming from the same social background as some of the military officers, they made their wishes known to the armed forces leaders well before the coup took place. However, other sectors of the bourgeoisie were much less enthusiastic about military rule. The fact that the armed forces arrested Jorge Batlle—a financier with long standing ties to international capital— illustrates that the military's relations with capital were complex if not confrontational. Finance capital seems to have been supportive of economic liberalization and structural adjustment but not at all enthusiastic about leaving the government in the hands of the military.[123] Uruguay's landowners showed surprising ambivalence if not hostility to military rule. The official Rural Federation (the class association of the landed elite) issued a statement in May of 1973 in which it "reaffirmed a profound faith in democracy and its institutions."[124] Large landowners did not, in general, "view the military's political or economic policy" as "being beneficial."[125] Though there was heterogeneity of opinion within the landowning classes, the establishment preferred

---

[121] The classic statement of this argument is Gulliermo O'Donnell, *Modernization and Bureaucratic Authoritarianism: Studies in South American Politics* (Berkeley: Institute of International Studies, University of California, 1979). For critical and incisive analyses of the model, see David Collier, *The New Authoritarianism*.

[122] Gillespie, *Negotiating Democracy*, makes this point about trade unions too.

[123] Handelman, "Labor-Industrial Conflict," 377.

[124] These are the words of the federation's president, published first in May before the coup and then again after the coup on 7 August 1973. See Rial, *Partidos Políticos*, 2:14.

[125] Handelman, "Labor-Industrial Conflict," 377.

to work as it always had, with the traditional party elites. Consequently, it showed support for "democratic and civil symbols" before and after the regime change.[126] Gerónimo de Sierra is correct in arguing that in Uruguay "it was not only the workers but important sectors in the middle class and even the bourgeoisie who rejected military authoritarianism."[127]

Economic crisis and class conflict certainly contributed to the atmosphere in which the coup took place but were not in themselves its "sufficient" cause. There were institutional and personal factors that played a contributing role, too. First, presidentialism and fixed-term elections deprived the legislature of a positive vote-of-no-confidence option that would have allowed for the democratic resolution of their impasse with the president. Second, the highly factionalized nature of the traditional parties, plus the related need for coalition governments, deprived the president of the solid support that consistent policy-making requires. Finally, on a personal level, neither Pacheco Areco nor Bordaberry were dedicated democrats.[128] If Gestido had lived or if Ferreira Aldunate had become president, the mix of crises and institutions summarized above might not have led to dictatorship.

Though all these factors contributed to the likelihood of dictatorship, the timing and the nature of what actually transpired was due primarily to factors related to the Uruguayan military. Military officers destroyed Uruguay's civilian government because they were emboldened by their past success, threatened by their future, and deluded about their popular support. The coup derived from these three factors.

The six-month victory over the Tupamaros was the success that drew the military deeper into politics. There is no evidence that the armed forces as an institution would have become an explicitly political actor if the Tupamaros had not engaged in armed struggle. The fact that the police (rather than the military) were charged with defeating the group indicates that the military's role was far from predetermined. The speed with which the military accomplished its mission contrasted dramatically with the slow achievements of elected politicians and undermined the government's credibility.

Incentives emanating from the international community emboldened the military, too. Deeply fearful of Cuban-style activity in Latin America and reeling from the shock of Allende's electoral victory in

---

[126] The federation's ties to the Blanco Party, which had a tradition of being more ruralist, were longstanding. See Kaufman, *Uruguay in Transition*, 43.

[127] "Introducción al Estudio," 572.

[128] González, *Political Structure*, 50

Chile, the United States made a substantial investment in training and equipment for counterinsurgency initiatives. U.S.–Uruguayan military ties had been strong for some time. Uruguay was second only to Brazil in the amount of aid it received from the U.S. in 1970, and aid increased as the Tupamaros appeared more threatening.[129] The defeat of the MLN-T brought an increase rather than a decrease in military initiatives, for the reigning security doctrine dictated that the battle against insurgency should embrace the whole set of institutions that gave rise to insurgency in the first place.[130] When the armed forces attempted to coerce a broader range of actors, they were met with greater opposition. González summarized the process succinctly: the military's "behavior and demands" proved "unacceptable for a civilian independent legislature and the first important rejection of the Army's demands produced the coup."[131]

The coup was precipitated by the legislature's refusal to deprive Senator Erro of his congressional immunity, but this act of defiance was simply the last of several incidents that threatened the military as an institution. In 1972, congressional criticism of the military's human rights violations had led five-hundred officers to sign a strong public statement condemning the legislature for the "unpatriotic smearing of the defenders of the nation."[132] Later, Colorado leader Amilcar Vasconcellos was charged with defaming the military when he criticized its treatment of Jorge Batlle. In February of 1973, Vasconcellos posed a threat once again when he exposed a document revealing an army plan to take over the state.[133] Still other legislators denounced corruption and lawlessness within the military itself.[134] Throughout Bordaberry's tenure in office there was a constant battle to find a defense minister who was worthy of the military's trust. Five different ministers filled the post in a period of only ten months.[135]

All these events and struggles were made more dramatic by what was going on in the rest of South America. Ties with the Brazilian military government had been growing stronger since the time of Pacheco

---

[129] Minello, "Uruguay: la Consolidación," 588. See also "Uruguay y Ahora, Que?" *Cuadernos de Crisis* 4 (1974): 10–11.

[130] See Rial, *Partidos Políticos,* 2:19; Junta de Comandantes en Jefe, *Las Fuerzas Armadas al Pueblo Oriental* (Montevideo: República Oriental del Uruguay, Junta de Comandantes en Jefe, 1976–1978).

[131] González, *Political Structure,* 43.

[132] Weinstein, *Uruguay,* 130.

[133] *La Opinión,* 7 October 1972, p. 1.

[134] Bari González of the Blancos was the most notable of these. See Kaufman, *Uruguay in Transition,* 29.

[135] Ibid., 32.

Areco. Ties with the Argentinean military had been growing stronger since the Ongania dictatorship years earlier. The fact that a civilian government had returned to power in Argentina and reestablished relations with Cuba exacerbated the military's sense of threat.[136] The coincidence of perceived threat and growing ambition on the part of the military proved lethal for Uruguayan democracy.

Added to this mix were misperceptions about citizen support for intervention. Some of these misperceptions were understandable. Civilian political elites sent mixed messages about what role the military should play in the resolution of the nation's problems. On the one hand, civilian leaders openly opposed an expansion of the military's powers, as illustrated by the incidents summarized above. On the other hand, politicians of various types courted the military in the hopes of getting them to remove Bordaberry, hold new elections, and thus help install a government more to their liking. The Broad Front was surprisingly reluctant to criticize the armed forces publicly, despite the military's notoriously harsh treatments of the MLN-T. The Left coalition focused its hostility on Bordaberry alone, mistakenly believing that "nationalist" and "progressive" forces would eventually dominate the military and force the president to resign.[137] This erroneous belief explains why Broad Front leader Liber Seregni publicly supported military intervention during a speech to the CNT on 9 February 1973.[138] The Left's illusions also explain why, even on the eve of the parliament's dissolution, the Broad Front senators uttered "not a single word" against the army's behavior.[139] Julio Maria Sanguinetti, a progressive leader of the Colorado opposition, concluded in retrospect that the "Uruguayan Left . . . encouraged the military advance."[140] But they were not the only force to do so. Ferreira Aldunate met with the commander in chief of the army in early February to ask that the military remove Bordaberry, install a government of national unity, and hold new elections.[141] These petitions for military intervention were not petitions for military dictatorship and were thus not wildly out of

[136] Kaufman suggests that the timing of the coup—just one month before Perón was to assume power in Argentina—was not coincidental. *Uruguay in Transition*, 16.

[137] Juan Rial cites the Communist Party newspaper, *El Popular*, as supporting military intervention from the Left. The Broad Front supported a left-wing military intervention as well, on February 9. See Rial, *Partidos Políticos*, 2:21, n. 17.

[138] Rial, *Partidos Políticos*, 2:20, from the Communist newspaper, *El Popular*, 11 February 1973.

[139] Kaufman, *Uruguay in Transition*, 30.

[140] *La Opinión*, 18 July 1973.

[141] Rial, *Partidos Políticos*, 2:21.

keeping with parliament's defense of democracy. The military, however, failed to recognize the distinction.

The people of Uruguay may have rejected even the idea of temporary intervention, but this went unrecognized too because of a misreading of what went on in the public sphere. Two events were key. The first took place in February 1973 when Bordaberry found himself bullied by the military over appointments. He made a public appeal for the defense of "democratic institutions" and was met with resounding silence. The demonstration he hoped for never materialized. Only a few supporters—including his ministers and their families—gathered outside his house. The backing he sought from the legislature was not forthcoming either. None of the parties made pronouncements or even spontaneous speeches on Bordaberry's behalf.[142] No one called for popular mobilizations, and when none appeared, the armed forces assumed that support for military rule was widespread. The military drew the same conclusion in June 1973 when the CNT organized a massive general strike and openly called upon the military to remove Bordaberry.[143] Both of these events reflected only a distrust of Bordaberry rather than a call for dictatorship, but this distinction escaped the military elites.[144] The armed forces closed the legislature five days later.

Conclusion

Ordinary people did not opt for dictatorship over democracy in Uruguay. The military toppled Uruguayan democracy. It did so largely to protect its own institutional interests. Though the military acted autonomously, civilian elites and civilian institutions had a decisive effect on how the armed forces calculated the cost of its action. Political elites were naive to expect that the military would simply step forward onto center stage, hold free elections, and then walk offstage, returning power to a civilian political class which had proved so obstreperous in

[142] Ibid., 1:57.

[143] Kaufman, *Uruguay in Transition*, 39, n. 69. See also Gillespie, *Negotiating Democracy*, 45.

[144] As Luis E. González put it, "Bordaberry was not a sincere democrat and was probably one of the most isolated presidents . . . since the birth of democracy. . . . [W]hen he attempted to stop the military in February 1973—nobody trusted him and accordingly, no one was willing to help him." *Political Structure*, 48. Ferreira Adulnate illustrated Bordaberry's credibility problem in the following description, "[Bordaberry was] always linked to the most anti-democratic currents of opinion: sympathizing with the Nazis in his youth; admiring Franco, supporting the 1933 coup d'état in Uruguay." "Introduction," x.

the past. Political elites were also naive in assuming that their failure to defend Bordaberry would not be interpreted as a go-ahead for anti-democratic action.

Behind these errors in judgment was a dysfunctional party system that muffled the voices of ordinary Uruguayans. In Uruguay, as in Brazil, there was not nearly as much voter polarization as imagined. Calculated with Sartori's own measures, the level of polarization in Uruguay in 1971 was comparable to those of France, Italy, and Finland in the same time period. The fact that none of these other countries underwent regime change indicates that this level of discord was not in itself intolerable.[145]

Uruguayans had a much higher tolerance for discord, disruption, and economic crisis than military elites believed. A careful analysis of public opinion and voting patterns reveals that their society was not vulnerable to the appeals of the revolutionary Left, that the extreme Right had miniscule support, and that the democratic Center was still strong. These facts were not appreciated because Uruguay's party system was not providing a clear reflection of the popular will. The combination of the double simultaneous vote, proportional representation, and an electoral law that awarded the presidency to the most popular party (rather than candidate) created strong incentives for internal party fragmentation. Party leaders allowed diverse and very small factions to use their party's name because every vote could be decisive and the competing party would accept the faction if they refused. What these abstractions meant in the real world was that the number of factions Uruguayan voters had to choose from multiplied dramatically. The number of Blanco lists for deputy increased from 126 in 1958 to 308 in 1971. The number of Colorado lists increased in the same period from 151 to 246.[146]

The system grew so complex that a voter in Montevideo in 1971 seeking to vote for one of the two traditional parties had 110 separate factions from which to choose. To make matters worse, "the ideological distance between certain factions of *different* parties . . . turned out to be smaller than what existed between factions *within* each party."[147] The party system was so complex that it became opaque. Pivotal actors could not use it as a window on the public will, so they constructed their vision from other materials. Military elites looked to highly polar-

---

[145] The calculations were done by Luis E. González and totaled .51. See *Political Structure*, 111.

[146] See Gillespie, *Negotiating Democracy*, 31, for the 1962 and 1966 figures as well.

[147] See González, *Political Structure*, 34; and González, "Continuity and Change," 142, emphasis added.

ized public spaces and to what seemed like a less opaque Left to craft their image of the popular will. What they saw provided both a push and pull toward dictatorship.

The sad irony is that ordinary Uruguayans had not defected from democracy in 1973. The problem, as González describes it, was simply that "political parties were no longer capable of performing their expressive functions transmitting . . . the desires of the electorate. . . . Not only did they not transmit the signals coming from the electorate, they obscured them." Democratic forces were, he believes, in the "majority" in 1972.[148] The opaque party system simply obscured the popular will.

The depth of ordinary people's attachment to democracy was made patently clear in the aftermath of the June *golpe*. The CNT called for a twenty-four-hour general strike, but support was so widespread that the strike was extended indefinitely. It took nearly two weeks and hundreds of arrests to finally break the strikers' resistance.[149] On July 9, as it became clear that the strike would soon be crushed, thousands of unarmed people flooded the streets of Montevideo to demand a restoration of civilian rule. The army and police shot into the crowd and arrested hundreds of protestors.[150] Public resistance to the dictatorship thus ended at gunpoint, and a new regime—a regime that only a small minority of Uruguayans desired—was finally born.

[148] González, "El sistema de Partidos," 79.
[149] Collier and Collier, *Shaping the Political Arena*, 656.
[150] *La Opinión*, 9 July 1973.

5

THE TRAGEDY OF DEMOCRACY IN CHILE

"I don't know why we need to stand by and watch a country
go communist due to the irresponsibility of its own people."
—Henry Kissinger[1]

"[We erred in] our inability to perceive the divisive, negative
and selfish tendencies that also existed in the hearts of the
people."
—J. Silva Solar[2]

THE PEOPLE OF CHILE are often blamed for the regime change that
brought dictatorship to their country in 1973. Though they are
rarely, if ever, accorded full responsibility for the events leading
to the September 11 military coup, Chileans are criticized by actors of
all sorts for shortcomings of all sorts. Henry Kissinger, secretary of
state of the United States, found Chileans irresponsibly drawn to the
communist Left. Julio Silva Solar, the Chilean Socialist leader, found
them selfishly and irrationally drawn to the fascist Right.

Ordinary Chileans were highly visible throughout the last years of
their nation's democracy, and the intensity of their political mobilization helps explain the ironic patterns of blame summarized above. The
intensity of popular mobilization also explains why the final act in the
drama of the breakdown of democracy in Chile was more violent and
more horrifying than that in either Brazil or Uruguay. The air attack
on the presidential palace and the violent death of the nation's freely
elected president, Salvador Allende, marked the culmination of a long
and bitter struggle between ideological opposites.

[1] These words were spoken in reference to Chile at a 27 June 1970 meeting of the
Committee of Forty, as quoted in Radomiro Tomic, "Christian Democracy and the Gov-
ernment of the Unidad Popular," in *Chile at the Turning Point*, ed. Federico G. Gil, Ricardo
E. Lagos and Henry A. Landsberger (Philadelphia: Institute for the Study of Human
Issues, 1979), 236.

[2] Reflecting on why Chilean democracy collapsed, Silva Solar also says that errors
were made in "attributing to the masses an ability to adopt and administer decisions
and to resolve problems by themselves." He bemoans the fact that the left-wing leadership was deluded by "a certain anarchist optimism" regarding those over whom they
supposedly had authority. "Errors of the Unidad Popular and a Critique of the Christian
Democrats," in Gil et al., *Chile at the Turning Point*, 320.

It is thus neither surprising nor wrong that references to polarization riddle analyses of Allende's years in power. In Parliament, in the press, and in public spheres of all sorts, Chile in 1973 seemed truly a nation of enemies. But how encompassing were the enemy camps and when did they begin to form? Does Chile in the early 1970s constitute a classic case of polarization?

Giovanni Sartori would answer this last question in the affirmative, for he uses the Chilean case to illustrate the merits of his polarization metaphor. The data he presents seem to indicate that Chilean voters were progressively attracted to parties on the extremes of the political spectrum. When we combine this image with knowledge of the notorious performance failures of Allende's government, it is easy to conclude that ordinary Chileans simply abandoned democratic institutions as soon as they yielded unwanted results.

This conclusion is appealing but erroneous. It has at least three flaws. First, the earliest and numerically most dramatic phase of polarization began well before performance failures became acute. Second, the magnitude of the shifts in party popularity between 1965 and 1973 is easily exaggerated. These shifts seem less dramatic and less extraordinary if put in historical perspective. Third, and most importantly, the shifts in party popularity that did occur were generally not the result of massive changes in the party loyalties of ordinary people. The changes that at first glance looked like polarization were usually not the result of vote switching but the result of changes in electoral laws and changes in the tactics of party elites.

Of all the South American cases examined in this study, the Chilean case comes closest to fitting the polarization model, but even this case falls short. What stands out as we sift through the historical evidence is the resilience of the political center, the stability of political identities, and the longevity of democratic discourse. As I shall explain below, it was the stability of voting patterns (and not their fluidity) that proved most problematic as Chilean democracy entered its last crisis. As party elites realized that they were unable to make any more significant incursions into enemy voting blocks at the polls, they began to encourage more confrontations in public space. Public polarization increased dramatically in the last months of the democratic regime, but this was the ironic result of an inability to polarize voters further.

Thus, in Chile, as in Brazil and Uruguay, polarization reached different levels of intensity in different political spaces. Making assumptions about the preferences of ordinary Chileans from observations of a highly polarized polity in the streets proves highly misleading. I explain the different modes of polarization below. My explanation begins with a discussion of the real and imagined polarization of voters.

An Overview of Congressional Voting Trends

The percentage of Chileans voting for parties at the polar ends of the Left-Right party spectrum grew between 1965 and 1973. This indisputable fact presumably explains why Sartori uses the Chilean case to illustrate "the dynamics of polarized pluralism."[3] Table 5.1 indicates how he makes his case.

Sartori divides Chile's congressional elections into historical groups and, dismissing the elections between 1945 and 1961 as "not very significant,"[4] draws our attention immediately to the period between 1961 and 1973. He concludes that by 1969, "it was very evident that the pulls of the system were overwhelmingly centrifugal, with the extreme Left going up to 32 percent and the Right (now united in the PN) regaining 21 percent."[5] Sartori sees the 1973 congressional elections as "confirm[ing] that polarization had destroyed whatever might formerly have been considered a Center area." He concludes that "on the sole ground of its center-fleeing polarization" it was "easy" to predict "that all the conditions of a democratic governance were rapidly dwindling."[6]

Electoral Trends prior to Allende

Closer attention to historical trends and to the political context behind these voting figures suggests that Sartori's claims are exaggerated. Focusing only on a few elections in a small time-period, Sartori unwittingly overstates the intensity of polarization and misleads us about its source. The 1969 election is truly a watershed in Chilean politics, but it needs to be analyzed in historical context to be properly understood. The four-year period running from 1965 to the election itself is rich in meaning but brief enough to be misleading.

Sartori is misled, for example, by the sudden increase in support for the Partido Nacional in 1969. He classifies the party as an extreme-right group and presents its 21 percent vote-share as ominous evidence of system polarization. This interpretation requires rethinking. The Partido Nacional came into being in 1965, when the Liberal and Conserva-

[3] Sartori, *Parties and Party Systems*, 163.
[4] Ibid., 162.
[5] Ibid.
[6] Ibid., 162–63.

TABLE 5.1
Congressional Elections in Chile, 1945–1973

	Communists (PCCh)	Socialists (PS)	Radical (PR)	Christian Dem. (PDC)	Liberal (PL)	Conservative (PCU)
1945	10.3	12.8	20.0	2.6	18.0	23.6
1949	—	9.3	21.7	3.9	18.0	22.7
1953	—	14.1	13.3	2.8	11.0	10.1
1957	—	10.7	21.5	9.4	15.4	13.8
	PCCh	PS	PDC	PR	PL	PCU
1961	11.8	11.1	15.9	22.2	16.6	14.8
1965	12.8	10.6	43.6	13.7	7.5	5.3
	PS	PCCh	PR	PDC	PN	
1969	15.1	16.6	13.4	31.1	20.9	
	PS MAPU Izq. Chr.	PCCh API	PR	PDC	Rad. Dem. Izq. Rad.	PN
March 1973	18.7	16.7	3.3	33.3	1.3	22.7
	1.3	1.3			0.7	
	0.7					

Source: Reproduced from Giovanni Sartori, *Parties and Party Systems: A Framework for Analysis* (Cambridge: Cambridge University Press, 1976), 161.

Notes: Any discrepancies between these data and those presented in Table 5.12 are resolved in favor of the latter. (The notes that follow are from Sartori's original table.): R. H. McDonald, *Party Systems and Elections in Latin America* (Chicago: Markham, 1971), 134. In 1973 the Popular Unity Front—PS, MAPU, PCCh, API—obtained 42.1 percent (an increase of six seats in the House and of two seats in the Senate), and the opposition (CODE) 56.2 percent of the vote. The 1973 percentages are computed from the allocation of the seats. The returns of 1949, 1953, and 1957 are highly incomplete (in 1953 as much as 48.7 percent of the vote is considered residual), but I follow McDonald for purposes of longitudinal comparability (the 1953 election produced a disturbing and ephemeral Ibanista majority). The major, unaccounted parties of the 1949–1957 period are PAL (Partido Agrario Laborista) and PSP (Partido Socialista Popular).

PS: Socialist Party; MAPU: Movement of United Popular Action (PCD split); Izq. Chr.: Christian Left; PCCh: Chilean Communist Party; API: Popular Independent Action; PR: Radical Party; PDC: Christian Democratic Party (since 1957; formerly National Falange); Izq. Rad.: Radical Left; Rad. Dem.: Radical Democrats; PN: National Party (merger of PL/PCU); PL: Liberal Party; PCU: Conservative Party.

tive Parties merged. Whether the combination of the Liberal and Conservative combination produced an "extreme-right" party at all is questionable in the first place,[7] but these groups truly did increase their

---

[7] Whether the Liberal Party fits the criteria for an extreme-right party may be questionable. Chilean scholars conclude that the party "contributed to developing more democratic consciousness" among the Chilean elite in the earliest years of competitive poli-

percentage of the poll between 1965 and 1969. The parties' share of votes in the Congressional elections jumped from a combined 12.8 percent in 1965 to an after-merger total of 20.9 percent.[8] In isolation, this appears to be an impressive gain, but if we look back to any election before 1965, the pattern is indisputably one of *loss*—and a *flight* from the Right. The Liberal and Conservative Parties garnered a combined total of 29.2 percent of the votes in 1957 and 31.4 percent of the votes in 1961. The National Party actually won *fewer* votes in the 1969 election than the Conservative Party won (running alone) twenty years earlier. The extreme Right was growing in electoral popularity as Chilean democracy entered its final crisis but this growth was not even a restitution of past levels of support.

The 1969 decline in support for the Christian Democrats is another component of the polarization model that has to be contextualized to be properly understood. The party's share of votes dropped precipitously between 1965 and 1969. This drop certainly represented a weakening of the political Center, but its implications seem less grave in the context of three facts. First, the party's drop in support followed a landslide victory in 1965. No party in Chilean history had ever amassed such a large share of congressional votes. Even when the Christian Democrats lost votes in 1969, their total was still higher than that of any other party in any legislative election since 1945.

Second, and relatedly, the centrist Christian Democrats outdistanced their nearest competition by some ten percentage points even after their 1969 loss. The Christian Democrats were still the largest party in the system (by a wide margin), and they still commanded twice the amount of support they had attracted in 1961. Seen through a wider historical lens, the party's 1969 loss looks very little like a devastating defeat.

This argument is reinforced if we consider that the loss followed four to five years of incumbency. This third contextual fact leads to the conclusion that the party's loss in 1969 was simply "the typical ebbing of a party in power."[9] If we use the preceding Alessandri government as our point of comparison, the conclusion rings true. Indeed, the parties

---

tics. The party's historical links with the Masonry, the liberal professions, and the bourgeoisie (rather than the landed aristocracy) made it decidedly different from the Conservative Party. See Germán Urzua Valenzuela, *Los Partidos Políticos Chilenos: Las Fuerzas Políticas* (Santiago: Editorial Jurídica Ediar-ConoSur, 1988), 288–89. For Liberal Party leaders' statements on the merits of democracy and universal suffrage, and for critiques of fascism, see the interviews in Sergio Guilisasti Tagle, *Partidos Políticos Chilenos*, 2d. ed. (Santiago: Editorial Nascimento, 1964), esp. 100–103.

[8] Note that the 1973 figures in Sartori's table represent seats and not votes. This is because parties contested the 1973 elections in coalitions.

[9] Paul Drake, *Socialism and Populism in Chile, 1932–52* (Urbana: University of Illinois Press, 1978), 312.

backing Alessandri suffered a much greater loss in popularity between 1961 and 1965 than the Christian Democrats did between 1964 and 1969.

The increase in support for left-wing parties *is* historically unprecedented even if examined with a wider historical lens. Both the Socialist Party and the Communist Party rose in popularity. Though the Socialists in 1969 were only recouping the percentage of the vote they had garnered in 1937 and 1945, the Communists' popularity in 1969 was at an historic high.[10]

The increase in support for left-wing parties was certainly real, but it was probably not the result of vote switching or of massive ideational change, as the polarization metaphor implies. It was very likely the result of the expansion of the Chilean electorate, instead.

Sartori, like many others, seems to assume that Chileans enjoyed universal suffrage throughout the period of his concern. He writes, for example, that Allende was elected by universal suffrage in 1970.[11] This is incorrect. Though the law on universal suffrage was passed (by the Christian Democrats) before Allende came to power, it did not come into effect until after Allende was elected. Chileans did not enjoy the right to universal suffrage until the municipal elections of 1971, and it was not until 1973 that Chile's legislative elections were open to all Chileans eighteen and over.[12] The growth of Chile's eligible electorate is depicted in table 5.2.

As these figures show clearly, Chilean democracy was highly exclusionary.[13] It was not until almost 1960 that even one-fifth of the population was registered to vote. The path toward a more inclusionary electoral system was traveled late and slowly. Voting rights were not extended to women until 1949. The single ballot (insuring the secrecy of the vote) was not instituted until 1958.[14] Voter registration did not become mandatory until 1962, and as mentioned above, the vote was not extended to illiterates and citizens over eighteen until 1970–71.

The expansion of the suffrage and the perception of polarization are closely related. It is not coincidental, for example, that Timothy Scully

---

[10] Valenzuela's data as shown in Scully "Reconstituting Party Politics in Chile" in Mainwaring and Scully, *Building Democratic Institutions*, p. 114.

[11] Sartori, *Parties and Party Systems*, 159.

[12] Law 17.284 extended voting rights to illiterates and to citizens above the age of eighteen. Though the law was passed on 23 January 1970, it did not come into effect until 4 November 1970, after the September elections that brought Allende to power. See Ricardo Cruz-Coke, *Historia Electoral de Chile, 1925–1973* (Santiago: Editorial Jurídica de Chile, 1984); and *Keesing's Contemporary Archives*, 1971, 18:24872.

[13] For an enlightening discussion of this point, see Karen Remmer, "Exclusionary Democracy," *Studies in Comparative International Development* 20, no. 4 (1985): 64–85.

[14] Prior to the government's printing of a single ballot, parties printed their own ballots. Since these were distinguished by color, voters' choices could be easily detected (and controlled). Scully, *Rethinking the Center*, 134.

TABLE 5.2
The Growth of the Chilean Electorate, 1953–1973

Year	Type of Election*	Total Population (000s)	Number of Registered Voters (000s)	Registered Voters as Pct. of Total Population
1953	C + M	6,462	1,100	17.0
1956	M	6,962	1,185	17.9
1957	C	7,137	1,284	18.0
1958	P	7,326	1,498	20.4
1960	M	7,689	1,762	23.0
1961	C	7,858	1,859	23.6
1963	M	8,217	2,570	31.3
1964	P	8,319	2,915	34.7
1965	C	8,584	2,921	34.0
1967	M	9,100	3,074	33.7
1969	C	9,566	3,245	33.9
1970	P	9,717	3,540	36.4
1971	M	9,879	3,792	38.3
1973	C	10,200	4,510	44.1

Sources: Cruz-Coke, *Historia Electoral de Chile, 1925–1973*, 38; Julio Heise González, *El Período Parlimentario* (Santiago: Editorial Universitaria, Universidad de Chile, 1982), 204, as presented in Timothy Scully, *Rethinking the Center: Party Politics in Nineteenth- and Twentieth-Century Chile* (Stanford: Stanford University Press, 1992) 143.

* C = Congressional; M = Municipal; P = Presidential.

dates the polarization of Chilean politics from 1958. It was only then, with the institution of the secret ballot, that less privileged Chileans could use elections as a meaningful forum of political expression. Coupled with the relegalization of the Communist Party, this change in electoral law was bound to affect the outcome of elections.

The fact that illiteracy began to drop during these same years was bound to affect elections as well. As literacy increased, and more Chileans qualified to vote, the electorate became not only larger but more socially diverse. Divisions that had been partially shrouded in the past simply became more visible as the electoral system became more inclusionary.

How much of what we see as polarization is really only an artifact of delayed inclusion? Without individual voting histories, we can never really know. We do know that Chile's electorate expanded by

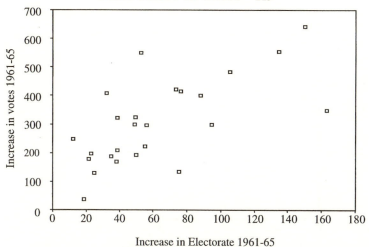

Increase in Electorate 1961-65

5.1. The expansion of the suffrage and the increase in votes for the Christian Democrats, 1961–1965. Figures represent percentage change and show the relationship between the variation in the votes for the Christian Democrats in each constituency and the increase in the electorate of the same constituency. Coquimbo is excluded because between 1961 and 1965 the electorate decreased. Asysén and Magallanes are excluded because in 1965 the Christian Democrats did not contest the elections in those two provinces. Santiago's electoral data are disaggregated into four constituencies. r = .668, significant at the .01 level (2-tailed test). N = 25. (*Source*: Germán Urzúa Valenzuela, *Historia Política de Chile y su Evolutión Electoral* [Santiago de Chile: Editorial Jurídica de Chile, 1992])

over one million people between 1961 and 1965 and that an additional 324,000 citizens exercised their right to vote in 1969. We also know that there is a strong statistical association between the growth of the electorate and the growth of support for particular parties. In the 1965 election, the expansion of the electorate seems to have worked to the benefit of the Christian Democrats.[15] The correlation between the growth in the Christian Democratic vote and the growth in the number of voters is illustrated in figure 5.1. There is no comparable statistically significant correlation for any other political party in the 1965 election.[16]

In the 1969 election, the expansion of the suffrage seems to have worked to the benefit of the Left. Figure 5.2 shows that what seemed

---

[15] The fact that the Christian Democrats picked up votes from both the moderate Right and from new voters is discussed in Atilio Borón, "Desarrollo Económico y Comportamiento Político," *Revista Latinoamericana de Ciencia Política* 1, no. 2 (1970): 236–87.

[16] The parties to the right of the Christian Democrats lost votes in 1965. For the Chilean Left, including Communists and Socialists, r = .301, but this is not statistically significant. See appendix to chapter 5, figure 5.A1.

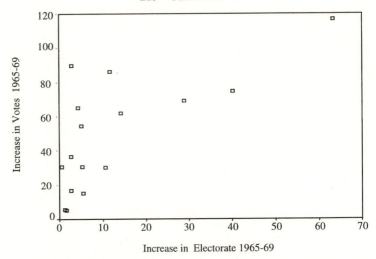

Increase in Electorate 1965-69

5.2. The expansion of the suffrage and the increase in votes for the Communists and the Socialists, 1965–1969. Figures represent percentage change and show the relationship between the variation in the votes for the Communists and the Socialists in each constituency and the increase in the electorate of the same constituency. Atacama, Arauco, Malleco, Cautín, Chiloé, and Santiago I and II are excluded because between 1965 and 1969 the electorate decreased. Talca, Maule, Cautín, Llanquihue, and Magallanes are excluded because neither the Socialists nor the Communists contested the elections in those provinces in either 1965 or 1969. Santiago's electoral data are disaggregated into four constituencies. $r =$ .668, significant at the .001 level (2-tailed test). $N = 17$. (*Source*: Valenzuela, *Historia Política de Chile*, 610, 612.)

like radicalization and polarization may well have been the result of making the electorate more inclusionary.[17]

Seen in the light of a dramatic 75 percent increase in the number of voters between 1961 and 1969, what seems most surprising about the increased support for the left-wing parties in 1965 and 1969 is not that it occurred, but that it occurred on such a small scale. An increase of only 8.8 percentage points in eight years is only a modest, and fairly gradual, gain. Seen in the proper historical context, it is remarkable that so few of the newly enfranchised voted for either the Communists or the Socialists.

A closer, more historically informed analysis of Chilean voting trends thus illustrates that vote switching in the late 1960s was not as dramatic

[17] The relevant statistics for the Christian Democrats and the National Party are $r =$ .347 and $r = -.007$, respectively. Neither of these correlation coefficients is statistically significant. See appendix to chapter 5, figures 5.A2 and 5.A3.

TABLE 5.3
Real Variations in Remuneration for Industry and
the Total Economy, 1959–1969

Year	Industry Remuneration Index	Total Economy Remuneration Index
1959	–1.0	1.4
1960	–2.0	2.2
1961	9.0	10.9
1962	4.4	0.9
1963	–7.9	–8.6
1964	2.5	–4.3
1965	10.9	13.9
1966	13.9	9.3
1967	9.9	8.6
1968	1.9	–1.4
1969	4.6	3.5

Source: Barbara Stallings, *Class Conflict and Economic Development in Chile, 1958–1973* (Stanford: Stanford University Press, 1978), pp. 250–51.

Note: Indices are calculated as the weighted average of the percent change in real wages for those earning the minimum wage, those earning the minimum salary, and those working in medium and large industries where remuneration was typically above the minimum.

as Sartori (and others) supposed. A close look at government performance illustrates that the vote switching and ideational change that did take place were brought on as much by policy success as policy failure. Chilean voters turned away from the Christian Democratic Party less because it suffered from policy paralysis than because it seemed successful in achieving so many of its farthest reaching policy goals.

The polarization that did occur during the Frei years *preceded* the onset of deep economic crisis. Indeed, by many standard measures Chile's economic performance in the mid- to late 1960s was fairly good. Levels of remuneration, for example, were not dropping as polarization occurred. This was true in the economy as a whole and in industry specifically. Table 5.3 tells the story.

Real remuneration in industry rose continuously, though unsteadily, from 1963 on. In the economy as a whole, it is interesting to note that the single two-year drop in remuneration was followed by a landslide victory for the *centrist* Christian Democrats. Thus, in the only brief period in which real wages fell, the Center expanded.

TABLE 5.4
Trends in Industrial Unemployment: Chile, 1958–1969

Year	1958	1959	1960	1961	1962	1963	1964	1965	1966	1967	1968	1969
Unemployment Rate in Percent	8.2	9.0	7.1	6.9	5.7	5.5	5.4	4.6	4.6	5.8	5.3	4.7

Source: Universidad de Chile, Instituto de Economia y Planificación, *Ocupación y Desocupación en Gran Santiago, 1958–1969*, as presented in Stallings, *Class Conflict*, 252.

TABLE 5.5
Inflation in Chile, 1958–1969: Annual Percent Increase in the Consumer Price Index

Year	1958	1959	1960	1961	1962	1963	1964	1965	1966	1967	1968	1969
Inflation	33.3	38.6	11.6	7.7	13.9	44.3	46.0	28.8	22.9	18.1	26.6	30.7

Source: Banco Central, *Boletín Mensual*, 1958–69, as presented in Stallings, *Class Conflict*, 247.

Trends in employment, like trends in remuneration, were fairly positive. Industrial unemployment rates were either stable or falling during the years when polarization supposedly began. As table 5.4 shows, unemployment was significantly lower in 1969 than in 1959.

Inflation was still a serious problem in the 1960s, and the rate of inflation was rising as the 1969 elections approached. Yet, as table 5.5 demonstrates, inflation was far below a historic high as polarization began. Even at its worst, the rate of inflation was nearly sixteen percentage points below what it had been when the Christian Democratic Party came to power.

Frei's modest success with remuneration, employment, and inflation was accompanied by a less visible but equally important rationalization of the administrative tax system.[18] The Christian Democrats reduced Chile's fiscal deficit from around 5 percent of GDP in 1964 to 1 percent of GDP in 1969. They achieved this reduction while extending social security coverage to almost 70 percent[19] of the active population and making dramatic improvements in access to education. In just five years, the government built three thousand new schools and increased school-age enrollments from under 60 percent to 70 percent.[20]

[18] The Christian Democrats' commitment to redistributive policies and the alienation this provoked on the Right is discussed in Joan E. Garcés, *Desarrollo Político, Desarrollo Económico: Los Casos de Chile y Colombia* (Santiago: Editorial Andres Bello, 1972). See p. 314 for data showing dramatic increases in the levying and collection of property tax between 1965 and 1970.

[19] Julio Faúndez, *Marxism and Democracy in Chile: From 1932 to the Fall of Allende* (New Haven: Yale University Press, 1988), 157.

[20] Kathleen Fischer, *Political Ideology and Educational Reform in Chile 1964–1976* (Los Angeles: UCLA Latin American Center, 1979), 46 and 54.

TABLE 5.6
Private Investment in Fixed Industrial Capital in Chile, 1965–1970

Year	Domestic Sources	Foreign Sources	Total
1965	205	83	288
1966	294	51	345
1967	92	149	241
1968	160	119	279
1969	160	102	262
1970	160	100	260

Sources: CORFO, Gerencia de Industrias, División de Planificación Industrial, Datos Básicos Sector Industria Manufacturero, Periódo 1960–1970, 1971, 17; Luis Pacheco, "Inversión Extranjera en la Industria Chilena" (Memoria de Prueba, Facultad de Ciencias Físicas y Matemáticas, Universidad de Chile, 1970), as reported in Stallings, Class Conflict, 248.

Note: Figures are in millions of 1965 escudos.

These positive trends demonstrate that the onset of a serious economic crisis had not become obvious when the poles of the political spectrum began to pick up votes. There is no clear evidence that policy failure drove vote switching. This said, it should be noted that the Frei government did have some serious policy failures. One was the resort to financing programs through the printing of money. Another was its inability to stimulate private-sector investment.[21] As table 5.6 shows clearly, private domestic investment declined rapidly during Frei's years in power.

The reasons for this decline are instructive, however, because they bring us to our earlier point about the policy success of the Christian Democrats. Traditional Chilean investors were scared off by the Christian Democrats' success in two policy areas. The first was in the area of agrarian reform. The second was in the creation and strengthening of civic life among Chile's disadvantaged.

The Christian Democrats' agrarian reform program had many deficiencies but the party did manage to expropriate three million hectares of property in less than five years.[22] This was the largest redistribution

[21] Faúndez, Marxism and Democracy, 155.
[22] Careful scholars have pointed out that the party sponsored the reform program "with differing degrees of enthusiasm and financial support" and that the program was directed toward the relatively privileged tenant farmers rather than landless workers. See Thomas Bossert, "The Agrarian Reform and Peasant Political Consciousness in Chile" Latin American Perspectives 7, no. 4 (1980): 8; also Tomic, "Christian Democracy," 215, and Brian Loveman, Struggle in the Countryside: Politics and the Rural Labor in Chile, 1919–1973 (Bloomington: Indiana University Press, 1976).

of property in Chilean history. It marked the expropriation of a full 15 percent of the nation's agricultural land.[23] The agrarian reform also marked a watershed in the Christian Democratic Party's relationship with Chile's landed elite. After the agrarian reform was passed, it was patently clear that the party of the Church was not the handmaiden of the wealthy. When this became obvious, the National Party captured the electoral benefits. Many wealthy voters who had been attracted to the Christian Democrats switched back to their original party.

The Christian Democrats' success in the area of social organization had dramatic implications as well. The most visible were those related to the organization of labor. The party was committed to expanding union representation throughout the country, and though its motivation may have been ambiguous, its success was not. There were only 2,000 agricultural workers in unions when the Christian Democrats came to power.[24] Two years later, the number had risen to 50,000. This dramatic increase was related to the party's dismantling of the legal barriers to rural unionization and to its willingness to provide government funds, infrastructural support, and legal status for new and previously existing organizations. By the time the Christian Democrats faced the electorate in 1969, the number of unionized rural workers had risen to over 110,000, constituting nearly half of the nation's rural workforce.[25] Organization paid off. Real wages for farmworkers doubled in six years.[26] The rapid growth of organized labor put Chile's landed elite on the defensive.

The Christian Democrats' success in the area of union mobilization was mirrored by success in civic organization more generally. The party's "popular promotion" campaign helped to create over twenty-thousand new civic groups, including neighborhood councils, youth organizations, and women's associations. Courses in community organization and improvement were offered to some seven-thousand citizens. All together, the members of these new groups numbered in the hundreds of thousands.[27]

This unprecedented organizational effort had multiple and unintended consequences. The new groups were intended (at least in part) to give the Christian Democrats a sure foothold in important sectors of Chilean society. They served this function to a point, but their other

---

[23] See Robert Kaufman, *The Politics of Land Reform in Chile, 1950–1970: Public Policy, Political Institutions, and Social Change* (Cambridge, Harvard University Press, 1972).

[24] Faúndez, *Marxism and Democracy*, 144.

[25] Scully, *Rethinking the Center*, 155.

[26] Solon Baraclough, "Agrarian Reform and Structural Change in Latin America: The Chilean Case," *Journal of Development Studies* 8, no. 2 (1972):163.

[27] Faúndez, *Marxism and Democracy*, 152; Tomic, "Christian Democracy," 215.

effects worked to the advantage of the Christian Democrats' competition. For the Right, these organizations were proof that the Christian Democrats truly were a threat to the old order. They provided an additional incentive for defectors to return to the Nationalist Party.[28] For the Left, these organizations opened up political spaces that could be used by Socialists and Communists as well. By raising people's consciousness and improving people's organizational skills, these civic groups lowered the costs of mobilization for any anti-traditionalist party speaking in the name of the disadvantaged. Communists and Socialists made important gains among groups that had been initially mobilized by the Christian Democrats. Left-wing Christian Democrats, such as those who formed the far-left MAPU, broke with the CD and took segments of the new organization's membership with them. MAPU eventually attracted 20 percent of the formerly Christian Democratic rural trade-unionists.[29]

The Christian Democrats' organizational efforts had repercussions throughout the political landscape, for they both represented and helped to stimulate a trend toward increased politicization across society. Chile's streets, factories, and farms became the scenes of increasing struggle as the Frei years wore on. Land seizures, building occupations, urban land invasions, and factory takeovers rose dramatically between 1965 and 1969. The public confrontations that we usually associate with the Allende years really began and then gained momentum during the period of Christian Democratic rule. Table 5.7 tells the story.

It was natural that the public drama of mobilization would have some effect on people's votes. But whatever electoral polarization existed was not driven by economic crisis. It was driven instead by a growing sense of disorder based on reciprocal and rational fears. The Right revived itself by pointing to the dangers inherent in the Christian Democrats' program and the party's inability to control the growing disorders resulting from the mobilization of the Left.[30] The Left expanded by using the changes in the political opportunity structure provided by Christian Democracy and by pointing to the revival of the Right. Thus, parties at both ends of the political spectrum used the mobilization of their polar opposite to gain electoral strength. To the extent that voters polarized at all, they did so less because of economic crisis than because of a crisis in public space.

---

[28] Cristobal Kay, "Agrarian Reform and the Class Struggle in Chile," *Latin American Perspectives* 5 no. 3 (1978): 128.

[29] Faúndez, *Marxism and Democracy*, 154. For more on MAPU, see MAPU, *El Primer Año del Gobierno Popular y El Segundo Año del Gobierno Popular* (Philadelphia: Institute for the Study of Human Issues, 1977).

[30] Faúndez, *Marxism and Democracy*, 153.

TABLE 5.7
The Growth of Political Mobilization in Chile, 1960–1970

Year	Number of Legal Strikes	Number of Workers Affected	Petitions	Number of Rural Strikes	Farm Seizures	Membership of Rural Unions
1960	257	88,518	60	3	—	—
1961	262	111,911	12	7	2	—
1962	401	84,212	21	44	1	—
1963	416	117,084	10	5	2	1,500
1964	564	138,474	31	39	2	1,658
1965	723	182,359	395	142	13	2,118
1966	1,073	195,435	526	586	18	10,647
1967	1,114	225,470	1,167	693	9	54,418
1968	1,124	292,794	1,852	684	26	76,356
1969	1,277	362,010	NA	1,127	148	103,635
1970	1,819	656,170	NA	1,580	456	140,293

Source: International Labour Organisation, *Yearbook of Labour Statistics* (Geneva: International Labour Office, 1967 and 1973), as reported in Francisco Zapata, "The Chilean Labor Movement under Salvador Allende: 1970–1973," *Latin American Perspectives* 3, no. 1 (1976): 85; Sergio Gomez, *Instituciones y Procesos Agrarios in Chile* (Santiago: Flacso-Clacso, 1982), 25 and 148.

Votes and Mobilization in the Allende Years

The mobilizational dramas that marked the Frei years increased in intensity and number after Salvador Allende won the presidential elections in September of 1970. Mobilization took a pendular form, as it had under Frei, but the pace of the process was quickened by the fact that the Socialist presidency gave unprecedented political opportunity to mobilizers on the Left. As the pace of public polarization picked up, a grave economic crisis set in. Chileans thus had unprecedented material reasons to polarize at the polls and unprecedented social pressures to take sides in a frenetic drama of mobilization. Given the context, it is not at all surprising that some sectors of the electorate switched loyalties and moved to the extremes of the party spectrum. Yet, a close examination of voting trends reveals two patterns of behavior that are completely at odds with what one would expect in a classic case of polarization: voting patterns evinced remarkable continuities across time, and the political Center remained remarkably resilient.

In Allende's Chile, as in our other cases, there were significant differences between citizen behavior in the streets and at the polls. I analyze these differences and their implications below.

TABLE 5.8
Strike Activity during the Allende Government

Year	Number of Strikes	Blue-Collar Workers	White-Collar Workers	Total Workers
1970	1,819	NA	NA	656,170
1971	2,709	182,770	119,628	302,398
1972	3,287	232,373	164,769	397,142

Source: Instituto Nacional de Estadísticas, Síntesis Estadístico, as reported in Stallings, Class Conflict, 247.

Polarization in Public Spaces

The political mobilization of the Allende years has already been the subject of a great deal of research. My purpose here is not to describe the mobilization in detail but to convey its dynamic and its breadth and in so doing demonstrate the intensity of the pressures to polarize.

Strikes emanating from trade unions plagued the regime from its earliest days, despite Allende's unambiguous personal commitment to improving the lot of Chile's working class. In the first two years of the Allende presidency, strike activity rose by approximately 170 percent. In 1972 alone, there were 3,287 strikes.[31] The figures in table 5.8 provide an introduction to the story of a beleaguered government.

These data show a dynamic of mobilization that was critically important in itself, but the political identity of the Chileans who mobilized was of equal if not greater significance. Strikes by industrial trade unionists and agricultural workers were only sections of a huge and chaotic canvas. The breadth of mobilization under Allende was unparalleled in Chilean history. Chileans from all classes, including citizens who had never engaged in any sort of protest activity before, took their politics into highly visible arenas.[32] The government was besieged by "groups from all walks of life."[33]

Rural Chile was the scene of intense politicization and rapid change. Strike activity in 1971 was even greater in the countryside than in the cities. Land seizures were even more disruptive than strikes and these increased rapidly, jumping from 456 seizures in 1970 to 1,278 seizures in 1971 alone.[34] Though the Popular Unity government did not support

---

[31] Arturo Valenzuela, Chile (Baltimore: Johns Hopkins University Press, 1978), 61.

[32] Women were among the most visible new groups to get mobilized. Radomiro Tomic claims that their mobilization was "unknown" before this time. "Christian Democracy," 232.

[33] Valenzuela, Chile, 62.

[34] Cristobal Kay, "Agrarian Reform and the Transition to Socialism," in Allende's Chile, ed. Philip O'Brian (New York: Praeger, 1976), 84.

land seizures, it was loath to stop them. Recognizing their newfound freedom from coercion, peasants and farm workers even seized rural government offices.[35]

Just as the Allende government proved unable to control politicization in the countryside, so it proved unable to manage conflict within the public sector. Strikes in this sector alone jumped 145 percent in a single year.[36] Since public-sector strikes were concentrated principally in urban areas, they were highly visible. Since they came from within the state apparatus, they were highly disruptive.

Strikes in the newly nationalized copper mines were especially costly in economic and political terms. The 1972 strike at the El Teniente mine ran from mid-April to early July and cost the government an estimated one million dollars per day in lost production.[37] The political costs of the strike grew when several thousand strikers accompanied their union leaders to Santiago to pressure Allende into concessions. In a classic example of pendular mobilization, the Central Workers' Federation organized a demonstration in favor of the government, while the opposition in its turn mobilized peasant, professional, and student organizations in support of the strikers.[38] What had started as a labor conflict in a remote province became a cross-class, bipolar, mass mobilization in the nation's capital.

The El Teniente strike was launched by Christian Democratic and Socialist unions,[39] but the government seemed unable to control the disruptive actions of workers of all sorts. In the gargantuan Chuquicamata copper mine, workers who had voted overwhelmingly for Allende in 1970 struck one hundred times in 1972.[40]

Just as the government found itself battling actors from the working class, actors from other classes joined the fray and took to the streets. One of the earliest and most important cross-class mobilizations took place on 1 December 1971 when 100,000 women marched through the streets of Santiago banging pots in protest against the government's economic policy. The action was called a *caceroleo*, after the Spanish

[35] Kay, "Agrarian Reform," 85. Allende's fruitless attempts to talk people out of wildcat property seizures are discussed and illustrated in Jorge Giusti, "Participación y Organización de los Sectores Populares en America Latina: Los Casos de Chile y Peru," *Revista Mexicana de Sociología* 34, no. 1 (1972), 44–45.

[36] Valenzuela, *Chile*, 62.

[37] Paul Sigmund, *The Overthrow of Allende and the Politics of Chile, 1964–76* (Pittsburgh, University of Pittsburgh Press: 1977), 210.

[38] Ibid., 211–12.

[39] Michael Fleet, *The Rise and Fall of Chilean Christian Democracy* (Princeton: Princeton University Press, 1985), 170.

[40] Tomic, "Christian Democracy," 227.

word for pots (*cacerolas*). Organized by a broad spectrum of women's associations connected with opposition parties, the demonstrators soon confronted a large group of pro-government activists who had been given a permit to demonstrate as well. Street-fighting broke out, the march was disbanded with force, and a state of emergency was declared. As the fate of the march became known, thousands of women all over Chile repeated the *caceroleo* in nightly protests. In Congress, the Christian Democratic delegation, egged on by the Nationalist Party, led a censure vote against Allende's minister of the interior, José Tohá, blaming him for the violence. It was to be the first of many debilitating censure votes.[41] On this and so many other occasions, mobilizations by one group soon encompassed others and then had broad and unforeseen ramifications.[42]

The mobilization that had the greatest effect on the economic and political solvency of the Allende government was a truckers' strike that began on 11 October 1972. It began far from Santiago, in the province of Aysen, as a private truckers' protest against government plans to establish a state-run trucking firm. The government jailed the strike leaders in an effort to control the spread of the disturbance, but the jailings had the opposite effect. The lead story in *El Mercurio* of October 12 wrote of death, serious injury, and four-hundred arrests.[43] On October 13, a broad range of professional associations sympathetic to the truckers declared a national strike. The Shopkeepers' Association, the Central Chamber of Commerce, taxi drivers, and most bus drivers stood united against the government. Both the National Party and the Christian Democrats backed the strike, and though most of the workers in the Christian Democratic industrial unions did not join the ranks of the strikers, 100,000 peasants did take anti-government action. Eighty percent of the nation's professional associations backed the strike as well. At its peak, between 600,000 and 700,000 Chileans joined the work stoppage.[44]

The strike produced chaos in the lives of ordinary people, which in turn produced new forms of organization to deal with the loss of services and goods. Workers' councils for supply and pricing, communal commandos to ensure the delivery and safety of scarce goods, and popular organizations of all sorts multiplied and grew stronger as a result

[41] Luis Maira argues convincingly that an escalating series of political trials was part of the tactical plan of the Right. "The Strategy and Tactics of the Chilean Counterrevolution in the Area of Political Institutions," Gil et al., *Chile at the Turning Point*, 259.

[42] Genaro Arriagada Herrera, *De la "Via Chilena" a la "Via Insurrecional"* (Editorial del Pacífico: Santiago, 1974), 167–69.

[43] *El Mercurio*, 12 October 1972, p. 1. The headline read, "Decretan Zona de Emergencia—Total e Paro de Camiones—Centares de Detenidos."

[44] Sigmund, *The Overthrow of Allende*, 186.

of the strike.[45] This ironic outcome exemplified the pendular mobilization that typified the Allende years. When a second truckers' strike was called in July of 1973, citizens in both camps were already primed for a long struggle. As the second strike entered its fifth week, the loss to the already staggering economy reached an estimated 100 million dollars.[46] The situation of hypermobilization was gravely exacerbated by the Central Intelligence Agency of the United States, which funded opposition groups and strikers throughout Allende's years in power.[47]

Outside funding, plus the almost rhythmic pattern of mobilization and countermobilization, contributed to an escalation of visible conflict across time. Confrontations between pro- and anti-government groups occurred almost daily in 1971, but by 1972 "mobilization had gotten out of hand."[48] It would be remembered as a year of "great offensives,"[49] when open and highly disruptive conflicts between masses of citizens became the "regular fare" of political life.[50]

In 1973, the pace and tumult of mobilization increased even further, and basic economic indicators plummeted to new lows. The indicators that the citizenry would feel most directly were all negative. Consumer prices rose an unprecedented 77.8 percent between 1971 and 1972. Between 1972 and 1973 the increase was 235.2 percent. The pace of inflation tripled in the months before the March election. The price pressures on Chilean consumers are illustrated in table 5.9.

Political mobilization caused productivity declines. These were especially problematic in consumer goods industries where ordinary people would feel them most directly. The value-added-per-worker in 1973 was lower than it had been in 1960.[51]

Strikes and uncertainty in the agricultural sector contributed to drops in food production. Food imports more than doubled between 1970 and 1972. In 1973, food imports rose by an additional 61.6 percent.[52]

---

[45] Maira, "The Strategy and Tactics," 270.

[46] Sigmund, *The Overthrow of Allende*, 234.

[47] The CIA's role in funding opposition trade unions, the mass media, and political parties is uncontested. The amount of money given to strikers for the perpetuation of the work stoppages remains the subject of some debate. See U.S. Congress, Senate, *Covert Action in Chile, 1963–1973*, Staff Report of the Select Committee to Study Governmental Operations with Respect to Intelligence Activities (Washington, D.C., 1975), and Nathaniel Davis, *The Last Two Years of Salvador Allende* (Ithaca: Cornell University Press, 1985).

[48] Valenzuela, *Chile*, 62.

[49] Tomic, "Christian Democracy," 233.

[50] Fleet, *Rise and Fall*, 128.

[51] Stallings, *Class Conflict*, 259.

[52] Consejo Interamericano Económico y Social, Comité Interamericano de la Alianza para el Progreso, *El Esfuerzo Interno y Las Necesidades de Financiamento Externo para el Desarrollo de Chile* (Santiago: Alianza para el Progreso, 1974), 2:4–14.

TABLE 5.9
Inflation in Chile, 1969–1973: Annual Percent Increase
in the Consumer Price Index

Year	Inflation (percent)
1969	30.7
1970	32.5
1971	20.1
1972	77.8
1973	235.2[a]

Source: Banco Central, *Boletín Mensual*, various years, as reported in Stallings, *Class Conflict*, 247.

[a] January-August only.

Shortages of all sorts of goods appeared and were exploited by the opposition in the popular press.[53] A survey carried out in 1972 (well before shortages reached their peak) found that 77 percent of middle-income Chileans found it "difficult" to procure household staples. For Chileans in general, the figure was 48 percent.[54]

Just as Chileans began to feel the vice of economic crisis tighten daily, it became more and more obvious that the national political elite was incapable of concerted, remedial action. Yet, concerted action was essential because the Popular Unity coalition controlled only the presidency. The opposition controlled the legislature and the courts. Party battles became institutional battles and problem-solving capacities nearly disappeared. The censure motion raised against the interior minister after the women's march precipitated many more censures as the sense of crisis mounted. The number of censure accusations made in 1972 was six times the historical average, and in 1973 it rose even higher.[55] As political elites became increasingly polarized, their capacities to actually legislate dropped precipitously. The data in table 5.10 shows how delays in approving national budget laws increased over time.

[53] For example, *El Mercurio's* front page article on the truckers' strike played on the shortages theme in its opening paragraph, despite the fact that the strike was less than 24 hours old and had probably not produced many shortages yet. *El Mercurio*, 12 October 1972, p. 1. *Ercilla's* coverage of food shortages and the protests they provoked ended with the suggestion that Allende resign or that the UP collaborate with the CD to find a solution. See *Ercilla*, 30 August–5 September 1972, pp. 9–12.

[54] The survey was conducted by Eduardo Hamuy and cited in James W. Prothro and Patricio E. Chaparro, "Public Opinion and the Movement of Chilean Government to the Left, 1952–72," *Journal of Politics* 36, no. 1 (1974): 34.

[55] Maira, "The Strategy and Tactics," 261.

TABLE 5.10

Delays in Approving the Budget Laws in Successive Administrations:
Chile, 1953–1972

President	Years	Number of Sessions Required to Approve Law	Average Number of Days over Deadline until Approval
Ibáñez	1953–1955	16	12.3
	1956–1958	25	3.0
Alessandri	1959–1961	19	16.3
	1962–1964	29	78.3
Frei	1965–1967	37	19.0
	1968–1970	55	113.3
Allende	1971–1972	60	167.3

Sources: Drawn from the *Boletines de Sesiones del Parlamento* (1952–73); Arturo Valenzuela and Alexander Wilde, "Presidential Politics and the Decline of the Chilean Congress," in *Legislatures in Development: Dynamics of Change in New and Old States*, ed. Joel Smith and Lloyd D. Musolf (Durham: Duke University Press, 1979), 209.

The number of sessions required to approve Allende's budget was twice the number required under Allesandri nearly ten years earlier. Frei (in keeping with the theme I developed earlier) had difficulties with a polarized and resistant legislature, too, but Allende's "days after deadline" figures exceeded even Frei's by approximately 50 percent. The legislature became less a place to make laws and cope with crisis than a source of crisis itself. On the eve of the March 1973 elections, national political elites were doing little to ameliorate polarization. On the contrary, their rhetoric alone was profoundly polarizing.[56]

The pressure on the Chilean people was historically unprecedented. Citizens who supported the Popular Unity government were justifiably fearful of a counterrevolution. Citizens who supported the opposition were equally justified in thinking that armed struggle might be initiated

[56] One of the highpoints in the rhetorical hostility came when *Ultíma Hora*, the official Socialist Party newspaper, printed an article calling Christian Democrat Jorge Fuentealba a "pimp" and a "whore" and then asking "the whores of Santiago to pardon [the paper] for comparing him to them." Years later, the rhetoric still had divisive effects. See Rodomiro Tomic, "The PDC during the Allende Years and Some Comments on the Origin of the Christian Democratic Left Wing," in Gil et al., *Chile at the Turning Point*, 336–37. Press coverage of the accusations and acrimonious language emanating from both sides of the political divide became so intense that General Prats, in his capacity as Allende's cabinet member, called a meeting of leading journalists to ask them for assistance in deescalating the rhetorical conflict. See *Ercilla*, 14–20 February 1973, p. 9.

TABLE 5.11
Percentage of the Vote Won by Left-Wing Candidates:
Presidential Elections in Chile, 1958–1970

Candidates	1958	1964	1970
Allende	28.5%	38.6%	36.6%
Zamorano Herrera	3.3%	—	—
Left Total	31.8%	38.6%	36.6%

Source: Cruz-Coke, *Historia Electoral de Chile, 1925–1973*, 108–12.

by forces on the Left. Chileans of all sorts were exhausted and expected that the economic crisis would just grow worse. If ever there were a situation that was ripe for electoral polarization, this was surely it.

It is remarkable that elections were held at all under these circumstances, but the most surprising aspect of the March elections was their outcome. Despite intense pressures to polarize, Chileans did not vote dramatically differently than they had in previous years. The continuities are best understood if we review each of the elections held in the Allende years.

Continuities at the Polls

From the time of Allende's own election through the congressional elections of March 1973, what stands out most is not polarization but continuity. Allende's successful race for the presidency in 1970 was misunderstood by many as evidence of a dramatic radicalization of the Chilean electorate. In fact, Allende won the 1970 elections with a smaller percentage of the vote than he had garnered in the elections of 1964. As table 5.11 illustrates, the percentage of the vote garnered by the Left varied only five percentage points between 1958 and 1970—despite dramatic expansions of both the national economy and the electorate.[57]

The absence of dramatic electoral swings explains why analysts of varied sorts argued against the idea that the Allende victory was the fruit of radicalization and polarization. Hugo Zemelman of the Chilean Communist Party cautioned that Allende won the elections despite "the lack of any real conquest of civil society."[58] Prothro and Chaparro

---

[57] In 1958, the vote for the Left was split between Allende and a former priest named Antonio Zamorano of Catapilco. Zamorano won 41,304 votes, or 3.3% of the total poll. For an informative discussion of his philosophy see Germán Urzúa Valenzula, *Historia Política Electoral de Chile, 1931–1973* (Santiago: Tamarcos-Van, 1986), 107–8.

[58] "The Political Problems of Transition: From the Assumption of Political Power to Revolutionary Power," in Gil et al., *Chile at the Turning Point*, 277.

(U.S.-based social scientists) concluded that the Popular Unity government came to power "without a corresponding increase in the ideological content or Left orientation of public opinion."[59] Where some analysts saw polarization, others saw a disturbing lack of change. This explains why a number of prominent left-wing leaders were shocked by Allende's victory. The leadership of the MIR failed to join the UP presidential coalition because even they assumed that Allende was bound to lose.[60]

The continuities that underlay the presidential election continued during the Allende years themselves, though the outcome of the April 1971 municipal elections suggested otherwise. The elections were the first national ballot after the Allende victory and were watched closely as a portent of future party trends. The outcome was seen as inspirational by some and ominous by others, for Popular Unity candidates won a "net increase of nine percent over the previous municipal election,"[61] and 50.86 percent of the valid votes.[62] The surge in support for the president's coalition was in part symptomatic of a longstanding Chilean tradition of coattail voting.[63] It was also the result of the fact that this was the first election in history in which illiterates and eighteen- to twenty-one-year-olds were allowed to vote. The fact that some 50 percent of the latter group failed to register at all indicated the limits of polarization, but all these important contextual factors were easily overlooked in the heat of party rivalry. As a key opposition leader described it in retrospect, "The Left's strong showing made their most determined adversaries aware that it was not impossible for Allende and the Unidad Popular to gain an absolute majority. As a result, the opposition decided to intensify its efforts and speed up its plans to block fulfillment of the Allende government's program."[64]

[59] "Public Opinion," 23.

[60] Both the MIR and the USP stayed out of the Popular Unity coalition in 1970 because their leaders assumed that Allende would lose the presidential elections for the fourth time. Drake, *Socialism and Populism*. 310.

[61] Valenzuela, *Chile*, 53, where he cites Arturo Valenzuela, *Political Brokers in Chile: Local Government in a Centralized Polity* (Durham: Duke University Press, 1977).

[62] *El Mercurio* (international edition), 5–1 April 1971, p. 8. Sigmund, *The Overthrow of Allende*, 143, explains that the left-wing candidates got 49.7 % of the vote, while the opposition got 48%. The remainder of the votes were either invalid or went to independents, but, counting only valid votes, the Left got an absolute majority.

[63] In the 1961 congressional elections, after the election of President Alessandri in 1958, the Conservative Party jumped from a low 3.8% of the votes achieved in 1957 to a high 14.8%. Likewise, after the election of President Frei in 1964, the Christian Democrats had a landslide electoral victory, going from 15.9% of the votes obtained in 1961 to 43.6%. See Nohlen, *Enciclopedia Electoral*, 255.

[64] Maira, "The Strategy and Tactics," 258.

Viewed out of context, the long-term meaning of the municipal elections was misread by figures on both sides of the political divide. Though the pressures to polarize were deliberately increased, the electorate proved much less malleable after the municipal elections than actors in the government and the opposition hoped. Despite all the turmoil in the streets and in the economy and even the assassination of a Christian Democratic leader in June, the 18 July 1971 by-elections in Valparaiso showed the electorate to be stable rather than changing. In almost every commune, the votes for opposition and government candidates were nearly an exact match with the previous election. The Christian Democrats and the Right increased their vote by a mere .24 of a percentage point. The Popular Unity gained a mere .3 of a percentage point.[65]

The one set of contests that suggested that the electorate was malleable occurred on 16 January 1972 in simultaneous by-elections, one for a senator representing the provinces of O'Higgins and Colchagua and another for a position representing Linares. Opposition candidates won handily in both contests. The National Party candidate (Sergio Diez) won 58 percent of the vote in Linares, while a Christian Democratic candidate (Rafael Moreno) won 52.7 percent of the vote in O'Higgins and Colchagua. Since the Popular Unity coalition had won the municipal elections in these latter districts the previous year, the poll was interpreted by both the government and the opposition as a decisive electoral swing away from the Left.[66] The election in Linares was seen as a swing to the Right. Whether the elections were evidence of polarization per se is ambiguous: a right-wing candidate attracted the support of centrist voters in Linares, but a centrist Christian Democrat drew the support of the Right (and some of the Left) in O'Higgins and Colchagua. The fact that there were two rather than three main candidates in each race made it difficult to determine whether candidate choices were the result of shifts in opinion or merely tactical voting.

It was thus with great uncertainty that political elites confronted the Chilean electorate in the early months of 1973. Would the unprecedented economic crisis and the unprecedented levels of public mobilization destabilize traditional voting patterns and boost polarization? If changes occurred, would they work to the advantage of the government, or would the pattern of change look more like the by-elections of 1972, proving advantageous to the opposition instead?

---

[65] *La Nación*, 20 July 1971, pp. 1–3. For an English language discussion, see Sigmund, *The Overthrow of Allende*, 149.

[66] See the coverage of the elections in *El Mercurio*, 15–17 January 1972, plus the Communist Party's report on the elections reprinted there.

TABLE 5.12

The March 1973 Congressional Elections in Comparative Perspective

Party	1949	1953	1957	1961	1965	1969	1973
Right							
Conservative	22.7	14.4	17.6	14.3	5.2	—	—
Liberal	19.3	10.9	15.4	16.1	7.3	—	—
National	—	—	—	—	—	20.0	21.3
Subtotal	42.0	25.3	33.0	30.4	12.5	20.0	21.3
Center							
Radicals	27.7	15.6	22.1	21.4	13.3	13.0	3.7
Christian Democrats	3.9	2.9	9.4	15.4	42.3	29.8	29.1
Agrarian Labor	8.3	18.9	7.8	—	—	—	—
Democrats	6.8	5.6	5.0	6.9	—	—	—
Subtotal	46.7	43.0	44.3	43.7	55.6	42.8	32.8
Left							
Socialists	9.4	14.2	10.7	10.7	10.3	12.2	18.7
Communists	—	—	—	11.4	12.4	15.9	16.2
Subtotal	9.4	14.2	10.7	22.1	22.7	28.1	34.9
Others	1.9	17.5	12.0	3.8	9.2	9.1	11.0
Total	100.0	100.0	100.0	100.0	100.0	100.0	100.0

Source: Adapted from Timothy R. Scully, "Reconstructing Party Politics in Chile," in *Building Democratic Institutions*, ed. Scott Mainwaring and Timothy Scully (Stanford: Stanford University Press, 1995), 114.

Notes: Values are in percent.

Despite unprecedented pressures to polarize, the results of the March 1973 congressional elections were similar in many respects to the results of the previous congressional poll in 1969. The only major changes were an increase of 6.8 points in the percentage of votes garnered by the Popular Unity coalition and a 9.3 percentage-point drop in support for the Radicals. The vote for the other major parties was almost unchanged. Table 5.12 illustrates the continuities.

The meaning of these figures cannot be understood without reference to the dramatic change in the size of the electorate. The number of people voting had increased by over 1,280,000 (or 53.2 percent) since 1969.[67] Given that both the Communist and the Socialist Parties presented themselves as parties of the previously disenfranchised, it is difficult to sustain the idea that the 6.8 percentage-point increase was the result of

[67] Cruz-Coke, *Historia Electoral de Chile*, 86–89.

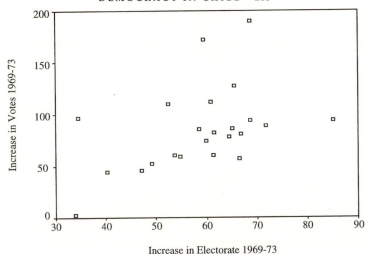

Increase in Electorate 1969-73

5.3. The expansion of the suffrage and the increase in votes for the UP, 1969–1973. Figures represent percentage change and indicate the variation in the electoral outcomes of UP parties in each constituency by the increase of the electorate in the same constituency. Linares is excluded because between 1969 and 1973 the electorate decreased. r = .453, significant at the .05 level (2-tailed tested). N = 23. (*Source*: Valenzuela, *Historia Política de Chile*, 598, 610, 621, 671.)

vote switching, as the polarization hypothesis would have us believe. The fact that the abstention rate dropped to 18.2 percent from a previous high of 25.1 percent in 1969 also suggests that the gain on the Left was not the result of vote switching but of the mobilization of previously inactive voters. These contextual facts suggest that Prothro and Chaparro were right to conclude that "the predominant feature" of political opinion on the Chilean Left was "immobilism rather than radical change."[68] Figure 5.3 shows the strong association between the increase in the size of the electorate and the increase in votes for the Left. There is no statistically significant association between increase in the size of the electorate and votes for the CODE, the opposition coalition.[69]

Analyzing votes in the Center and Right leads to further questions about the dynamics of polarization in Chile. The centrist Christian Democrats were not "enfeebled" during the Allende years, as polarization theory would suggest. To the contrary, they remained "a formidable electoral force" and maintained their place as Chile's largest single

[68] Prothro and Chaparro, "Public Opinion," 29.
[69] The relevant correlation for the CODE is .379, which is not statistically significant. See appendix to chapter 5, figure 5.A4.

TABLE 5.13
Chileans' Party Preferences, 1970–1973

| | Party Preference in Percentage | | | | | | | | |
Survey Date	MIR-MAPU	PS	PCCH	PDC	PN	PYL	None/Indep.	Others	DA/DK
Aug. 1970	—	11.7	6	21.2	10.9	—	35.8	7.7	6.6
April-June 1972	1.8	25.5	7.6	21.3	7.2	0.6	27.1	3.9	5
Feb. 1973	2.5	24.1	9.9	32.1	9.2	0.3	9.5	4.9	7.4

Source: Eduardo Hamuy, CEDOP Studies, Inter-University Consortium for Political and Social Research, Ann Arbor, Michigan, 1970–73, various issues.

Question asked: Of the current political parties and movements, which comes closest to your ideas? MIR = Movimento de Izquierda Revolucionaria; MAPU = Movimiento para Acción Popular Unitario; PS = Partido Socialista; PCCH = Partido Comunista de Chile; PDC = Partido Demócrata Cristiano; PN = Partido Nacional; PYL = Patria y Libertad.

party in the parliamentary elections of 1973.[70] The party had lost support since 1965 but it still had twice as many votes as it had in 1961.[71] The fact that the party maintained its vote support in 1973 was particularly remarkable given the pressures to polarize and the level of polarization in the streets. Yet this is precisely what happened. The Left picked up many of the votes of the previously disenfranchised, and the largest party of the Center held. Even analysts who used the polarization metaphor themselves saw the 1973 elections as "a picture of continuity" where "there was no dramatic shift in the bases of [party] support" and "overall change was slight."[72]

The surprising resilience of the Center was reflected in opinion polls as well as votes. Though the percentage of Christian Democrats who placed themselves to the right of the Center rose somewhat between 1972 and 1973, the vast majority did not move toward either pole and "a centrist orientation [in self-placement] still prevailed."[73] More significant, the percentage of Chileans choosing the Christian Democrats as their preferred party *rose* during the Allende years. As table 5.13 illustrates clearly, the Center *gained* support as public polarization increased and the regime entered into crisis.

[70] Scully, *Rethinking the Center*, 167.

[71] Ibid., 169. Here Scully also critiques Sartori, saying that the "hegemonic center party can hardly be described in the terms Sartori suggested as a 'passive, rather inert, and all in all an immobile kind of aggregate.' Rather, the center in Chile constituted a strong political protagonist with considerable initiative capacity."

[72] Valenzuela, *Chile*, 86.

[73] These trends were uncovered by Eduardo Hamuy and presented again in Fleet, *Rise and Fall*, 161.

TABLE 5.14
Percent of People in Favor of Selected Parties

Survey Date	Percent Expressing Favorable Attitude toward Selected Parties									
	PS	PCCH	PDC	MIR	Extr. Right (PYL)	PN	PR	PIR	PL	PC
Mar. 1966*	18.9	8.2	58	—	—	—	17.5	—	9.7	12
May 1967**	21.1	16.4	56.9	—	—	19.1	16.7	—	—	—
Apr.-June 1972**	47.3	32.3	40.5	14	11.6	23.8	20.7	16.8	—	—
Feb. 1973**	39.8	29.4	44.3	15	10.2	27.7	22.4	27.7	—	—

Source: Eduardo Hamuy, CEDOP Studies, various issues.
Question asked: Can you tell me if you have a "favorable" or "unfavorable" opinion about the following parties and movements?
PS = Partido Socialista; PCCH = Partido Comunista de Chile; PDC = Partido Demócrata Cristiano; MIR = Movimento de Izquierda Revolucionaria; PYL = Patria y Libertad; PN = Partido Nacional; PR = Partido Radical; PIR = Partido de Izquierda Radical; PL = Partido Liberal; PC = Partido Conservador.
* = Very Favorable or Favorable; ** = Favorable.

The resilience of the Center is further confirmed by the polling data presented in table 5.14. When asked to classify their attitudes toward the major political parties, respondents were more favorable to the Christian Democrats than to any other party. The Socialist and Communist parties had substantial support too, but their support was dropping precipitously. Contrary to what the polarization hypothesis would predict, support for the Christian Democrats was rising.

A Surge in Public Polarization

Because Chilean voters failed to polarize at the polls, the March elections failed to break the deadlock in the Chilean legislature. Producing only minor changes in the balance of forces in Congress, the March poll confirmed that the legislative arena would not provide a setting for the resolution of the political standoff. With a stalemate in the legislature, the activities of groups in other arenas became a singular focal point for political activity. There was an escalation of violence and sedition,[74] and a perceived decrease in police intervention.[75]

In April, an ill-timed government initiative to standardize school curricula in public and private schools brought yet more actors into the streets, including church groups, middle-class parents who had not been mobilized before, and hordes of anti-government secondary stu-

[74] Valenzuela, *Chile*, 87.
[75] Maira, "The Strategy and Tactics," 267.

dents.[76] An April 26 rally of secondary students degenerated into a riot, which was predictably countered with a demonstration by the pro-government workers' federation.

Actors across the political spectrum recognized that the "value" of mass organizations "increased once the possibilities for compromise vanished and the political system was paralyzed."[77] Mobilization had been "supplementary to institutional political processes in the past," but the weakening of institutionalized processes meant the strengthening of "extra-legal strategies and solutions."[78] PDC and UP relations became one of direct confrontation "by any means."[79]

Denunciations of arms caches and armed groups on both the Left and the Right became more and more common in the aftermath of the March elections. The country came to believe that armed confrontation and insurrection were practically inevitable.[80] It was this threat of armed struggle and the concomitant threat to the military as an institution that brought about the demise of Chilean democracy.

The fact that the September 11 coup was preceded by intense oppositional mobilization led many observers to conclude that ordinary Chileans had abandoned their loyalty to democratic institutions and embraced dictatorship instead. This is only a half-truth. Though some Chileans did defect from democracy (and others were never loyal to democracy in the first place), the majority of ordinary Chileans did not seek the institutionalization of military dictatorship in 1973. The data presented in table 5.15 illustrate the point. When asked, in February 1973, if a military government were desirable for Chile, nearly 70 percent of the respondents said no.

Another poll taken only weeks before the coup showed that "*more than 70 percent of the respondents opposed military intervention.*"[81] The bluster of the National Party and the hordes of demonstrators clamoring for the government's resignation had succeeded in drown-

[76] Jorge Tapia Valdes, "The Viability and Failure of the Chilean Road to Socialism," in Gil et al., *Chile at the Turning Point*, 314.

[77] These are the words of Luis Maira, reflecting on the increased importance of left-wing mass organizations.

[78] Fleet, *Rise and Fall*, 166.

[79] Tomic, "The PDC during the Allende Years," 330. Tomic notes that this phase was the last of three, and that it began only after the March elections. In a first phase (lasting from Allende's election through July 1971), the CD had what Tomic describes as a "clear desire to support the government." The fact that the Christian Democrats ratified Allende's presidency in Congress when they might well have refused to do so (and thereby made Alessandri president) indicates that the CD was indeed cooperative as the UP government began.

[80] This is a translation of the thoughts of the Christian Democrat Genaro Arriagada, *De la "Via Chilena,"* 312.

[81] The survey is published in *Ercilla*, 22–28 August 1973, pp. 18–19. For references, see Valdes, "The Viability and Failure," 315; and Valenzuela, *Chile*, 132.

TABLE 5.15
Support for the Establishment of a Military Government in Chile

Survey Date	For	Against	Other Answers	DK/DA
Apr.-June 1972	16.7%	77.6%	0.6%	5.1%
Feb. 1973	25.7%	68.2%	1.9%	4.2%

Source: Eduardo Hamuy, CEDOP Studies, April-June 1972 and February 1973.
Question asked: Do you think that Chile should have a military government?

ing out the voices of ordinary Chileans. Nearly three out of four were willing to either support or simply tolerate the UP government until the next round of elections.

Those who supported military intervention varied in both their motives and perceptions. There were certainly many Chileans who constituted a disloyal opposition even before Allende's election. Those who supported Patria y Libertad would surely have been in this camp. But there were others who supported intervention as only a temporary measure, expecting that the military would simply remove the existing government from office and call new elections. These expectations were not inconsistent with Chilean history.

The Chilean military had interrupted elected rule only three times in 140 years and had always turned power back to civilian authorities in a matter of months.[82] The fact that Allende himself had invited military officers to join his cabinet on two occasions illustrated that the constitutionalist integrity of the Chilean armed forces was widely accepted, even on the Left. In November 1972 Allende named military men to head the Ministries of Interior, Mines, and Public Works, hoping that their presence would guarantee both the restoration of public order and the integrity of the March 1973 elections.[83] Though the neutrality of the armed forces grew more questionable as time wore on,

[82] Valenzuela, *Chile*, 98; and Fleet, *Rise and Fall*, 167. Both these authors draw the same conclusion.

[83] Fleet, *Rise and Fall*, 82. In the short run, the move was successful because the government and the opposition "viewed the military as impartial arbiters." Sigmund, *The Overthrow of Allende*, 188. Though he argues that the armed forces were eventually not neutral, Alain Joxe writes that economically hegemonic forces in Chile "did not have the necessary command of the armed forces" at the time Allende came to power and that, on the contrary, the ultra-right's assassination of General René Schneider led the military "to reaffirm . . . that the constitution was the only valid norm." "The Chilean Armed Forces and the Making of the Coup," in *Allende's Chile*, ed. Philip O'Brien (New York: Praeger: 1976), 260. Other references to the impartial image of the armed forces appear in Tomic, "Christian Democracy," 233.

Allende was still willing to appoint military men to key cabinet positions as late as 9 August 1973.[84]

The view that the military would be the protector of elected government was sadly mistaken. It underestimated the power of the fundamentally anti-democratic elements within the institution. But the fact that such a broad spectrum of the Chilean people saw the military in a "constitutionalist" role makes "support for military intervention" difficult to interpret. There can be little doubt that such support was anti-democratic, in that it violated the legitimacy of free elections. But it would be wrong to see support for military intervention as synonymous with support for an outright military dictatorship. Given the role that the military had played in Chilean history, it is likely that some citizens supported military intervention as a means of *preventing* left-wing dictatorial rule.[85]

Political elites in the opposition had panicked people into believing that left-wing dictatorship was a real possibility. Inflammatory language from a sector of the left-wing elite made their task easy. The idea that military intervention was a means of preventing dictatorship was based on the same mistaken line of reasoning that spun out in Brazil and Uruguay. In Chile, as elsewhere, it was very much the fabrication of polarized political elites. Political elites in both the government and the opposition consistently interpreted the political voice of their opponents as a call to all-out war. They also demonized their opponent camp, identifying them with only their most extremist elements. UP defenders too often characterized the opposition as fascist, despite the clear numerical dominance of the Christian Democrats.[86] UP opponents too often constructed the heterogeneous and divided Allende government as a beachhead for Marxist-Leninist dictatorship.[87] It was this latter construction that lay at the foundation of calls for military intervention. The violation of electoral principles was rationalized as a defense of other democratic principles embodied in the Chilean constitution.

[84] Sigmund, *The Overthrow of Allende*, 225.

[85] Valenzuela, *Chile*, 98; and Fleet, *Rise and Fall*, 167.

[86] For examples, see almost any edition of *Ultima Hora*. For an extended and influential summary of the Christian Democrats' reactions to the "fascist" label, see Patricio Alwyn Azócar "Dos Años de Destrucción," *Política y Espíritu* 28, no. 336 (1972): 23–37.

[87] For example, both the Christian Democrats and the National Party were quick to publicize Carlos Altamirano's insistence that the March 1973 elections not be seen as a plebiscite on the Chilean revolution. "We have not submitted the Chilean revolution to a plebiscite," he stated, "Revolutions are not made with votes." *Ercilla*, 14–20, February 1973, p. 15. The statement was constructed as a negation of democratic principles and an indication that Altamirano rejected Allende's vision of a democratic road to socialism. See *Ercilla*, 20–26, September 1972, p. 7, for Christian Democrat Fuentealba's promise to block the UP if they continue "to take the road that tramples on democracy."

The fact that both the government and the opposition consistently accused the other of being a threat to democracy shows that the currency of democratic discourse still had great value in 1973. If ordinary Chileans had defected from democracy en masse, politicians' appeals for popular support would have been cast in other language. Instead, laudatory references to democracy riddled the discourse of both camps.[88]

The value attached to democratic discourse was related to the value attached to democratic procedure. On 8 September 1973, the regional heads of the Christian Democratic Party issued an official document proposing that the government deadlock be resolved through the disbanding of both the executive and Congress and the holding of new elections. The fact that the largest party in Chile saw elections as a means of resolving Chile's crisis on the eve of the coup illustrates that pivotal elites maintained a commitment to basic democratic procedures very late in the game.[89]

In Chile, as in our other cases, the military was the only force that was both necessary and sufficient for the coup, but, commanding officers in every service were "committed constitutionalists" until "the very end."[90] Their position was reinforced not simply by a long history of constitutionalism but by more contemporary events: the assassination of General Rene Schneider at the hands of the Chilean ultra-right on October 25 of 1970 "sealed the neutrality" of the armed forces for "at least two years" and led to the "rejection of any attempt" at a coup d'etat.[91] The

---

[88] See Manuel Garretón and Tomás Moulian, "Procesos y Bloques Politícos en la Crisis Chilena 1970–1973," *Revista Mexicana de Sociología* 41, no. 1 (1979): 159–204, for examples of how the Nationalist Right used democratic discourse to attract the Christian Democrats and "to hide its true version of political order." See especially p. 196. A book by Claudio Orrego Vicuña on the general strike exemplifies the discourse I describe. It begins with a dedication to the heroes of the "arduous democratic fight" (p. 7), and continues with many references to the "totalitarian forces of the Unidad Popular" (p. 11). Claudio Orrego Vicuña, *El Paro Nacional: Via Chilena contra el Totalitarismo* (Santiago: Editorial Pacífico, 1972). Even the military junta rationalized its intervention with reference to democratic institutions. "The military repeatedly cited a resolution adopted in the Chamber of Deputies in August 1973 which claimed that the Popular Unity government had violated the Constitution." Arturo Valenzuela and Alexander Wilde, "Presidential Politics and the Decline of the Chilean Congress," in *Legislatures in Development: Dynamics of Change in New and Old States*, ed. Joel Smith and Lloyd D. Musolf, (Durham: Duke University Press, 1979), 189.

[89] Sadly, *El Mercurio*'s report on the meeting focused only on their demand for Allende's resignation, rather than the electoral solution they proposed. See *El Mercurio*, 9 September 1973, p. 32. The proposal had been presented by Eduardo Boeninger, the rector of the University of Chile, who had used the same solution to solve the deadlock with the University Council early in 1972. See Sigmund, *The Overthrow of Allende*, 239.

[90] Valenzuela, *Chile*, 99. General Prats and Admiral Montero resisted intervention until the last moment. General Ruiz Danyau of the air force seems to have yielded "more readily to pressure."

[91] Tomic, "Christian Democracy," 219.

senior officers' reluctance to support a move against the democratically elected government was evident late in the regime's tenure when they crushed a coup by right-wing junior officers on June 29. At a meeting organized by the top fifteen officers in the country on June 30, "it was clear that any talk of military insurrection was simply out of the question."[92] This was less than seventy days before the coup took place.

What finally caused the military to intervene? Here the parallels with the Brazilian and the Uruguayan cases are clear, for in Chile, as elsewhere, it was a threat to the military as an institution that proved decisive. Various sources indicate that preparations for the coup did not begin until "the arms issue had become a central concern."[93] The real and imagined build-up of weaponry on both sides of the political divide was an unambiguous threat to the military as an institution. Right-wing officers used this threat as the foundation for what would eventually be a coup coalition. It was this and not the will of the Chilean people that was decisive in military decision-making.

When military intelligence discovered plans for left-wing sailors' revolts in Talcahuano and Valparaiso, the right-wing officers' ominous projections about Marxist insurrection were verified. Though the revolts were scotched before they even began, the discovery seemed to confirm rumors that the revolutionary Left had succeeded in infiltrating the armed forces. When the executive committee of the Popular Unity Federation issued a statement supporting the insurgent sailors, the threat to the military as an institution grew greater. Though Allende disassociated himself from the statement almost immediately, the federation's position posed what was seen as an unbearable threat.[94] The military launched its attack on the presidential palace a week later.

Conclusion

The polarization metaphor holds in Chile if we apply it to what happened in Parliament and public space. In the more private world of the ordinary citizen, the metaphor breaks down. In this case, as in our others, democracy collapsed despite the preferences of most citizens. A contextualized history of the period illuminates three important

---

[92] Valenzuela, *Chile*, 100, citing Arturo Fontaine Aldunate, "Como Llegaron las Fuerzas Armadas a la Acción del 11 Septiembre de 1973," *El Mercurio*, special supplement, 11 September 1974, pp. 16–27.

[93] Sigmund, *The Overthrow of Allende*, 288.

[94] Ibid., 236–39. Naval intelligence accused three prominent left-wing leaders of inciting the revolt. They were Socialist senator Carlos Altamirano, MAPU deputy Oscar Garreton, and MIR leader Miguel Enriquez.

themes about popular polarization: one about economic performance, one about political parties, and a third about public space. The first theme is that economic performance and the polarization of the electorate are only weakly linked. Chilean voters did not abandon democratic parties when hard times set in. The polarization of the electorate was never as great as many claimed, and the polarization that did occur began in the Frei period, well before the onset of economic crisis. One pole of the Left-Right spectrum did pick up votes during the Allende years, but the gain was made by a ruling coalition whose economic performance was disastrous. The polarization metaphor fits uneasily in that voting had no punitive content: it was the poorly performing ruling party that gained ground.

The fact that the ruling party gained votes at all in the context of a ruined economy illustrates the limits of economic voting arguments. Though the Popular Unity coalition had certainly made efforts to improve the lives of disadvantaged Chileans, many of the material gains made in the early Allende years had been eroded by hyperinflation and general chaos by the time of the March elections. If voters defected because of economic performance failures, they surely would have defected in 1973, but evidence of defection is very weak. The disjuncture between immediate material interests and voting preferences was so obvious that it was noted by actors from various positions on the political spectrum.[95] The disjuncture between the regime's material performance and its voting base might explain why "the predominant feature of Chilean political opinions" on the Left was "immobilism rather than radical change."[96] People began the Allende years with an affinity for a certain political party and maintained that loyalty regardless of economic performance.

The second theme that the Chilean experience brings to light is that strong political parties are not sufficient to guarantee either the accurate reading of citizens' preferences or the longevity of democracy itself. The common wisdom is that strong parties are essential for linking citizens to democratic institutions and for interpreting and channeling citizens' demands.[97] Strong parties are thought to be key to the consolidation of

---

[95] While Zemelman, of the Communist Party, points out that Christian Democrats were "radicalized not according to their objective, material interests but in conformity with their ideological and partisan commitment," Tomic, of the Christian Democratic Party, argued that the UP's attempts to "buy support" with redistributive policies failed. Zemelman, "The Political Problems of Transition," 291; Tomic, "Christian Democracy," 231.

[96] Prothro and Chaparro, "Public Opinion," 29.

[97] For a lively review of some of the current literature on parties, see Sheri Berman, "The Life of the Party," *Comparative Politics* 30, no. 1 (1997): 101–22.

democracy,[98] and Chile's political parties ranked among the strongest on the continent. They were characterized as "decisive for the functioning of the government"[99] and "more relevant to national decision-making" than anywhere else in Latin America.[100] They seemed to function as textbooks suggest they should: "disciplining representatives, channeling citizens' demands and mobilizing political support."[101] Their role in political and social life was "such an undeniable reality" that their "existence was thought to be non-problematic."[102]

Despite the dramatic differences in their component parts, the Chilean party system was like the Brazilian in that it failed to convey the full resilience of centrist opinion. In Brazil, it was the multipolar and opaque nature of the party system that obscured centrist sentiment. In Chile, the party system had different and seemingly more helpful attributes, but it failed nonetheless. Chile's party system was considerably more transparent because it came closer to the simpler bipolar model and banned no important political parties. Most significantly, the extension of the franchise to illiterates eliminated a major source of uncertainty.

Ironically, Chilean party leaders *made* their party system opaque and obscured the enduring popular commitment to democracy through their own resort to polarized alliances. As elites polarized at the top of the party system and formed the UP and the CODE, their rhetoric eclipsed the moderate and pro-democratic sentiment that still existed at the base of both camps. Important commonalities of opinion were easily forgotten as elites consistently identified their opposition with its most strident and extremist elements. But commonalities did exist in at least two key areas. The first was in the general commitment to procedural democracy discussed above. The second was in the profound rejection of command socialism. Even citizens who supported the socialist transformation of Chile rejected socialism's most radical forms: only 4.3 percent supported a Cuban or Russian model. Only 15.2 percent supported Marxist-Leninism. The overwhelming majority of "pro-socialist" citizens supported rights-based, democratic forms of socialism that were

---

[98] As Mainwaring and Scully put it, " It is difficult to sustain modern mass democracy without an institutionalized party system. The nature of parties and party systems shapes the prospects that stable democracy will emerge, whether it will be accorded legitimacy and whether effective policy-making will result." Introduction, *Building Democratic Institutions*, 2.

[99] Tomás Moulian, *La Forja de Ilusiones: El Sistema de Partidos, 1932–1973* (Santiago: Universidad ARCIS: Facultad Latinoamericana de Ciencias Sociales, 1993), 63.

[100] Ronald H. McDonald, *Party Systems and Elections in Latin America* (Chicago: Markham Publishing Company, 1971), 166.

[101] Moulian, *La Forja de Ilusiones*, 63.

[102] Adolfo Aldunate, Angel Flisfisch, and Tomás Moulian, *Estudios Sobre el Sistema de Partidos en Chile* (Santiago: Facultad Latinoamericana de Ciencias Sociales, 1985), 10.

TABLE 5.16

Types of Socialism Favored by Chileans, February 1973

Type of Socialism	% of All Respondents	% of Those Who Desire Socialism	N
Democratic Models*	29.7	68.3	224
Marxist-Leninist	6.6	15.2	50
Cuban-Russian	1.9	4.3	14
Others	5.3	12.2	40
Subtotal	43.5	100.0	328
Don't Know	3.4	—	26
Reject Socialism	53.1	—	400
All Respondents	100	—	754

Source: Eduardo Hamuy, CEDOP Studies, February 1973.

* Includes those in favor of Chilean-style Socialism, Allende-style Socialism, Communitarian Socialism, and Class-equality Socialism.

probably not radically different from the redistributive projects supported by many Christian Democrats. Table 5.16 illustrates how moderate the ordinary proponents of Chilean socialism actually were.

Chile's highly institutionalized political parties had both the incentives and the capacity to obscure these commonalities and to focus on differences instead.[103] Their electoral alliances gave them the incentives to demonize their opposition in the feverish struggle for votes. Their institutional resources gave them the capacity to reach broad sectors of the public and convince them that their accusations were true. Party media were well developed, party organizations played an important role in associational life and party leaders were truly national (rather than regional) elites. Thus, an escalation of hostility at the top of the party system had immediate ripple effects.

The polarization of elites was closely related to the polarization in public space. The third theme emerging from the Chilean experience is that public polarization obscured cross-camp commonalities and the resilience of the Chilean Center. Ironically, the intensity of public polarization also derived from party strength. Party institutions so pervaded civic life that when activists chose to mobilize they could do so with relative ease.[104] Yet, mobilizational capacity proved to be a double-

---

[103] Though the article emphasizes the differences between the three party blocks, Frédéric Debuyst and Joan E Garcés point out the details of the "common ideological space" shared by the UP and the Christian Democrats in "La Opción Chilena de 1970: Analisis de los Tres Programas Electorales," *Revista Latinoamericana de Ciencia Política* 2, no. 2 (August 1971): 318.

edged sword, for it gave each camp's political opposite an exaggerated image of the other camp's strength. The ironies of high mobilizational capacity were most obvious when the left-wing elites nearly succeeded in mobilizing a sailors' revolt. It was the incursion into the space of the armed forces that finally provoked the military intervention.

Neither strong political parties nor a highly organized civil society were sufficient to sustain Chilean democracy. On the contrary, when elites chose to polarize in a situation of high organization, the outcome was disastrous. Though institutional strength and a high profile in civil society were short-term assets for individual parties, they were liabilities for democracy itself. The clamor of polarization in parliament and the streets drowned out the democratic voices of ordinary Chileans on both sides of the political divide.

[104] Maurice Petras and James Zeitlin made this connection some time ago. See "The Working Class Vote in Chile," *British Journal of Sociology* 21, no. 1 (1970): 28.

Appendix to Chapter 5

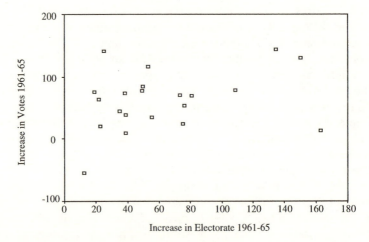

5.A1. The expansion of the suffrage and the increase in the votes for the Communists and the Socialists, 1961–1965. Figures represent percentage change. Coquimbo is excluded because between 1961 and 1965 the electorate decreased. Tarapaca, Antofaga, Atacama, Talca, Maule, and Llanquihue are excluded because neither the Socialists nor the Communists contested the elections in those provinces in either 1965 or 1969. Santiago's electoral data are disaggregated into four constituencies. $r = .301$ (not significant). $N = 21$. (*Source*: Valenzuela, *Historia Política de Chile*, 598, 610.)

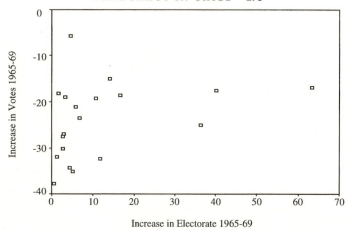

Increase in Electorate 1965-69

5.A2. The expansion of the suffrage and the increase in the votes for the Christian Democrats, 1965–1969. Figures represent percentage change and show the relationship between the variation in the votes for the Christian Democrats in each constituency and the increase in the electorate of the same constituency. Atacama, Arauco, Malleo, Cautín, and Santiago I and II are excluded because between 1965 and 1969 the electorate decreased. Aysen and Magallanes are excluded because the PDC did not contest the elections in those provinces in either 1965 or 1969. Santiago's electoral data are disaggregated in four constituencies. $r = .347$ (not significant). $N = 19$. (*Source*: Valenzuela, *Historia Política de Chile*, 610, 621.)

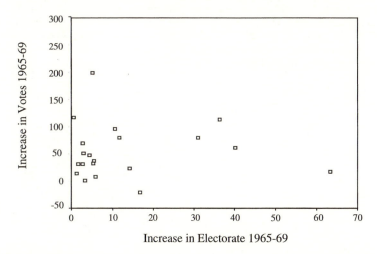

Increase in Electorate 1965-69

5.A3. The expansion of the suffrage and the increase in the votes for the National Party, 1965–1969. Figures represent the relationship between the variation in the votes for the National Party in each constituency and the increase in the electorate of the same constituency. Atacama, Arauco, Malleco, Cautín, Chiloé, and Santiago I and II are excluded because between 1965 and 1969 the electorate decreased. Magallanes is excluded because the predecessors of the National Party (Conservatives and Liberals) did not contest elections in this province in 1965. Santiago's electoral data are disaggregated in four constituencies. $r = -.007$ (not significant). $N = 20$. (*Source*: Valenzuela, *Historia Política de Chile*, 610, 621.)

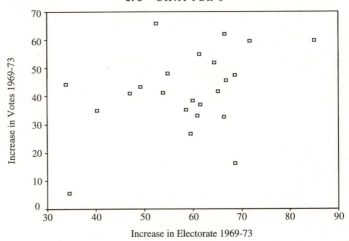

5.A4. The expansion of the suffrage and the increase in the votes for the CODE, 1969–1973. Figures represent the relationship between the variation in the votes for the CODE in each constituency and the increase in the electorate of the same constituency. Linares is excluded because between 1969 and 1973 its electorate decreased. In order to compute the variation in the electoral outcomes between 1969 and 1973 of the two coalitions that contested the 1973 elections (UP and CODE), we aggregated the 1969 electoral returns. The sum of the electoral outcomes obtained by Communists, the Socialists, the Social Dmocrats, Popular Socialist Union, plus half of the returns of the Radicals were considered the 1969 basis of the UP coalition; the sum of the performance of the National Party, the National Democratic Party, the Christian Democrats, plus half of the returns of the Radicals were instead considered the 1969 basis of the CODE coalition. Finally, cases in which a party did not contest both elections are also excluded. $r = .379$ (not significant). $N = 23$. (*Source*: Valenzuela, *Historia Política de Chile*, 621, 671.)

6

THE VIOLENT DEATH OF DEMOCRACY

IN ARGENTINA

THE PRESIDENTIAL ELECTION of Héctor Cámpora in March of 1973 brought thousands of jubilant Argentines into the streets in celebration. Cámpora, a sixty-two-year-old dentist and longtime Peronist Party loyalist, had won by a landslide, garnering over 49 percent of the national vote in a field of nine competitors. His victory was all the sweeter because this was the first time his party had been allowed to compete in a free election in over twenty years. The Peronist, or Justicialista, Party, as it was officially called, had been proscribed since 1955, when a military coup ousted the government of Juan Perón.[1] The last truly free national elections were thus those that brought Perón himself to power in 1951.

Since the 1955 regime change, Argentina had suffered at least seven military coups.[2] Elected governments had come to power in 1958 and 1963, but never as a result of fully inclusive elections and never long enough to finish their first full term. The March 1973 election led many to believe that a profound change had come about and that democracy would finally endure. As a key figure in the political elite put it at the time: "It is only possible to strengthen democracy if it is practiced. . . . Now there is no lie; the fiction is ended. The election, of exemplary honesty, has produced the government that the people have wanted. . . . The election is a triumph of all Argentine people. . . . With the full exercise of the Constitution, there is no reason that might ever

---

[1] The order for proscription came from General Pedro Aramburu, who took control of the military government two months after Perón's ouster. Aramburu allowed neo-Peronist parties such as the Partido Laborista and the Union Popular to compete in elections, knowing that they only had bases in the interior of the country and hoping they would fracture the Peronist camp. James McGuire, "Political Parties and Democracy in Argentina," in Mainwaring and Scully, *Building Democratic Institutions*, 213.

[2] The count depends on whether one includes successful and unsuccessful coups and whether one counts events internal to the military itself. The coups cited here include the deposition of Lonardi by Aramburu in November 1955, the unsuccessful coup by Peronist military officers in June 1956, the ouster of Frondizi after the elections of 1962, the armed struggle within the military between the Colorados and the Azules in September 1963, the ouster of civilian president Illia in June of 1966, the ouster of Onganía in 1970, and the ouster of Levingston in 1971.

justify a coup d'etat." These might well have been the words of someone in the victorious camp, but they are all the more significant for
being the words of the vanquished instead. They were spoken by General Alejandro Lanusse, the leader of the military government that was
devolving power on newly elected civilian rulers.[3] His attitude boded
well for the future of the new government, as did the magnitude of
the Peronist victory itself. Argentina's new executive had solid majorities in the newly elected legislature. The March 1973 elections had
gained the Peronist coalition 145 of the 243 seats in the lower house
and 39 of the 73 seats in the Senate.[4] All but one of the nation's governorships were won by the Peronists as well. Cámpora, unlike Allende,
would not have to wrestle with the problems of divided government.

Despite this seemingly positive start, Argentina's democracy came
to a tragic end. In March of 1976, military officers ousted the constitutional government and went on to establish one of the most brutal military dictatorships in Latin American history.

Though the ousted leaders, headed by Isabel Martínez de Perón,
were the legal descendants of the Cámpora government, they had few
protectors. No one within the military rose in their defense, and their
civilian supporters seemed confined to small sectors of the trade-union
movement.[5] The same streets and plazas that were sites of celebration
just three years before were calm or empty. The day after the coup,
production records rose to new highs, absenteeism vanished and the
trains kept to their timetables."[6] The press ran headlines reading "Everything is Normal Throughout the Country"[7] and reported that the
people of Argentina were "heaving long sighs of relief."[8]

The brevity of the democratic interlude and the swift success of the
March 1976 coup make it easy to conclude that Argentines were somehow not "ready" for democracy in the mid-1970s. Journalistic and
scholarly assessments of Argentine political culture are replete with
critiques of popular beliefs and behavior. As a journalist in an influential weekly put it in April of 1976, "Argentina is a difficult country to

---

[3] Lanusse gave this speech at the Colegio Militar on 19 May 1973. His reference to
there being no need for a coup is especially significant given his audience. See complete
text reprinted in Samuel Baily, *The Durability of Peronism*, Special Studies Series (Buffalo:
Council of International Studies, State University at Buffalo, 1975), 38–41.

[4] These seats were won by a coalition of parties called the Frente Justicialista. The
elections are discussed in greater detail later in this text and in Horacio Eichelbaum, *De
Nuevo el Parlamento* (Buenos Aires: La Bastille, 1974), 117–26.

[5] The 62 Organizations, a group of Peronist unions, publicly repudiated the Argentine
press for "campaigning" for a coup in a "synchronized" manner. *La Opinión*, 24 March
1973, p. 10.

[6] *Review of the River Plate*, 31 March 1976, 414.

[7] *La Nación*, 26 March 1976, p. 14.

[8] *Review of the River Plate*, 31 March 1976, 414.

govern . . . because her citizens seem to lack the knack of teamwork [and because] they are given to mob behavior rather than human society."[9] Scholars of a variety of sorts drew similarly unflattering conclusions. Gino Germani wrote extensively about the "irrationality" of the Argentine masses.[10] Seymour Martin Lipset used Argentina as a case study for his theory of working-class authoritarianism,[11] and hosts of other foreign scholars pointed out an Argentine affinity for personalism and caudillismo.[12] When the highly respected Guillermo O'Donnell wrote that the military coup of 1966 had the "support of, or at least the acquiescence of, a considerable part of the popular sector,"[13] it was easy to conclude that history had simply repeated itself.

To what extent did the failure to defend the constitutional regime reflect popular defection from democracy? To what extent did it reflect an embrace of dictatorship born of polarization? The extreme Left and the extreme Right were certainly active and polarized in the three years before the military coup, but a deeper and more historically contextualized analysis of the years before 1976 shows that ordinary Argentines were less culpable than they might initially have seemed. A closer look at the drama of failed democracy in Argentina shows that Left-Right polarization was limited to small sets of people whose activities were not supported by ordinary Argentines, that labor mobilization was supported by larger segments of society (but that this support was independent of a Left-Right divide), that the workings of the Argentine party system are not captured by a bipolar unilinear model or by a model based on economic performance failures, and, finally, that Argentina's political Center did not weaken as the constitutional government went into crisis. Key civilian leaders drew closer together in the last months of the regime. The dynamic of the party system was not centrifugal, as the polarization metaphor would hold, but centripetal instead.

In Argentina, as in our other South American cases, the emergence of dictatorship was not the fruit of popular defection but the fruit of a longstanding conflict between the Argentine military and the decidedly unpopular forces of disorder. These themes are woven into the narrative below.

[9] *Review of the River Plate*, 9 April 1976, 455–56.

[10] *Política y Sociedad en una E'poca de Transición: de la Sociedad Tradicional a la Sociedad de Masas* (Buenos Aires: Editorial Paidos, 1962), 239–52. Germani does state that the "irrationality" of Argentines was not as great as the irrationality of Italians and Germans who supported Fascism (p. 251).

[11] Lipset, *Political Man*, esp. 173–76.

[12] For a widely read, fairly recent example from two British scholars, see Susan and Peter Calvert, *Argentina: Political Culture and Instability* (Pittsburgh: University of Pittsburgh Press, 1989).

[13] *Bureaucratic Authoritarianism: Argentina, 1966–1973* (Berkeley: University of California Press, 1988), 40.

Politics in Public Space

Hopes were high as Héctor Cámpora assumed the presidency in 1973, but anxiety was high as well, for Argentina's new democracy was being born in decidedly hard times. To start with, none of Argentina's immediate neighbors provided a model of stable democracy as the Peronistas came to power. Brazil's inchoate democracy had collapsed nine years before, Chilean democracy was under siege, and Uruguayan democracy was already the target of a partial military intervention.

Adding to the experiment's unfavorable regional context was an unfavorable experiential context in which political violence and direct action were not only increasingly common but successful as well. One could argue, in fact, that the new democracy was a product of violence, for the process of liberalization that had brought it into being was triggered by a series of urban insurrections. Starting from a 1969 worker-student alliance in the city of Córdoba, the insurrections built around hostility toward the economic stabilization measures of the Onganía dictatorship. The *Cordobazo*, as the insurrection came to be called, provided clear and costly evidence that the authoritarian formula for rule was not effective either for economic policy-making or for the preservation of order.[14] The riots dealt "a devastating blow" to the autocratic regime, making it obvious to General Lanusse and others that "the passive consensus" that the government needed to rule "had disappeared," if in fact "it ever existed."[15] Onganía was ousted by his fellow officers in 1970, marking the third time in less than a decade that direct action and mobilization campaigns had destabilized governments.[16] When another wave of bloody riots challenged the government of Onganía's successor in March of 1971, General Lanusse himself took control of the presidency and began the military's return to the barracks.[17]

[14] At the peak of the insurrection, workers and students controlled a 150-block area of ᷄ Córdoba. Eventually the police and armed forces reclaimed control, but with 30 dead, 500 wounded and 300 in detention. The Cordobazo "marked the beginning of the end for the Argentine Revolution" against Perón. See Daniel James, *Resistance and Integration: Peronism and the Argentine Working Class, 1946–1976* (New York: Cambridge University Press, 1988), 222; also Daniel Villar, *El Cordobazo* (Buenos Aires: La Historia Popular, 1971).

[15] Alejandro Lanusse, *Mi Testimonio* (Buenos Aires: Lasserre, 1977), xviii–xx. Wayne S. Smith, "The Return of Peronism," in *Juan Perón and the Reshaping of Argentina*, ed. Frederick C. Turner and José Enrique Miguens (Pittsburgh: University of Pittsburgh Press, 1983), 98.

[16] Peter Ranis, "View from Below: Working-Class Consciousness in Argentina," *Latin American Research Review* 26, no. 2 (1991): 135, argues that an alliance between trade unionists and political Peronism destabilized governments in 1962 and 1965 as well.

[17] Onganía's successor was General Roberto Levingston, who had refused both legalizing political parties or allowing elections for four years.

TABLE 6.1
Guerrilla Operations in Argentina, 1969–1973

	Number of Incidents	% of Total
Theft of Arms	278	15.80
Attacks on Property	210	11.94
Seizures	200	11.37
Bombings	855	48.61
Kidnappings	85	4.83
Hijackings	2	0.11
Deaths	129	7.34
Total	1,759	100.00

Source: Contemporary press reports, as compiled by Maria José Moyano in *Argentina's Lost Patrol: Armed Struggle, 1969–1979* (New Haven: Yale University Press, 1995), 56.

The success of insurrections in Córdoba and elsewhere emboldened the proponents of violence throughout the country. Young guerrilla groups akin to the Tupumaros in Uruguay became increasingly active. The kidnapping and eventual murder of ex-president General Pedro Aramburu in May of 1970 marked the beginning of a long and bloody stream of attacks on prominent figures within the coercive apparatus of the state. A group called the Montoneros gained great notoriety for the execution of Aramburu, but other armed groups such as the FAL, the FAP, the FAR, and the Descamisados were operating as well.[18] The largest of the guerrilla groups was the ERP, the People's Revolutionary Army. Together, these organizations carried out over 1,750 separate operations between 1969 and 1973. Table 6.1 shows what forms the guerrilla actions took.

Bombings were the most obvious and dangerous threat to public space, and it was ominous that the most prevalent forms of guerrilla action were bombings and arms thefts. Ominous too was the role that rioting had taken on in Argentine society. Between 1 January 1969 and Cámpora's 24 May 1973 inauguration, well over eight-hundred riots broke out. Each was covered in the national media (often on television), and most took place in densely populated urban areas where thousands of Argentines could see them firsthand.[19]

[18] These acronyms stand for the Liberation Armed Forces, the Peronist Armed Forces, and the Revolutionary Armed Forces, respectively. The Descamisados took their name from the phrase Perón used to describe the poor working men of Argentina—the shirtless ones.

[19] Moyano, *Argentina's Lost Patrol*, 66.

TABLE 6.2
Percent of Public Believing That the Military Should
Leave Power, July 1972

City	Percent
Buenos Aires	87
Córdoba	90
Rosario	92

Source: From a poll conducted by Instituto IPSA, S.A., in July 1972, as recorded in Wayne S. Smith, "The Return of Peronism," in *Juan Perón and the Reshaping of Argentina*, ed. Frederick C. Turner and José Enrique Miguens (Pittsburgh: University of Pittsburgh Press, 1983). The data from this poll can be obtained from the Roper Center, University of Connecticut, Storrs, CT 06268.

The origins of the new democracy were decidedly ambiguous, for the intense and violent politicization of public space could be understood in at least two ways. Was it essentially a means of fighting authoritarian rule and bringing about democratization? Or was it, instead, aimed at bringing about a social revolution and thus bound to continue even after authoritarian forces retreated from power?

Public opinion polls suggested that ordinary Argentines sought democratization and not revolution. Though they might have accepted military intervention with passivity in 1966, as O'Donnell suggested, they were openly hostile to military government by 1972. A nationwide poll conducted less than a year before Cámpora's election reveals overwhelming support for democratic rather than military rule. Table 6.2 shows that only a small minority of Argentines backed the continuation of military government.

The fact that these poll results were published in a newspaper with a decidedly mainstream, rather than dissident, readership shows that the rejection of authoritarianism had itself become mainstream. Surveys conducted by José Miguens in the two months prior to Cámpora's election show that democracy and democratic institutions had broad support in 1973. A full 93.7 percent of respondents thought elections were either useful or indispensable. A full 80.1 percent believed that an elected Congress would aid "in carrying the country forward," and 72.4 percent believed that political parties would do the same.[20] Ninety-two percent of the people surveyed said they would accept the results of an

[20] The confidence ordinary people had in Congress and political parties contrasted dramatically with what the military would later term "black parliamentarism." See Edward Gibson, *Class and Conservative Parties: Argentina in Comparative Perspective* (Baltimore: Johns Hopkins University Press, 1996), 81.

election even if the winning candidate were opposed to their ideas.[21] The more enlightened elements of the Argentine officer corps were patently aware of popular support for democratization. General Lanusse was motivated by this awareness himself. Reflecting on Argentina in the early 1970s he wrote: "The military could not go against the opinion of the vast majority of the nation indefinitely. . . . The only intelligent alternative was to reestablish legitimate government, and thus permit the spiritual repair of the armed forces and the consolidation of order."[22]

Would Cámpora be able to build on democratic sentiment and quell disorder? Many reasoned that he could, arguing that Argentines had turned to violence only because the two alternative political formulas that dominated Argentine politics since 1955 allowed them no other choice. Since the coup against Perón in 1955, Argentina had alternated between periods of dictatorship and periods of severely restricted democracy. Since peaceful party politics were ineffectual during dictatorship and degraded during periods of restricted democracy, Argentines were forced to use noninstitutional means of political expression. Argentines had turned to violence because viable alternatives were not available. Lanusse was referring to precisely this in his speech to the military academy: only a democracy can produce democrats.

Structural arguments for optimism were reinforced by changes in the behavior of key political elites. Political leaders seemed more cooperative and conciliatory in the early 1970s than ever before. At the initiative of the centrist Radical Party (UCR), all the major political parties in the country had joined together on 11 November 1970 in an initiative called La Hora del Pueblo. It aimed at reestablishing free political parties, setting a firm date for free elections, and, most significantly, "overcoming the Perón/Anti-Perón antimony."[23] Levingston, who was president at the time, ignored the initiative, but Lanusse, his successor, supported it and stated publicly that he too sought to "overcome the animosities of the past."[24] He chose Mor Roig, the Radical leader who had held the highest office in the last freely elected Congress, to be minister of the interior and to orchestrate free elections. Though plans for a national unity government never materialized, there was an undeniable and very public reconciliation between the leader of the Justicialista Party, Juan

---

[21] These data were collected between 29 December 1972 and 3 January 1973 in the City of Buenos Aires, Greater Buenos Aires, Rosario, and Córdoba. The sample size was not reported. See table 6.7.

[22] *Mi Testimonio*, 43 and 134.

[23] Marcelo Luis Acuña, *De Frondizi a Alfonsín: La Tradición Política del Radicalismo* (Buenos Aires: Centro Editor de America Latina, 1984), 201.

[24] *La Nación*, 24 March 1971, p. 1. The headline read, "The Junta Took Control of the Government to Reestablish the Democratic System."

Perón, and the leader of the Radicales, Ricardo Balbín. Perón talked with Balbín at length during his return to Argentina in November of 1972, and both leaders verified their reconciliation. As Perón put it in a Peronista publication, "We are in agreement with the Radicals. As Balbín himself has just said, as soon as we free ourselves from the yoke of military rule, our parties will unite to solve the problems of the country."[25]

Despite seemingly strong underpinnings, any optimism that democrats felt as Cámpora took power was seriously misplaced. The chaos in public space increased with Cámpora's rise to power. Guerrilla action did not die down as the elections approached, and even after Cámpora's victory, concerted campaigns of disruption continued. Between the March 11 elections and Cámpora's inauguration on May 25, guerrillas organized five murders of military personnel, twenty-one kidnappings, twelve bombings, eight weapons thefts, seven assaults on military posts, and sixteen shootings.[26]

The presidential inauguration provided a forecast of things to come. Left-wing youth seemed to be "in control of [both] the government and the city of Buenos Aires."[27] The military personnel who had assembled for the inaugural parade were so abused by the crowd that the parade and the procession to the National Cathedral had to be cancelled.[28] As night fell, the chaos grew worse. A crowd of twenty-thousand assembled in front of Villa Devoto Prison and demanded the freedom of the political prisoners inside. As inmates draped ERP and Montonero banners from the prison windows, youth groups made frenzied phone calls to the new president. Cámpora, whose own sons and nephews were active on the radical Left, gave in to the crowd's demands. Within a few hours, hundreds of prisoners, including guerrillas convicted of murder, streamed back into Argentine society.[29] On May 27, the newly elected Congress approved the amnesty with no significant opposition.[30]

---

[25] *Mayoría*, 14 January 1973, as recorded in Liliana de Riz, *Retorno y Derrumbe: el Último Gobeirno Peronista* (Mexico: Folios, 1981), 47.

[26] Ambrosio Romero Carranza, Alberto Rodríguez Varela, and Eduardo Ventura, *Manual de Historia Política y Constitutional Argentina, 1776–1976* (Buenos Aires: AZ Editora, 1977), 393.

[27] Smith, "The Return of Peronism," 125.

[28] *Review of the River Plate*, 31 May 1973. The crowd was so wild and unpredictable that they even beat up a Chilean soldier who had come with the delegation of Socialist president Salvador Allende.

[29] Cámpora's familial links to young people on the far left explains why he was known as *el Tío* (the Uncle). These links also explain many of his ministerial choices. For the all-important post of interior minister, he chose the thirty-one-year-old Esteban Righi, a friend of his sons and nephews. For an excellent overview of this period, see Smith, "The Return of Peronism."

[30] *Review of the River Plate*, 31 May 1973.

Ironically, it was the long-awaited homecoming of Juan Perón that confirmed Cámpora's inability to maintain order. Perón had been in exile since his ouster in 1955. Though he went back to Argentina briefly to help negotiate the transition to democracy in 1972, the day of his permanent and triumphant return was set for 20 June 1973. Millions of loyal Peronistas assembled to greet Perón at the Ezeiza airport outside of Buenos Aires. Officials estimate that some three million people (meaning 12 percent of the Argentine population) traveled to the site. An eyewitness described the scene years later as "una cosa oriental" ("something Asian") in that the scale of the crowd was so vast that it had no duplicate in the West.[31] The crowd contained the whole spectrum of Argentines identified with Perón, but the banners and chants of the younger Peronistas were especially noteworthy, for they celebrated Perón as "un viejo Montonero" ("an old Montonero") and thus linked the party's leader to both armed struggle and the "patria socialista."[32] Much to the horror of nearly everyone assembled, armed struggle broke out among rival factions of the waiting crowd. Weapons of all sorts—including machine guns—were fired at close range. Some twenty people died and over four-hundred were wounded.

Perón (whose plane had landed elsewhere) made an impassioned speech the next day in which he made his identity and his preferences patently clear. "We are Justicialistas," he affirmed, and thus *we raise a banner that is equally distant from both of the dominant imperialisms. . . .* There are no new banners in our . . . ideology. . . . Those who naively think they can take control of our movement are wrong. . . . I counsel [these] enemies to desist because when the patience of the people runs out they seek revenge." Perón was decidedly not a Montonero—and he did not condemn those who took up arms against the Left. José Ignacio Rucci, the leader of the Peronist labor federation, paid to have Perón's speech printed in all the major newspapers. But he added a simple headline, and with it an implicit warning, "This is What We Believe In and We Will Defend it on Any Terrain."[33] Less than four weeks later, Cámpora was forced to resign. Rucci announced his assessment of the change in the clearest of terms, "Se acabó la joda" ("The screwing around is over").[34]

[31] For a vivid and detailed account of Cámpora and his government, see Miguel Bonasso, *El Presidente Que No Fue* (Buenos Aires: Planeta, 1997). The information presented here is from pp. 532–33.

[32] Liliana de Riz, *Retorno y Derrumbe* (México: Folios Ediciones, 1981), 64–65.

[33] These are the words of Perón and Rucci as recorded in Bonasso, *El Presidente*, 550. The literal translation of Rucci's headline is "This is our flag . . ." ("Esta es Nuestra Bandera . . .")

[34] *La Opinión*, 17 July 1973, as reported in de Riz, *Retorno y Derrumbe*, 66.

Democracy had certainly not yielded the positive results that many had hoped for. Though there was no economic downturn, guerrilla groups continued to disrupt the social order. In 1973, they launched 203 operations before Cámpora's inauguration and 205 afterward.[35] They murdered a trade union leader named Dick Kloosterman on the eve of the inauguration,[36] and openly threatened Rucci himself with murder on numerous occasions. In ominous reference to Augusto Vandor, a predecessor of Rucci's who had been murdered by guerrillas in 1969, they chanted, "Rucci, traitor!/You'll meet the fate of Vandor!" Kidnappings made the use of public space risky for many, and these too did not abate. On the contrary, a partial list of individuals kidnapped between the announcement of elections and the ouster of Cámpora includes (in addition to a former chief of naval intelligence) top executives from ITT, the Bank of Boston, Kodak, British-American Tobacco, Coca-Cola, Roberts, and Firestone.[37]

Given these facts, it is astounding that Cámpora's government was not the target of a military coup. In keeping with my argument that Argentine democracy had a devoted constituency even under conditions of duress, the country's civilian government attempted a self-correction. Consistent with the popular commitment to electoral democracy expressed in opinion polls, new elections were deemed the optimal solution to the problem of disorder. Both civilian and military elites eschewed the option of a military coup, and free presidential elections were held in September 1973. Perón himself stood as the Justicialista candidate and won nearly 62 percent of the vote. Argentine democracy got a second chance.

Public Space under Perón

The great majority of Argentines looked upon Perón's presidency with hope and optimism. As an informed eyewitness said at the time, "Almost 90 percent of the electorate [was] prepared to back him [and he] stood an excellent chance of winning the support of the Armed Forces. . . . [Thus], for the first time in history, a president might operate from a foundation based on a consensus of all three poles of Argentina's power structure: the Peronists representing the working class;

[35] Moyano, *Argentina's Lost Patrol*, 36.

[36] The murder took place in La Plata on 22 May 1973. A. Romero Carranza et al., *Manual de Historia*, 395.

[37] Moyano, *Argentina's Lost Patrol*, 59. The list of executive kidnappings includes only those with the highest ransoms. Moyano calculates that the guerrillas gained nearly thirteen million dollars in ransom with these attacks.

the UCR representing the middle class[;] and the Armed Forces, the final guarantors of the . . . state."[38]

With a broad consensus behind him, Perón moved swiftly to quell the disorder in public space throughout Argentina. In his homecoming address, he had spoken of the "inalienable right to live in peace and security" and of the government's "unavoidable obligation to secure this right."[39] Now, he cited this obligation as justification for a series of policy changes.

The first major change came on September 24 with the banning of the ERP, the country's largest guerrilla group. Perón had won the elections only a day before and had not formally assumed office but was eager to send a strong signal through provisional president Raúl Lastiri. The ERP sent a signal of its own by murdering José Rucci (and his driver) the very next day.[40]

Simultaneous to the banning of the ERP, Perón appointed General Miguel Angel Iníquez chief of police and gave him a mandate to end guerrilla activity at all costs. Even the more conservative, non-Peronist press took these initiatives as proof that Perón sought "peace."[41]

Perón supplemented these early changes with controls on the media. He signed laws that forbade newspapers from mentioning the ERP or publishing any of the organization's documents. He got the Justicialista Party Council to censure three Peronist Youth publications in October and then in April 1974 shut down two of these publications altogether.[42]

Perón's campaign to undercut the power of the Left among younger Argentines also involved changes in the administration of universities. Under Cámpora, Argentine universities had been centers of left-wing activism, as in Uruguay, Chile, and Brazil. In fact, left-wing students and faculty seized all the departments at the state universities of Buenos Aires and La Plata only three days after Cámpora assumed office.[43] Perón dismissed many of the administrators named by the former government and instated new, more conservative leaders.[44] He also dis-

---

[38] From an interview with the influential journalist Heriberto Kahn in Smith, "The Return of Peronism," 136.

[39] *La Opinión*, 22 June 1973, p. 1.

[40] Lester A. Sobel, *Argentina and Peron, 1970–75* (New York: Facts on File, 1975), 95.

[41] *Review of the River Plate*, 29 September 1973, p. 478.

[42] These were *El Descamisado* and *Militancia*. Both were closed by order of the Ministry of the Interior on April 8 and 9.

[43] Moyano, *Argentina's Lost Patrol*, 71. The situation paralleled the situation in our other South American cases and does not warrant lengthy description here.

[44] One of the most important changes took place at the University of Buenos Aires, where he named Vicente Solano Lima, a man "known for his right-of-center attitudes," rector. Guido di Tella, *Argentina under Perón, 1973–76: The Nation's Experience with a Labour-Based Government* (New York: St Martin's Press, 1983), 62.

missed Cámpora's minister of education and installed his own, a relatively conservative man who had held the post under Perón's second presidency.[45]

On 25 January 1974, in the aftermath of a bloody guerrilla assault on a military tank garrison, Perón introduced hard-line anti-terrorist legislation. It expanded federal police powers, outlawed "illicit" political associations, criminalized the "incitement to violence," and doubled prison sentences for kidnappers, conspirators, and armed extremists.[46] Perón "intervened" in the governments of a number of Argentine provinces to insure that his campaign against the guerrilla movement would be carried out as planned. Backed by the Act of Obligation to National Security, he secured the resignation of elected leftist governors in six of the nation's most troubled provinces, including Buenos Aires, Córdoba, Mendoza, Santa Cruz, Salta, and Catamarca.[47]

The final and most controversial aspect of Perón's attempt to restore order in public space involved the operation of the Argentine Anti-Communist Alliance. Better known as the Triple A, the organization operated as an ultra-right direct action squad, publishing death lists, threatening labor activists, and even eliminating the regime's left-wing opponents. Perón was not a founder of the organization and it was not officially sponsored by the state, but it emerged during his presidency (on 21 November 1973) and was the brainchild of López Rega, an ultra-right figure who had once been Perón's secretary and was then (ironically) minister of social welfare.[48]

Perón's efforts were lauded in the national press. Even media, such as the *Review of the River Plate*, that catered to decidedly non-Peronist sectors of society were reporting that "violence in Argentina had dropped by 80%" since Perón came to power. They quoted the minister of the interior as attributing the drop to the existence of "real democracy," and concluded that his assessment was "undoubtedly true . . . no government supported by more than 60% of the electorate can be anti-democratic."[49]

Troubling continuities lay behind the appearance of change. Despite Perón's efforts, violence in public space continued almost unchecked. Radicalized Argentines simply "refused to accept the defeat that the downfall of Cámpora represented."[50] Bombings, armed attacks, assas-

---

[45] The new minister was Oscar Ivanissevich. Di Tella, *Argentina under Perón*, 71.

[46] Sobel, *Argentina and Peron*, 103.

[47] Ronaldo Munck, with Ricardo Falcón and Bernardo Galitelli, *Argentina from Anarchism to Peronism: Workers, Unions and Politics, 1855–1985* (London: Zed Books, 1987), 193.

[48] Moyano, *Argentina's Lost Patrol*, 80–83.

[49] *Review of the River Plate*, 21 November 1973, p. 773.

[50] Moyano, *Argentina's Lost Patrol*, 69.

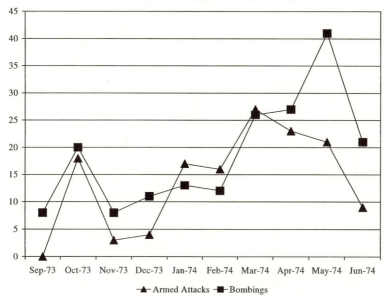

6.1. Bombings and armed attacks during the presidency of Juan Perón, September 1973–June 1974 (*Source*: Author's content analysis of *La Nación* daily issues, September 1973–July 1974.)

sinations, and kidnappings were no less likely at the end of Perón's presidency than at its beginning. The data in figures 6.1 and 6.2 tell the story.

Strike levels proved as resilient as the level of violence in public space. Building on a social pact initiated during the Cámpora government, Perón had hoped to bring down the strike level and restore a more attractive investment climate. His hopes were never realized. In May 1974, a month before his death, strikes in Buenos Aires and Córdoba reached a record high. On the national level, the average number of strikes per month was actually rising when Perón finally died on July 1. Table 6.3 gives an overview of the trends.

Public Space under Isabel Martínez de Perón

With Perón's death, his widow, Isabel Martínez de Perón, rose to the presidency. Though she had almost no formal education and had never held an elected position before, Isabel had been Perón's choice for vice president and was thus the constitutional heir to his office. Because she had none of her husband's leadership qualities and no personal base of support within the Peronista Party or movement, Argentines of all sorts

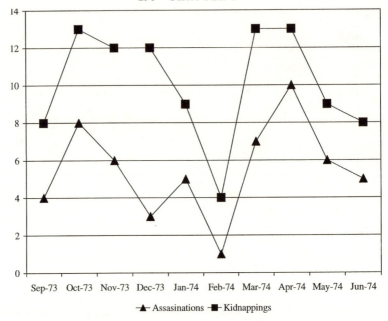

6.2. Kidnappings and assassinations during the presidency of Juan Perón, September 1973–June 1974. (*Source*: Author's content analysis of *La Nación* daily issues, September 1973–July 1974.)

were pessimistic as Isabel assumed office. Their pessimism was amply justified on the economic front, for the new government proved helpless in the face of skyrocketing inflation. Concerning the maintenance of public order, Isabel's government did as well or better than her husband's. As figure 6.3 illustrates, incidents of armed struggle and collective violent protest actually decreased between 1974 and 1976.

Isabel derived little or no political legitimacy from the decrease in violence. Two reasons explain why. First, violence remained at an extremely high level. It was even higher than in 1971, when the chaos in the nation's streets and factories had caused the last regime change. Argentina's exhausted citizenry may not even have been aware that violence was decreasing. Second, citizens were aware that Isabel's government was participating in an increasing amount of violence itself. Figure 6.4 illustrates the variations in what Maria Moyano calls "enforcement violence"—the violence directed toward guerrillas and the Left in general.

Shrouded in extralegality, enforcement violence eroded government legitimacy. All sorts of media carried stories of the Triple A and of the sinister López Rega, on whom Isabel depended for advice. The govern-

TABLE 6.3
Strikes during the Presidency of Juan Perón, October 1973–June 1974

Strikes in Greater Buenos Aires and Córdoba							
Month	12/73	1/74	2/74	3/74	4/74	5/74	6/74
Number	72	109	90	104	85	123	107

Monthly Average of Strikes Nationwide		
June–September 1973	October 1973–February 1974	March–June 1974
30.5	30.8	39.0

Source: Elizabeth Jelin, "Conflictos Laborales en la Argentina, 1973–1976," *Revista Mexicana de Sociología* 40 no. 1 (1978): 457.

ment's open association with paramilitary groups was seen by most as a sign of weakness rather than a sign of legitimating efficacy.

Even the more traditional sectors of society saw the danger in imposing order by force. As a disapproving editorial in *La Nación* put it in November of 1974: "The government's move toward the Right may turn out to be dangerous in that the reaction to subversion may grow irrational and our sense of equilibrium may be disturbed. . . . They say that fascists are frightened liberals. . . . In fact, a right-wing dictatorship can be the consequence . . . of despair."[51]

The record of the government in quelling strikes was as problematic as its record with quelling violence. Table 6.4 shows that there were fewer strikes under Isabel's government than under its predecessor, but strikes declined because of a highly coercive crackdown on union dissent.

Isabel used the Law of National Security to declare strikes for higher wages illegal and to threaten and intimidate strike leaders. She used the Law of Professional Associations to discipline and to take outright control of dissident unions. Dissident leaders recognized, as they themselves put it, that "their day was over" and that "the situation could not get worse."[52] The attack on uncooperative unions was "long, hard and head-on."[53]

[51] *La Nación*, 10 November 1974.

[52] From a study of trade union militants by I. M. Roldan de Reuter, *Sindicato y Protesta Social en Argentina, un Estudio de Caso: el Sindicato de Luz y Fuerza de Córdoba*, as cited in Juan Carlos Torre, *Los Sindicatos en el Gobierno 1973–1976* (Buenos Aires: Centro Editor de America Latina, 1983), 118.

[53] Details of Isabel's policy and a discussion of the "intervened" unions are available in Elizabeth Jelin, "Conflictos Laborales en la Argentina, 1973–1976," *Revista Mexicana de Sociología* 40, no. 1 (1978): 441.

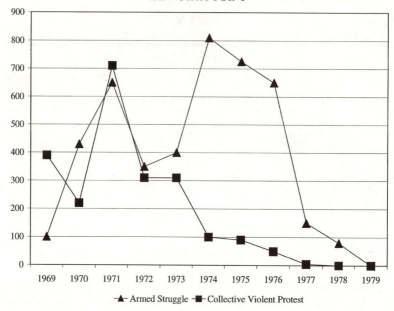

-▲- Armed Struggle -■- Collective Violent Protest

6.3. Incidents of armed struggle and collective violent protest, 1969–1979. (*Source*: Contemporary press reports, as compiled by Maria José Moyano, *Argentina's Lost Patrol: Armed Struggle, 1969–1979* [New Haven: Yale University Press, 1955], 90).

The attack was only effective in a narrow sense. Workers found an alternative means of expressing dissent through absenteeism. Absenteeism reached as high as 20 percent under Isabel.[54] Strikes of long duration and great drama hit vital sectors of the Argentine economy anyway.[55] These notorious strikes plus a general strike called on 27 June 1975 overshadowed any achievements on the labor front. The general strike was called by the Peronista federation itself and marked the first time the Peronist unions ever confronted a government of their own party. The strike broke out over the government's attempts to use wage controls as a means of stemming a staggering 100 percent annual inflation rate. Eight thousand workers marched on the government palace to make the unions' case. Isabel succumbed to union pressure and granted the three concessions the unions wanted most: a substan-

---

[54] Patricia M. Berrotarán and Pablo A. Pozzi, "Diez Años de Lucha 1966–1976," in *Estudios Inconformistas Sobre la Clase Obrera Argentina: 1955–1989*, comp. Patricia M. Berrotarán and Pablo A. Pozzi (Buenos Aires: Ediciones Letra Buena, 1994), 38.

[55] Strikes in the town of Villa Constitución were typical of these. They paralyzed steel production and lasted for two months. See Sobel, *Argentina and Peron*, 146.

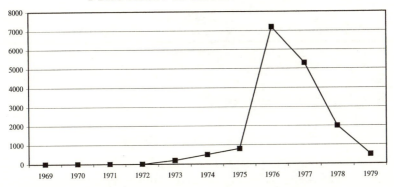

6.4. Incidents of enforcement violence, 1969–1979. (*Source*: Contemporary press reports, as compiled by Moyano, *Argentina's Lost Patrol*, 94.)

tial increase in wages, the dismissal of the economics minister who argued for austerity in the first place, and the ouster of López Rega. The combination of coercion, vacillation, and unpredictability proved lethal for the government's credibility on this and many other occasions. Francisco Manrique, the leader of the Federal Party, voiced the opinions of many on March 23, as rumors of an imminent coup swept the country, "We are witnessing the burial of a government that has already died."[56] The widespread sense that the executive had become a power void was captured in the witticism that circulated in the aftermath of the coup: "Seizing the presidential palace was never so easy—this time there was no one inside."[57]

Politics in Private Spaces

There can be little doubt that Argentine politics were chaotic when the military launched its coup on March 26. Likewise, there can be little doubt that the coup was greeted with relief and resignation rather than resistance. But the chaos in Argentina's public spaces should not be mistaken for societal polarization, and the silence that greeted the coup should not be mistaken for defection from democracy. A careful look at how ordinary people were voting and reasoning enables us to make important distinctions.

[56] This is a quotation from a widely publicized interview. For more, see Pablo Kandel and Mario Monteverde, *Entorno y Caída* (Buenos Aires: Editorial Planeta, 1976), 212.

[57] This is my translation of the original, which runs, "Nunca antes había sido tan fácil para las fuerzas armadas ocupar la Casa Rosada. No había nadie en ella." De Riz, *Retorno y Derrumbe*, 144.

TABLE 6.4
Strikes during the Presidency of Isabel de Perón, July 1974–March 1976

July-Oct. 74	Nov-Mar 75	Apr.-June 75	July-Aug. 75	Sept.-Jan 76	Feb.-Mar. 76
22.5	11.6	24.7	33.0	31.2	17.0

Source: Jelin, "Conflictos Laborales," 457.

Politics in Polling Places

Rather than reflecting polarization and democratic defection, Argentinian electoral behavior reveals continuity rather than dramatic change, concentration rather than fragmentation, and a strengthening rather than a weakening of support for the political Center. That these trends would manifest themselves at a time of unquestionable performance failure is remarkable.[58]

Ordinary people in Argentina, like their counterparts in our other South American cases, were fairly steadfast in their loyalties to certain parties and politicians. We see this clearly if we compare the vote that Juan Perón received in his penultimate run for the presidency in 1951 with the vote that he received when he finally ran again in September 1973. Despite the passage of over twenty years and the incorporation of millions of new voters who were too young to participate in the 1951 poll, the outcomes of the two races were surprisingly similar. Perón won 63.5 percent of the vote in 1951 and 61.8 percent of the vote in 1973.[59] Figure 6.5 shows the strong continuities in support for Perón at the provincial level. Despite decades in exile and continual changes in government, Perón's popularity in 1951 was an excellent predictor of his popularity in 1973.[60]

We see the same continuity if we analyze the strength of the vote for Ricardo Balbín over time. Balbín, as the leader of the Radical Party, was Perón's major opponent in both the 1951 and the 1973 elections. Figure 6.6 shows that the continuities in support for Balbín were, like those for Perón, surprisingly strong. These patterns are not surprising to those with an understanding of the intensity of party loyalty in Ar-

---

[58] Carlos Waisman deems all the governments of the 1973–1976 period "spectacular failures." See Larry Diamond, Juan Linz, and Seymour Martin Lipset, eds., *Democracy in Developing Countries: Latin America* (Boulder: Lynne Reinner, 1989), 82.

[59] Dieter Nohlen, ed., *Enciclopedia Electoral Latinoamericana y del Caribe* (San José: Instituto Interamericano de Derechos Humanos, 1993), 44–45.

[60] For a detailed discssion of the continuities in support for Perón across classes and regions, see Dario Canton and Jorge Raul Jorrat, "El Voto Peronista en 1973: Distribución, Crecimento Marzo-Setiembre y Bases Ocupacionales," *Desarrollo Económico* 20, no. 7 (April–June 1980): 71–92.

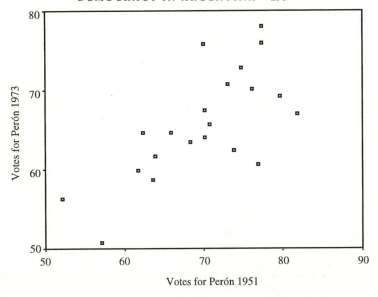

6.5. Vote support for Juan Perón in presidential elections, 1951 vs. 1973. Figures represent percent of votes for Perón in each province. Excludes provinces of La Pampa and Tierra del Fuego (which did not exist in both time periods) plus the province of San Juan (with less than 200,000 votes), where small regional parties became dominant after the proscription of Justicialismo. $r = .706$, significant at the .001 level (2-tailed test). $N = 21$. (*Source*: Rosendo Fraga and Graciela Malacrida, *Argentina en las Urnas 1916–1986* [Buenos Aires: Editorial Centro de Estudios Unión para la Nueva Mayoría, 1989], 49–243; and Rosendo Fraga, *Argentina en las Urnas 1931–1991* [Buenos Aires: Editorial Centro de Estudios Unión para la Nueva Mayoría, 1992]).

gentine society. In the period under study, one's identification as a Peronista or as a Radical was often inherited and carried throughout one's life, reinforced by a myriad of personal associations.[61] The millions of people who turned out to welcome Perón at Ezeiza airport were testimony to continuity rather than change.

The continuities discussed above were reinforced by continuities in electoral laws. In all our other cases, the discontinuities that were easily mistaken for vote switching and voter polarization were often the result of changes in electoral laws instead. Changes in party support

[61] Writing of the 1990s, James McGuire emphasizes continuities, too. Pointing to the fact that no elected president has come from outside the Peronist or Radical Parties, he goes on to say that the "current party system is similar in many ways to the configuration that has existed for decades." He also writes of the strong subcultures that sustain each party. "Political Parties and Democracy in Argentina," 224–26.

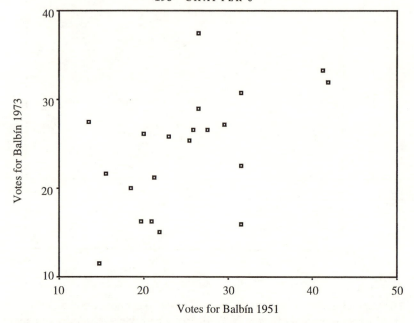

6.6. Vote support for Balbín in presidential elections, 1951 vs. 1973. Figures represent percent of votes for Balbín in each province. Excludes provinces of La Pampa and Tierra del Fuego (which did not exist in both time periods) plus the province of San Juan (with less than 200,000 votes), where small regional parties became dominant after the proscription of Justicialismo. r = .538, significant at the .05 level (2-tailed test). N = 21. (*Source*: Fraga and Malacrida, *Argentina en las Urnas 1916–1989*; and Fraga, *Argentina en las Urnas 1931–1991*, 49–243.

emerged when new rules brought new voters into the electoral system. Argentina, unlike all our other South American cases, had no major changes in electoral laws during the period under study. Male suffrage had been universal since 1912, women had gotten the vote (under an earlier Perón presidency) in 1947, and voting had been obligatory for over sixty years.[62] Aside from new voters who were just reaching voting age, parties had no new bases for recruitment. The continuity of electoral law minimized the changes that were mistaken for polarization elsewhere.

The nature of the party-system change that did occur undercuts the utility of the polarization model as well. Our previous discussion of public disorder shows that the Cámpora presidency was, by standard

[62] Luigi Manzetti, *Institutions, Parties, and Coalitions in Argentine Politics* (Pittsburgh: University of Pittsburgh Press, 1993), 31.

TABLE 6.5
Presidential Election Results, March 1973 and September 1973

March 1973			September 1973		
Candidates (Pres./Vice Pres.)	Party/ Coalition	Percentage of Vote	Candidates (Pres./Vice Pres.)	Party/ Coalition	Percentage of Vote
H. Cámpora/V. Solana Lima	FREJULI	49.6	J. D. Perón/I. Perón	FREJULI	61.9
R. Balbin/E. Gamond	UCR	21.3	R. Balbín/F. de la Rua	UCR	24.4
F. Manrique/R. Raymonda	APF	14.9	F. Manrique/R. Raymonda	APF	12.1
O. Allende/H. Sueldo	APR	7.4	J. C. Coral/ F.J. Páez	PST	1.6
E. Martinez/L. Bravo	AFR	2.9			
J. Chamizo/R. Ondarts	Fuerza Nueva	2.0			
A. Ghioldo/R. Balestra	PSD	.9			
J .C. Coral/N. Schiapone	PST	.6			
J. Ramos/J. Silvetti	FIP	.4			

Sources: *La Nación*, 25 September 1973; James W. McGuire, "Political Parties and Democracy in Argentina," in *Building Democratic Institutions: Party Systems in Latin America*, ed. Scott Mainwaring and Tim Scully (Stanford: Standford University Press, 1995), 242.

Notes: In March 1973, the total number of votes was 11,918,975. In September 1973, the total number of votes was 12,077,422 and the total number of registered voters was 14,334,253, with a voter-turnout rate of 84.25 percent.

FREJULI = Justicialista Front; UCR = Radical Civic Union; APF = Federalist Popular Alliance; APR = Revolutionary Popular Alliance, AFR = Republican Federal Alliance; PSD = Social Democratic Party; PST = Workers Socialist Party; FIP = Popular Left Front.

criteria, disastrous. Yet what happened between the elections that brought him to power and the elections in September? Cámpora's miserable performance should have caused party fractionalization, but the opposite occurred. The number of candidates dropped from nine to four, and the range of ideological options narrowed. Table 6.5 shows that the changes between the March and September elections were of a centripetal rather than a centrifugal nature. The parties on the extreme ends of the Right-Left political spectrum did not even bother to field candidates. The Fuerza Nueva and the AFR dropped out on the far Right, while the FIP and the PSD dropped out on the far Left. By standard measures, the party system was growing more rather than less consolidated.

The party system was also growing less rather than more polarized. Though the supposed incentives for polarization were certainly evident, people did not transfer support to parties on the Left and Right political extremes. If the Peronist Party identity were not so durable, the coalition that brought Cámpora to power would surely have been punished at the polls for poor performance. Left-wing defectors had the option of voting for the Marxist PST and the candidacy of J. C. Coral. Right-wing defectors had no truly right-wing voting option, and this, in itself, is a significant sign of the lack of polarization. But the only party that might have been considered right of center actually lost votes, and this is a sign of the lack of polarization too. The APF dropped around 2 percentage points in the polls, and the Marxist PST garnered under 2 percent of the vote overall. The one unambiguously centrist party, the UCR, *increased* its share of the vote in the presidential poll. The 3 percentage-point increase was not dramatic, but there is certainly no evidence that the Center grew weaker in the chaotic year of 1973.

The outcome of the election was in keeping with the tone that most of the nation's political elite set during the campaign itself. As the press reported it, no coup is "being talked about. . . . The Army, the Navy and the Air Force are playing the part of mere spectators."[63] Though guerrilla violence continued up to the election and beyond, there was no violence deriving from the campaign itself. Ordinary people were politically "exhausted." Far from being hypermobilized, they were described as viewing the elections with "complete indifference."[64] The news stories that dominated the media at the time of the campaign concerned the bombing of a military barracks, the reorganization of the Young Peronistas, a change of agricultural policy, and the September 11 coup in Chile. The campaign itself was so tame that it received relatively little attention.[65] One of the nation's most influential journalists saw the campaign as evidence that stable democracy was no longer "a dream." "This election" he wrote, "was preceded by the most civilized campaign that I can remember. . . . Argentina has grown up a great deal. . . . Violence has been morally overwhelmed by a convergence of wills within the winning party and by the cordial relations between the Peronistas and the Radicals. . . . Democracy has given birth to the image of a constitutional and stable Argentina"[66]

The new electoral law drawn up on the eve of the transition to democracy provided that Argentina have simultaneous legislative, gubernatorial, and presidential races. Thus, there were no national elections after those of 1973. There was one gubernatorial race held in the province of Misiones in April of 1975, however, and this gives us a second reading of voting behavior—in at least a subset of the elector-

---

[63] *Review of the River Plate*, 22 August 1973, p. 258.
[64] *Review of the River Plate*, 11 September 1973, p. 363.
[65] *La Opinión*, 20 September 1973, p. 10.
[66] Mariano Grondono, *La Opinión*, 25 September 1973, p. 1.

ate. The Misiones case supports the argument that the political Center held strong. Despite the chaos of the Cámpora regime and a full nine months of chaotic government by Isabel Perón, it was the centrist UCR that gained the most votes in Misiones between 1973 and 1975. The UCR garnered 26.7 percent of the vote in the first round of gubernatorial elections in 1973. The party won 39 percent in the second round one month later, and then by April 1975 a full 43 percent of the vote.[67] Careful Argentinean analysts estimate that 20 percent of the votes picked up by the centrist Radicals came from the Right, that 10 percent came from the Tercera Posición, and that 10 percent came from voters who had not participated in the 1973 elections.[68]

The Peronists won the Misiones election in the end, proving once again that survival was not closely linked to governmental performance. But their victory was a triumph of the Center as well, for the mainstream Justicialistas who dominated the local list were challenged by left-wing Peronistas under the name of the Partido Auténtico. The Auténticos, or the Authentic Ones, obtained only 9,000 votes vs. over 74,000 for the mainstream FREJULI, proving that ordinary people were not backing the revolutionary tendency in any great number. According to the commentary in *La Opinión*, the vote showed that "the truculent folklore of the revolutionary Left was better for scaring the aunts of the young, than for attracting popular majorities."[69]

All told, the Misiones elections suggested that the party system was converging on some sort of democratic Center. The minister of the interior asserted that the elections "demonstrated that everyone had faith in democracy, in the republican form of government, and above all in the people themselves."[70] The press wrote of the imminent evolution of a two-party system where third parties would soon have a "choice between submission, desperation or disappearance."[71] Voters were, most certainly, not polarizing in April 1975.

Public Opinion

The nonpolarized voting patterns described above reflect the general profile of Argentine public opinion in the 1970s. The data are far from

---

[67] Rosendo Fraga, *Argentina en las Urnas 1931–1991* (Buenos Aires: Centro de Estudios Unión Para la Nueva Mayoría, 1992), 153.

[68] Manuel Mora y Araujo and Ignacio Llorente, "Misiones 1973–1975: A la Búsqueda de las Bases Sociales del Comportamiento Electoral," in *El Voto Peronista*, ed. Mora y Araujo and Llorente (Buenos Aires: Editorial Sudamericana, 1980), 517.

[69] *La Opinión*, 15 April 1975, p. 16.

[70] *La Nación*, 14 April 1975, p. 10.

[71] *La Opinión*, 15 April 1975, p. 12.

ideal, but those that exist suggest that anti-democratic forces on either the extreme Right or the extreme Left had very little support among ordinary Argentines.

It is essential to remember that the regime that was founded in 1973 had its roots in a massive, pro-democratic mobilization. Middle- and lower-class citizens played an active public role in the defeat of the military government and took all the physical and economic risks that opposition to dictatorship involves.[72] Public opinion had an undeniable effect on Lanusse's decision to allow free elections. He believed that "the immense majority of Argentines associated legitimate government with popular elections," and that Argentina would have to democratize or "fight a civil war."[73] On the eve of the democratization, pollsters estimated that fewer than 10 percent of the population believed either that the armed forces were "in a condition to hold power" or that "the country would have fallen into chaos" without the military government. Over 70 percent of the population openly opposed the continuation of military rule.[74] This political commentary from *La Nación* indicates the breadth of support for elected government in January 1973: "Little by little the country has turned massively to [support elections]. Now, one hardly hears any voices opposed to holding elections or to the transmission of power to whomever wins."[75] As a well-placed official in the U.S. Embassy put it, the "single overriding issue in the elections . . . was . . . sending the military back to the barracks and on that, Peronistas, Radicals and most other parties were in full agreement."[76]

The fact that support for elections emerged when the nation was still under a formal state of siege is highly significant.[77] Though it was widely recognized that right-wing parties had no hope of electoral victory,[78] the expression of the popular will was still seen as a solution to discord.

[72] Leonardo Senkman, "The Right and Civilian Regimes, 1955–1976," in *The Argentine Right*, ed. Sandra McGee Deutsch and Ronald H. Dolkhart (Wilmington: SR Books, 1993), 132. Senkman points out that the military ceded power to civilians at other times merely of its own volition, without overt pressure from mobilization.

[73] Lanusse, *Mi Testimonio*, 238.

[74] Frederick C. Turner, "Argentina through Survey Research," *Latin American Research Review* 10, no. 2 (1975): 92. The surveys were conducted by Opiniómetro.

[75] *La Nación*, 28 January 1973, p. 8.

[76] Smith, "The Return of Peronism," 119.

[77] The coincidence of the state of siege and the elections is discussed in *La Opinión*, 6 January 1973.

[78] This theme emerged frequently in the mainstream press. See, for example, *La Opinón* 11 March 1973, p. 1.

The outcome of the election was widely interpreted as a repudiation of military rule and a wholesale rejection of regimes "lacking representation and based on force."[79] Despite the fact that the military had overseen the transition, the official candidate of the armed forces, Brigadier Ezequiel Martínez, got only 2.5 percent of the vote. The two centrist parties, the UCR and the center-right AF, garnered a total of 36.3 percent of the vote.[80] The big winner, of course, was FREJULI, the Justicialista coalition. Though, as I explain below, the Peronists are not easily fitted into a Left-Right spectrum, no one could claim that their victory was the victory of an extreme. On the contrary, analysts found "few major differences in the programs of the two major parties."[81] Cámpora's willingness to name Radicals to his cabinet indicated that the parties were not, in fact, too ideologically distant.[82] The March elections seemed to indicate the opposite of polarization. As the CGT leadership wrote in a newspaper advertisement titled "Only One Winner: The People," "The verdict at the polls has shown that we want a future where sterile conflicts and historically-rooted passions will disappear forever."[83]

The desire to distance the country from destructive political passions manifested itself in other settings as well. Public support for terrorism was highly ambiguous, when it existed at all, and soon disappeared altogether. The support that sectors of the public extended to groups engaging in armed struggle emerged during the period of dictatorship when guerrillas were using violence against a regime that was based on coercion. We are unable to know how much of this early support derived from the desire for a regime change at all costs or from a desire for retribution for past wrongs.[84] We do know that public support for political violence and for the guerrillas dropped markedly after democratization and that "the vast majority of Peronists and non-Peronists alike recoiled from the violence on both sides."[85] Though poll-

---

[79] Smith, "The Return of Peronism," 125, quoting *La Opinión*, 13 March 1973.

[80] The UCR earned 21.3 percent of the vote, while Manrique's AF got 15 percent. Manrique is classified as a right-wing populist by Alberto Ciria, "Peronism Yesterday and Today," *Latin American Perspectives* 1, no. 3 (1974): 35. I classify him as center-right because of his populism and because he left the Lanusse camp early in the transition, finding it too conservative. See Smith, "The Return of Peronism," 118–19.

[81] Smith, "The Return of Peronism," 119.

[82] *La Opinión* 26 January 1973, p. 8.

[83] *La Opinión*, 17 March 1973, p. 7

[84] Moyano makes this point convincingly and illustrates it by explaining how the Montoneros gained prestige from the murder of Aramburu. His murder was thought to be justified by some because of the role he played in the ouster of Perón, the exhumation of Evita's corpse, and the persecution of Peronistas. See Moyano, *Argentina's Lost Patrol*, 97.

[85] James McGuire, *Peronism without Perón: Unions, Parties, and Democracy in Argentina* (Stanford: Stanford University Press, 1997), 159. Ironically, and tragically, the leadership

sters estimate that some 30 percent of the public believed that violence had been necessary for the creation of an electoral democracy, the majority of Argentines (59 percent) did not believe that even this was true.[86] Well before Perón was elected, even the more conservative press was reporting on the dramatic drop in support for armed struggle. An article in the *Review of the River Plate* insisted, "Neither the ERP nor other guerrilla organizations enjoy the support and complicity of the people at large any more . . . they are outlaws and will be fought by popular sentiment."[87] By August of 1973, "terrorism did not enjoy a high degree of support." Over two-thirds of the public gave "no support whatsoever" to groups seeking armed struggle.[88] Ricardo Balbín and others emphasized the vast political distance between the proponents of violence and ordinary Argentines. As he put it, "We have an unbeatable army to fight against subversives, and that's the people, our people. . . . The people will triumph over subversives because they are not living in a microclimate. . . . They are longing for peace and work and these people will triumph."[89] Moyano's very careful study of armed groups and their supporters makes the essential point: "Support for the Montoneros and the ERP . . . was given only when the groups attacked property rather than people. . . . When the extreme Left had turned decidedly towards kidnapping and murders, public sympathy dropped."[90] Public sympathy for the ideology of the revolutionary Left was low, too, and this diminished the possibilities of polarization even further. When asked, "Who is to blame for the situation of Argentina today?" respondents to a large random-sample survey conducted in 1973 gave the answers recorded in table 6.6.

Relatively few of the respondents blamed the actors most often blamed and attacked by the revolutionary Left. A majority of Argentines blamed either the armed forces or the Argentine people them-

---

of the guerrilla movement seemed oblivious to popular sentiment. McGuire quotes Mario Firmenich, the leader of the Montoneros, saying that armed combat with the Peronist government might leave "five thousand cadres less, but how many masses more?" (p. 158).

[86] Roberto Pereira Guimarães, "Understanding Support for Terrorism through Survey Data: The Case of Argentina, 1973," in Turner and Miguens, *Juan Perón*, 208, citing a poll done by Frederick C. Turner in August and September 1973. The remainder of respondents either did not know or did not answer.

[87] *Review of the River Plate*, 29 June 1973, p. 956.

[88] Guimarães, "Understanding Support," 200.

[89] Carlos Giacobone, ed., *Ricardo Balbín: Discursos Políticos-Parlamentarios* (Buenos Aires: Cámara de Diputados de la Nación 1986), 39. From a speech on 8 October 1974.

[90] *Argentina's Lost Patrol*, 41. Daniel James also found that the guerrillas "were largely isolated from the working class who formed the central subject of their radical rhetoric." *Resistance and Integration*, 247.

TABLE 6.6
Who Is to Blame for the Situation of the Country?

Politicians	14.2%	Cattle Oligarchy	4.9%	Union Leaders	3.3%
Military	29.6%	Foreign Capital	8.1%	Other	3.3%
Ourselves	24.9%	Businessmen	1.2%	DK/NR	10.1%

Source: Surveys conducted by José Miguens between December 1972 and February 1973, Centro de Investigaciones Motivacionales y Sociales, Archivo Miguens-Colecciones Especiales, Biblioteca Max von Buch, Universidad de San Andrés.
$N = 500,000$.

selves for the nation's problems. Though 14.2 percent of all respondents blamed professional politicians instead, foreign capital was blamed by fewer than 8.1 percent of survey respondents. The cattle oligarchy and businessmen combined were blamed by a meager 6.1 percent. In a truly polarized polity, many respondents would have blamed unions too, but unions were blamed by only 3.3 percent of all respondents.

The problems that voters found most important were related to economic development rather than distribution. A society with a broad constituency for social revolution would have ranked distributive issues as most important. Yet, as table 6.7 illustrates, a strong majority of the population ranked development and price stability as more important than either salary increases or the expansion of social benefits.

Even the poorest income cohort in the country ranked high prices as more important than wage increases. For the second poorest cohort, salary increases ranked slightly higher than inflation, but both of these issues were deemed substantially less important than economic development. These polls suggest that the constituency for social revolution was very small, even among the poorest Argentines.

Argentina's Multidimensional Party System and Its Implications

The subject of the extreme Left brings us naturally to a discussion of the Argentine party system and the Left-Right spectrum more generally. One of the central reasons that ordinary Argentines did not behave as polarization theory would predict is that the Argentine party system was multidimensional. There was no single, unilinear, Left-Right party spectrum. There were certainly Argentines whom we might classify as leftists or rightists, but they were often in the same party. The Justicialista Party was a broad tent with longstanding factions on the Left and Right. Though its policies immediately before the death of Perón were usually characterized as center-left, its com-

TABLE 6.7
Which of These Problems Do You Care about Most?

	Economic Development	Inflation	Higher Salaries	Job Security	Better Benefits	Better Housing	Better Education	DK/NR
Total Respondents	44.4	17.5	16.1	6.8	4.4	3.3	5.8	1.1
Income Level								
I	68.5	5.6	3.6	5.2	3.1	—	11.9	2.1
II	56.6	6.6	11.8	4.1	5.8	0.6	9.4	3.3
III	42.0	17.4	20.1	6.6	4.7	2.7	4.1	1.8
IV	18.1	32.7	23.1	7.4	8.0	6.4	4.3	—

Source: Surveys conducted by José Miguens between December 1972 and February 1973, Centro de Investigaciones Motivacionales y Sociales, Archivo Miguens-Colecciones Especiales, Biblioteca Max von Buch, Universidad de San Andrés.
Note: Income Levels are as follows: I = High Income, II = Medium High, III = Medium Low, IV = Low Income. Values are in percent.

position and voting base embraced the broadest possible spectrum of ideologies and classes.[91] Its rural base of support derived from traditional conservatism, while its urban base of support drew from moderate and leftist circles in the working class.[92] As James McGuire and others have noted, the ideological distances within the Peronista Party were greater than the distance between the Peronistas and the Radicals.[93] The largest party in the country could, thus, not be fitted on the Left-Right spectrum.

Regional parties could not be fitted easily on the Left-Right spectrum either. The deep divisions between Buenos Aires and the rural provinces were an important source of political identity that sometimes trumped those of class and ideology.[94] The "provinciales," as regional parties were known, operated with "an ideology that was not at all

[91] Eichelbaum, *De Nuevo el Parlamento*, 103.

[92] Peronism was weak in the better-off rural areas and weak in urban areas where the service sector was more important than the industrial sector. For an expertly documented discussion of the diversity of the party and the varied sources of its vote support, see Manuel Mora y Araujo, "Las Bases Estructurales del Peronismo, " in Mora y Araujo and Llorente, *El Voto Peronista*.

[93] "Political Parties and Democracy in Argentina," 226.

[94] For a discussion of regionalism and its political implications, see Edward Gibson, *Class and Conservative Parties: Argentina in Comparative Perspective* (Baltimore: Johns Hopkins University Press, 1996), esp. 221. Ronald McDonald describes the "profound" political importance of Argentine regional identity in *Party Systems and Elections in Latin America* (Chicago: Markham Publishing, 1971), 98.

clear, . . . behaving as a mass that took different positions from week to week."[95]

Journalistic and scholarly accounts of Argentine politics were replete with references to polarization, but the term usually referred to the divide between Peronists and non-Peronists rather than the divide between Left and Right. For decades, this was the political division that seemed to matter most.[96] In the 1946 elections, for example, Perón's party was opposed by a bizarre alliance embracing Communists, Socialists, Conservatives, and Radicals. The divide between Peronists and non-Peronists was so meaningful that virtually every major party that was not associated with Perón joined the Unión Democrática alliance.[97]

The division around Peronism affected individual parties as well as electoral alliances. In 1956, for example, the Radical Party became severely divided over whether Peronist laws and programs should be preserved under a new government. The debate led to a permanent party split. The Radical Party divided in two with the Intransigents (UCRI), led by Frondizi, seeking continuity with Peronismo, and the UCR, led by Balbín, seeking a reversal. Though the Peronist-Radical polarization diminished sharply as the democratic experiment began, the party system could still not be fitted on a unilinear spectrum because of the heterogeneity of the Justicialistas and the importance of regional parties.

The multidimensionality of Argentina's party system and the uniquely heterogeneous nature of the Peronist Party itself had serious implications for trade unions and for the mobilization of workers more generally. In the countries where public polarization grew most intense, trade unions were closely linked to parties of the Left. In these countries, class polarization and party polarization reinforced one another in public space.

In Argentina, relations between trade unions and the Left were highly problematic between 1973 and 1976, and thus labor mobilization took a peculiar form. The Argentine labor movement had been captured by Perón in the 1940s and had been what he called the "backbone" of Peronismo ever since. When the party was proscribed in 1955, the trade unions became the embodiment of the movement itself. The unions managed to survive over two decades of non-Peronista government and many years of military dictatorship, but not without cost

---

[95] Eichelbaum, *De Nuevo el Parlamento*, 130.

[96] Ruth Berins Collier and David Collier write that "the struggle between Peronists and Anti-Peronists . . . was the central tension in Argentine politics from 1955 until at least 1970." *Shaping the Political Arena* (Princeton: Princeton University Press, 1991), 349.

[97] McGuire, "Political Parties and Democracy in Argentina," 210.

to the reputation of their leadership. Accused of being insufficiently militant (at best) and the corrupt stooges of capital (at worst), the established union leaders found themselves increasingly challenged by a new cohort of militants emerging in the new industrial sectors after 1969.[98] As leftists inside and outside the Peronist camp sought to wrest control of the labor movement from the old guard, union officials found themselves facing not simply wildcat strikes but physical threats as well. Rather than working together, the Peronist unions and the most visible sector of the Argentine Left killed one another instead. Left-wing guerrillas insisted "on the physical extermination" of the official union leadership[99] and murdered CGT head Augusto Vandor in 1969, CGT leader José Alonso in 1970, CGT head José Rucci in 1973, and building workers' head Rogelio Coria in 1974, as well as many others.[100] For their part, defenders of the old guard were responsible for uncounted deaths on the extreme Left, beginning with the Ezieza massacre.

In addition to contributing to the extraordinary level of violence, divisions between the institutionalized labor movement and the Left forced each group to ratchet up its demands in an attempt to secure the loyalty of rank-and-file trade unionists. The competition for rank-and-file support helps explain why unions of all sorts engaged in what O'Donnell called praetorian action.[101] Though trade union demands certainly fueled hyperinflation and made "a significant contribution to the pre-coup climate,"[102] there were limits to how long trade unions could play the praetorian role, and there is much to suggest that these limits had already been reached before the coup took place. To begin with, the government campaign against the Left within the labor movement had already decimated opposition leadership and diminished the immediate incentives to ratchet up demands.

Second, Peronists and non-Peronists alike were beginning to realize that the Argentine working class would not be easily recruited by either left-wing trade unionists or left-wing parties. Among trade unionists, even the Juventud de Trabajadores Peronistas "never became a

[98] For a skillful and detailed analysis of the challenge from the Left in Córdorba, "the site of the most modern industries," see James Brennan, *The Labor Wars in Córdoba, 1955–1976* (Cambridge: Harvard University Press, 1994), 212 and 209–304.

[99] The term comes from the Montoneros themselves. For this and a good discussion of the Left–CGT rivalry, see Marcelo Cavarozzi, *Peronism and Radicalism: Argentina's Transition in Perspective* (Washington: Latin American Program, Wilson Center, 1986), esp. 40.

[100] Munck et al., *Argentina: From Anarchism*, 192.

[101] Di Tella concludes that competition was "at the root of the unrest in the large factories," particularly in Córdoba. *Argentina under Perón*, 65.

[102] Ibid., 79.

major tendency in the labor movement,"[103] "never acquired industrial muscle," and ruined its chances of winning future "influence in the bastions of the working class by shooting its leaders."[104]

On the electoral front, it became clear by the end of 1973 that the working class was still firmly in the Peronista mainstream. The majority of Argentina's poor and working classes had longstanding links to the Peronist Party and these proved much more durable than many leftists expected. As Daniel James points out, "Many of the basic elements of the leftist rhetoric had already found echo in the Peronist experience [and] it was meaningless to expect workers to simply abandon a tradition and experience which they felt was their[s]." The need "for a more formal leftism symbolized by left-wing political parties"[105] was not at all clear, and thus the Left faced a formidable recruitment task. The fact that the Peronistas were running the "system" (with a large legislative majority) made the recruitment task of the anti-system Left especially difficult.

The majority of workers voted for Perónism in 1946, and the majority (69 percent) continued to do so in 1973. Estimates suggest that the proportion of lower-class Argentines voting for the Left was no more than 2.2 percent and that working-class people were seven times more likely to vote for the centrist Radical Party than for any Left competitor.[106] The need for the Peronists to ratchet up demands decreased as it became clear that competition was weaker than originally imagined.

The third factor that limited the likelihood of sustained mobilization was simple exhaustion. Trade unions had been mobilized since 1969. They mobilized first in opposition to the dictatorship, then in a highly competitive period during Cámpora's presidency, again in support of Perón's election, and, finally, in opposition to the austerity programs of Isabel Perón. The cycle of protest was bound to wind down as fatigue set in.[107]

The fact that Argentine unemployment was remarkably low during this period contributed to fatigue as well. In Greater Buenos Aires, for example, unemployment dropped below 3 percent in 1975 and was

[103] Munck et al., *Argentina: From Anarchism*, 192.

[104] Richard Gillespie, *Soldiers of Perón: Argentina's Montoneros* (Oxford: Clarendon Press, 1982), 139. The JTP did gain control of the State Workers' Association and in Buenos Aires had influence among the Bus Drivers and Gas Workers.

[105] James, *Resistance and Integration*, 264.

[106] José Enrique Miguens, "The Presidential Elections of 1973 and the End of Ideology," in Turner and Miguens, *Juan Perón*, 160–62.

[107] For evidence, see Brennan, *The Labor Wars*, 297, where he writes that after July 1975, the "exhaustion of the politically charged atmosphere" led to a decline in leftist influence and mobilizational power.

only around 4.8 percent when democracy collapsed.[108] The armies of unemployed men that had been so important for mobilizations in Italy and Germany were absent in Argentina. The time and energy it took to cope with skyrocketing inflation detracted from the likelihood of mobilization too. Oscar Landi described this period as one in which civil society seemed to be "institutionally empty," because inflation forced everyone to focus on their own urgent needs.[109]

These factors help explain why so many observers believed that the trade union movement was already weakened when the military launched its coup. Analysts concluded that three years of Peronist government had put "the working class on the defensive,"[110] that the "labor movement was divided and demoralized," and that "the working class had already withdrawn from the scene."[111] The evidence that unions were indeed failing in their praetorian role and no longer a powerful source for polarization grew stronger as the March coup approached. When the CGT called for a demonstration against an attempted military coup in December 1975, few workers heeded the call. When the organization called for strikes and slowdowns, it became clear (to union leaders and outsiders alike) that "the mobilizational climate was missing."[112] Even the more conservative press wrote, less than two weeks before the coup, that unions had "lost [their] capacity of leadership of the masses."[113] In the last days of the regime, the most visible figure in the trade union movement persuaded the CGT to drop its opposition to the government's stabilization plan, arguing that "hardline attitudes" and mass mobilization would bring down the regime.[114] Trade union mobilizations certainly shook the government, but they did not topple it. In any case, most ordinary Argentines were not part of the trade union movement at all. Over 66 percent of the workforce watched union activities as outsiders.[115]

[108] Luis A Beccaria, "Los Movimientos de Corto Plazo en el Mercado de Trabajo Urbano y la Coyuntura 1975–78 en la Argentina," *Desarrollo Económico* 20, no. 78 (July–September 1980): 156.

[109] Oscar Landi, "La Tercera Presidencia de Perón," *Revista Mexicana de Sociología* 3 (1978): 1402.

[110] Elizabeth Jelin, "Labour Conflicts under the Second Peronist Regime: Argentina 1973–1976," *Development and Change* 10, no. 2 (April 1979): 249.

[111] Munck et al., *Argentina: From Anarchism*, 203. Landi dates labor's last intervention as the 1975 general strike and emphasizes that this was defensive. He insists that, by 1976 "labor had already left the scene." "La Tercera Presidencia," 1407–8.

[112] Horacio Maceyra, *Cámpora, Perón, Isabel* (Buenos Aires: Centro Editor de América Latina, 1983), 151.

[113] *Review of the River Plate*, 12 March 1976, p. 295.

[114] *Review of the River Plate*, 23 March 1976, p. 359.

[115] Robert L. Ayres, "The 'Social Pact' as Anti-Inflationary Policy: The Argentine Experience since 1973," *World Politics* 28, no. 4 (July 1976): 477, estimates that between 35 and

Argentina's Steadfast Center

The relations between the Radical Party and the ruling Justicialistas were as unique as the relations between Argentina's trade unions and the Left. A polarizing system would not have had a steadfast Center, but the Radical Party was certainly this. Indeed, it stood fast in two ways. First, as already discussed, its vote support was stable and even expanding despite the larger system crisis. Second, its loyalty to the principles of democratic government endured until the coup itself. Ricardo Balbín, the leader of the Radicals, was the embodiment of the loyal opposition. Unlike his counterparts in any of our other cases, he never called for a coup.

From the first days of the democratic transition through the last days of the regime, Balbín compromised with his old Justicialista adversaries in the interests of democracy. As early as 1970, with the formation of the Hora del Pueblo coalition, he pledged to force an end to the proscription of Peronism and to support the outcome of free elections no matter which party proved victorious. This initiative reflected the change in the attitudes of Perón, but it also embodied the Radicals' recognition that democracy could be attained only through the complete political integration of the Peronistas.[116] The Radicals' initiation of the Hora del Pueblo pact "foreshadowed the emergence of an institutionalized party system" and the end of an era in which Radicals and Peronists saw themselves as majoritarian movements.[117]

Though Balbín and the Radicals lost both sets of elections in 1973, the UCR did not waver in its commitment to the democratic system. Balbín ended his once acerbic criticism of Perón, and, as discussed above, the two leaders made much of their newfound solidarity.[118] The pacts between these long-time rivals promised a diminution of the partisan fighting that had divided the nation for decades.[119] The bond between the two party leaders became so strong that many expected Perón to ask Balbín to be his vice president. The decrease in the Radical-Peronist polarization did not increase the polarization of the Left and Right. On the contrary, conciliation emerged to prevent Left-Right

---

42 percent of the labor force was unionized in 1973. The second figure is probably the inflated estimate of the unions themselves. See Calvert and Calvert, *Argentina*, 54.

[116] Cavarozzi, *Peronism and Radicalism*, 40.

[117] James McGuire, "Political Parties and Democracy in Argentina," 219.

[118] Guillermo Makin, "The Argentine Process of Demilitarization: 1980–83," *Government and Opposition* 19, no. 2 (Spring 1984): 235.

[119] Luigi Manzetti, *Institutions, Parties and Coalitions in Argentine Politics* (Pittsburgh: Univeristy of Pittsburgh Press, 1993), 94–95.

polarization. This point was made frequently in the press where the two party leaders were deemed "the architects of Argentine unity."[120]

Even when Perón died and the regime went into deeper crisis, Balbín came forward again and again in affirmation of democratic legality. In October 1974, he publicly told the troubled Isabel that his party would defend her, because "you are the President of the Republic and . . . thus represent the consequence of the people's will in a civilized, democratic country."[121] In April of the following year, he publicly affirmed the party's desire for "permanent [democratic] institutions" and insisted, "We are against coups and coupmakers. We are sick of dictators and dictatorships. . . . May the people vote in 1977, all the people."[122] Even as the regime drifted into chaos, Balbín did not incite polarization. On the contrary, with the support of key figures like the Peronista minister of the interior, Alberto Rocamora, he backed a Grand Coalition to keep democracy alive. Announcing the plans, Balbín emphasized the parties' "common roots." Rocamora went a step farther and spoke of their "convergence."[123] The Grand Coalition was such an attractive idea that the Communist Party backed it too. Rather than polarizing, party elites in Argentina came together. Balbín, the leader of the largest opposition party played a key, consensus-building role. In a televised address to the nation on March 16 he insisted: "The will to talk exists. . . . I have spoken with men from all the political camps. . . . There is a common denominator that wants to save our institutions . . . that wants to collaborate . . . because it is the civilized, the democratic and the Argentine way. . . . There is still time. . . . The institutions of the Republic will never be abandoned by the UCR."[124] Balbín and the vice president of the Justicialista Party were working out a program for a common front on the eve of the military intervention.[125]

The Radicals' steadfast commitment to the continuation of democracy had important implications. First, it meant that the national legislature was only rarely a platform for inciting larger popular mobilizations. There were moves to impeach the president (which failed because

---

[120] See a long article on the end of the old polarization and the moderate spectrum of party opinion in *La Opinión*, 3 February 1973, p. 13. The quotation is from *Review of the River Plate*, 20 July 1973, p. 86.

[121] From a speech at the Casa de Gobierno, 8 October 1974, as quoted in Giacabone, *Ricardo Balbín*, 39–40.

[122] From a speech during the special elections in Misiones, as quoted in Giacabone, *Ricardo Balbín*, 42.

[123] Acuña, *De Frondizi a Alfonsín*, 208.

[124] From a televised speech on March 16, as quoted in Giacabone, *Ricardo Balbín*, 47.

[125] The press reported long meetings between Balbín and Deolido Bittle on March 19 and March 22. See, for example, *Review of the River Plate*, 23 March 1976.

the Justicialistas always voted in the president's defense), but since the major opposition party sought to defuse rather than exacerbate conflict, the tone of elite discourse was less incendiary than in our other cases.

This difference reinforced the effects of other aspects of the Argentine political landscape and substantially reduced the level of collective polarization. In many of our other cases (most notably Brazil and Chile) we saw the phenomenon of pendular mobilization, with groups on opposite ends of the political spectrum demonstrating against one another in an alternating pattern. In Argentina we saw less of this kind of collective polarization for three reasons.

First, the actors that should have mobilized the collective opposition to the extreme Left were ill suited to the task. The Argentine Right did not have a vocation for party development or for collective mobilization of a more general sort.[126] The large landowners who supplied Argentina with most of its foreign exchange (and food) were "indifferent or hostile to party politics" and "had never forged ties to a party (or parties) capable of winning fair elections."[127] Conservative political parties existed in Argentina, but they were small and confined to provincial regions. No conservative parties capable of playing a significant role in the political process existed in either the province or the city of Buenos Aires. Conservative elites certainly wielded power through informal networks in the state and the military, but "as a rule [they] avoided party politics" and "tended to disdain the practice of mass mobilization."[128]

The effects of this disdain for mass mobilization were reinforced by the peculiar qualities of the official Argentine Catholic Church, which engaged in little overt political activity during the period under study. The hierarchy maintained "a premeditated silence" on the political situation at hand, and there was not even "a glimpse of a dominant line" in the Catholic community as a whole. Argentine lay-Catholics were so weakly organized that they were simply not "capable of exerting a noteworthy influence on the sociopolitical order."[129]

---

[126] This point was made shortly before the beginning of the democratic experiment by Torcuato DiTella in "La Búsqueda de la Fórmula Política Argentina," *Desarrollo Económico* 11, (1971–1972): 42–44. See also Atílio Borón, "Becoming Democrats? Some Skeptical Considerations on the Right in Latin America," in *The Right and Democracy in Latin America*, ed. Douglas Chalmers, Maria do Carmo Campello de Souza, and Atílio Borón (New York: Praeger, 1992), 75–77.

[127] McGuire, "Political Parties and Democracy in Argentina," 201–2. For a more historical discussion of divisions, see Dietrich Rueschemeyer, Evelyne Huber Stephens, and John D. Stephens, *Capitalist Development and Democracy* (Chicago: University of Chicago Press, 1992), 178–79.

[128] Gibson, *Class and Conservative Parties*, 67.

[129] Antonio O. Donini, "Religion and Social Conflict in the Perón Era," in Turner and Miguens, *Juan Perón*, 92 and 85.

TABLE 6.8
Business Executives and Their Sense of Identification with Others

Group	Sense of Agreement/Identification Score
Peasants, farmers	51.5
Workers	57.9
Labor Union Leaders	41.0
Armed Forces	34.7

Source: Frederick C. Turner, "Entrepreneurs and Estancieros in Perón's Argentina: Cohesion and Conflict within the Elite," in Turner and Miguens, *Juan Perón*, 227.

Note: Responses based on the prompt, "You probably feel . . . that you agree more with some groups than with others, in other words, that . . . some people represent you better, and that they think more like you." Scores are 0–49 for groups who think less like respondents, 50 for lukewarm agreement, and 51–100 for groups that think like respondents.

The business community might have been a source of pendular mobilization, but its internal divisions prevented it from playing this role. One of the main divisions derived from the fact that a good number of businessmen actively supported the Peronist Party, and this made mobilizing anti-government activities more difficult. A second complication arose from the fact that the General Economic Confederation, or CGE, which represented small- and medium-scale industrialists, signed social pacts with both Cámpora and Perón and was thereby complicit in government policy-making. The Argentine Industrial Union represented the larger and more modern firms in the economy and it was not a signatory to any pacts, but it had neither the force of numbers nor the political inclination to engage in the sort of mobilizational activity that mass polarization involved.

Coupled with these organizational divisions were ideological inclinations that also hampered the community's mobilizational capabilities. Survey research suggests that most business executives did not identify with the military. As table 6.8 illustrates, business executives felt they had less in common politically with members of the armed forces than with workers, peasants, and even labor leaders.

This sort of evidence is far from conclusive, but it is not out of keeping with impressions gained from other sources. The Argentine business community was surprisingly comfortable with the transition to democracy in 1973. When the military confirmed the date of free elections and promised to cede power to whichever party won, the stock market remained unchanged. A moderate downturn after the victory of Cámpora a few months later was reversed in a single day.[130]

Investment decisions in these early days paralleled voting decisions. Pollsters estimated that over 32 percent of upper-class voters chose to vote for the centrist Radical Party in March of 1973 and that over 10 percent voted for the victorious Peronistas. The respective percentages for upper-middle-class voters were 22 percent and 29 percent.[131] The remainder of the votes of the upper and upper middle classes went to personalist or regional parties. The far Right gained very few votes because no ideological alternative to the reformism of the two largest parties had credibility.[132]

A reading of the business press confirms that the community was not uniformly anti-democratic, even after years of chaos. As late as January 1976, an editorial in a publication that catered to the wealthiest elements of the agricultural export sector read: "[Argentina's problems] cannot be put right by the impeachment of Isabel. It is not a new general that the country needs. It is a new spirit . . . of acceptance of laws, respect for political order . . . of conciliation towards those who think differently."[133]

These ideas were far from universal among the business elite, and there can be no doubt that individual businessmen joined a coup coalition very early in the breakdown process. The point being made here is that the nature of the business community made *collective* mobilization extremely difficult and thus made the sort of pendular polarization we saw in other cases unlikely. A successful employers' strike was launched late in February 1976, but it was the first of its kind in national history.[134] The business press reporting on the strike described it as "a mass movement . . . *in the making*,"[135] but the fact that the movement took years to begin and was still in an emerging state only weeks before the coup is of great significance.

Even if right-wing parties and business groups had been seriously engaged in mass mobilization, it is likely that the simple fear of vio-

---

[130] *La Opinión*, 25 January 1973. After the date of the elections was chosen, the front page headline in *La Opinión* read, "No Reaction in the Stock Market."

[131] These data are from surveys conducted in January and February 1973. The sample is of 1,265 voters who had decided on their choice of party. See Miguens, "The Presidential Elections of 1973," 161.

[132] Landi, "La Tercera Presidencia," 1406.

[133] *Review of the River Plate*, 9 January 1976, pp. 14–15.

[134] The strike was organized by a new association called the Permanent Assembly of Employers Associations. Its founders were centered in the Sociedade Rural Argentina and the Argentine Chamber of Commerce. For more, see Landi, "La Tercera Presidencia," 1406; and Munck et al., *Argentina: From Anarchism*, 201.

[135] *Review of the River Plate*, 27 February 1976, p. 255, italics added.

lence would have discouraged pendular polarization anyway. Vivid memories of Ezieza and the ubiquity of bombings and political murders must have made the risks of participating in any demonstrations seem especially high.[136] In any case, there were relatively few counter-demonstrations launched by even conservative, much less far-right, forces. As had long been the case, "conservative responses to the challenges of mass politics became increasingly dependent upon the coercive . . . power of the state."[137] The Right proved unable to polarize the legislature and eschewed polarization in the streets. It turned instead to direct action of the deadliest sort.

Despite its long association with praetorianism, the feature that distinguishes the Argentine case is that it did not undergo a Left-Right *societal* polarization. Polarization took place, but it was limited to what Balbín and others aptly described as "micro-climates" within a much larger political environment. The labor movement was the only movement with significant numerical support, yet it had no clear position on the Left-Right spectrum. Its most deadly enemy was the armed Left itself. Its class enemy failed to mobilize publicly until just a few weeks before the regime collapsed.

The blame heaped upon ordinary Argentines for their defection from democracy is exaggerated. Groups on the Left and Right did polarize, but they were numerically small. They made up what later became known as the two terrorisms—one of the Left and one of the Right. The battle that raged in public space was waged by two terrorisms, not by two sections of Argentine society. The battle began well before the economy collapsed and continued on its own trajectory independent from labor mobilizations.[138] The pace and nature of guerrilla activity bore no clear relationship to standard measures of economic performance, and economic indicators were surprisingly good during the years that labor and student mobilization were on the rise. The Argentine economy entered a severe crisis in 1975, and this certainly worked to the advantage of those who wanted to topple the regime, but, as table 6.9 indicates, the years of the highest mobilization were those when economic performance was relatively good.

---

[136] In 1975 alone, there were 564 civilian deaths related to guerrilla violence emanating from the Left or Right, according to the Asamblea Permanente por los Derechos Humanos. See Deborah Norden, *Military Rebellion in Argentina* (Lincoln: University of Nebraska Press, 1996), 59.

[137] Gibson, *Class and Conservative Parties*, 70.

[138] As Oscar Landi put it, "The activities of armed groups became increasingly autonomous from the behavior and struggles of the social forces they claimed to represent." "La Tercera Presidencia," 1402.

TABLE 6.9
Basic Economic Indicators: Argentina 1969–1976

Year	Total Growth Rate in %	Growth Rate in Manufacturing in %	Growth in Agriculture and Livestock (1970= 100)	Gross Investment (1968= 100)	Unemployment Rate in Greater Buenos Aires in %			Export Volume in US 1970 $ (millions)	Inflation in %
					April	June	Oct.		
1969	8.8	10.84	92.1	120.4	4.1	4.8	4.0	—	8.8
1970	4.9	6.32	100	127.9	4.8	4.7	5.0	1,773	12.2
1971	4.9	9.64	94.7	141.3	5.7	6.3	6.9	1,723	34.9
1972	3.5	5.97	89.7	148.8	7.4	6.4	5.8	1,597	58.9
1973	5.8	6.35	97.4	146.8	6.1	5.5	4.5	1,811	61.2
1974	6.3	6.1	106.3	152.5	4.2	3.4	2.5	2,008	23.3
1975	−1.3	−2.8	104.6	141.5	2.4	NA	2.8	1,740	182.5
1976	−2.8	−4.48	106.3	132.7	4.8	4.5	4.0	2,200	443.2

Sources: Official Argentine government documents as cited in Adolfo Canitrot, *La Viabilidad Económica de la Democracia: Un Análisis de la Experiencia Peronista 1973–1976*, Estudios Sociales, no.11 (Buenos Aires: Centro de Estudios de Estado y Sociedad, 1978), 22–24, 26, 29; International Monetary Fund, *International Financial Statistics Yearbook* (Washington, D.C.: International Monetary Fund, 1981), 64–65.

The battle between the two terrorisms was bloody and deep in its implications, but it did not involve great numbers of people. An editorial appearing just a few weeks before the regime collapsed conveys an image of a society that is far from mobilized: "There is a profound economic crisis which is not being reflected in hungry mobs, or armies of the unemployed, business bankruptcies on a massive scale or other outward manifestations. . . . We are living . . . without much evidence of disaster."[139] The polarization in Argentina embraced only selected groups and not huge swathes of society as a whole.

A Scheduled Execution

Rather than being the culmination of societal polarization, the death of democracy took the form of a scheduled execution in defense of the military as an institution. On Christmas Eve 1975, General Jorge Videla, the head of the armed forces, addressed a group of soldiers fighting guerrillas in the province of Tucumán and announced that "those who were charged with solving the country's problems" had exactly

[139] *Review of the River Plate*, 12 March 1976, p. 293.

ninety days to show their capabilities.[140] The speech was widely interpreted as an ultimatum, and as the ninety-day period drew to a close,
the press was replete with references to an impending coup. Rather
than be subdued, left-wing guerrillas stepped up their activities—even
exploding a bomb at army headquarters 150 meters away from Videla
himself.[141] The armed forces made their move precisely on schedule,
removing Isabel from the Casa Rosada by helicopter in the dead of
night on March 24.

The most remarkable aspect of the coup was its timing. Why had
the military waited so long to intervene? There had been talk of a coup
since at least April 1973, when a spate of military officers were success-
fully targeted by guerrillas in the aftermath of Cámpora's election.[142]
In July 1974, a larger coup-coalition formed immediately following the
death of Perón. Yet, the three branches of the military delayed official
discussions on the terms of intervention until October of 1975.[143] More
surprisingly, they actually reversed a right-wing military coup
launched on December 18, despite the fact that the coup was otherwise
unopposed.[144] The armed forces were unmistakably slow to topple the
civilian regime.[145]

The military's reluctance to intervene is rich in implications. If citizen mobilization had been sufficient cause for intervention, the military would have seized power under Cámpora or under the government of Isabel during the 1975 general strike, when mobilization was
relatively high. If pressures from transnational capital had been suffi-

[140] Félix Luna, *Golpes Militares y Soluciones Electorales*, (Buenos Aires: Editorial Sudamericana, 1983), 156; de Riz, *Retorno y Derrumbe*, 142.

[141] If Videla had not been held up in traffic, he would have been killed by the bomb.
La Opinión, 22 March 1976, p. 9. *Review of the River Plate*, 23 March 1976.

[142] Admiral Hermes Quijada was gunned down in the middle of Buenos Aires on 30
April 1973. A short time earler, Admiral Berisso had been killed and Admiral Aleman
had been kidnapped. Cámpora was in Madrid at the time of the Quijada murder and
this would have facilitated a coup, but no coalition materialized. *Review of the River Plate*,
11 May 1973, p. 659.

[143] The committee worked out a detailed plan, including the name of the future minister of the economy. See Norden, *Military Rebellion*, 53.

[144] Luna, *Golpes Militares*, 150. The leader of the coup was air force brigadier Jesus
Capellini. He immediately offered Videla control of the operation (and the inchoate
junta), so the latter's reaction to the coup was not related to rivalry. See Gerardo L.
Munck, *Authoritarianism and Democratization: Soldiers and Workers in Argentina 1976–1983*
(University Park, Penn.: Pennsylvania State University Press, 1998), 50.

[145] I am not the first person to note this. See, for example, di Tella, *Argentina under
Perón*, 81; and Munck et al., *Argentina: From Anarchism*. See also Norden, *Military Rebellion*, 50, who notes that the military forged its coup coalition only after impeachment
had failed. She argues too that the institutional cohesion of the armed forces was the
military's "predominant consideration" (p. 51).

cient cause for intervention, the *golpe* might have come in May or June of 1973, when property occupations and the kidnapping of business elites were both rampant.[146] It would surely have come in the summer of 1975, when the economy was in a tailspin and organized labor peaked in its influence on economic policy. Argentine capitalists were a heterogeneous group, as illustrated above, but there was always a powerful core that was ready to join a coup coalition.

The story told here does not challenge the common wisdom that the coup against the elected government of Isabel Perón was carried out in defense of capitalism. There can be little doubt that the mobilization of labor and the emergence of revolutionary groups on the Left were perceived as threatening to the Argentine business elite, or that threatened capitalists used longstanding contacts in the military and the state to demand a regime change, or that the military intended to eliminate these threats as soon as it assumed power.

This said, the timing and nature of the coup suggest that the military moved on its own schedule and in its own interests. Our literature tends to emphasize the civilian elements of coup coalitions, but their military elements are of equal if not greater importance. Argentine democracy fell to military elites, not to civilians. The military coup-makers did not topple the civilian government until it was in the military's institutional interests to do so. These interests required, first, that the intervention could proceed without any significant opposition from the military itself and, second, that it could proceed without significant overt civilian resistance. Building a unanimous coup-coalition in the officer corps took time because the military was still recovering from the experience in government that made it call for elections in the first place. General Lanusse had just convinced his fellow officers that it was not in the military's institutional interests to rule Argentina. Now the opposite argument had to be made, and it could not be made convincingly until the alternatives to direct rule had been exhausted. Two alternatives were tried. The first involved granting the armed forces the power to fight subversion, unconstrained by normal civil-rights laws. The second alternative involved the military actually joining the government, thus combining the expanded powers of the first alternative with ministerial powers. Juan Perón implemented the first alternative. Isabel Perón expanded the first and then implemented the second when she appointed Colonel Vicente Damasco minister of the interior in August of 1975. Both alternatives failed in that the military was still unable to quell the violence emerging from guerrilla action.

---

[146] Within twenty days of Cámpora's assuming office, a full 176 factories were occupied. Munck et al., *Argentina: From Anarchism*, 189.

The second alternative proved especially damaging, because it provoked serious divisions within the officer corps over the merits of participation itself.[147]

As alternatives to direct rule were tested, the military's failure to defeat the left-wing insurgency provoked autonomous armed action on the Right from the Triple A and other groups. If the military were simply a servant of capital, or of anti-democratic right-wing civilians more generally, the emergence of the Triple A would have been seen as a positive development, but the military was much more autonomous than many analysts realized. They actively participated in the ouster of López Rega in July of 1975, and they did so for institutional reasons.[148] The emergence of right-wing paramilitary groups was a grave blow to the military as an institution, for it meant that its "monopoly of force" had been lost to *two* opposing groups.[149]

The ouster of López Rega did not impair the operation of right-wing vigilantism. Thus, the military had a double incentive for intervening; but the second institutional condition for toppling the government was not yet met. How could the coup-makers assure reluctant officers that ordinary civilians would not offer overt opposition? Lanusse had argued that the military faced a choice between democracy or civil war. Were those still the only viable alternatives now? Here, as in all our cases, the military faced great uncertainty. On the one hand, the overwhelming mandate given to the ruling Peronist Party was a strong disincentive for intervention. On the other hand, the opacity of the political spectrum within the party made it difficult for anyone to know how much of the mandate reflected support for democracy per se. The mandate of the Radical Party was only slightly less ambiguous. This was a party of democrats, but did the citizens who voted for the Radicals (or for the other non-extremist parties) view Isabel's government as democratic? Since fear and economic crisis had brought opinion polling to a near standstill, information on these key questions was not readily available. The fact that there were no national elections after 1973 prevented an updating of information too.

The air force coup launched on 18 December 1975 allayed the military's uncertainty, for no civilian group offered resistance of any sort. It is not coincidental that Videla presented his ultimatum on the heels of this event. The military could now move forward to protect its inter-

---

[147] Munck, *Authoritarianism and Democratization*, 54.

[148] The press reported not only that the military backed the ouster of López Rega but that they pressured Isabel into firing him with an official report linking him to the Triple A. See Sobel, *Argentina and Peron*, 149.

[149] Landi, "La Tercera Presidencia," 1402.

ests with the essential preconditions met. The interests of the military coincided with the interests of the propertied civilians in the coup coalition in that the prospect of social revolution was equally horrifying to both groups. But the military did the bidding of no civilian forces. As final proof of the autonomous nature of the coup, the junta leaders broke all precedents and appointed no civilians to any major posts in the new government.[150]

Rethinking Popular Passivity

The subject of the new government brings us full circle, back to the question of how we should understand popular passivity in the face of the coup. Exhaustion and physical fear explain a great deal in this case, as in our others. But there are two specific reasons why we should not equate popular passivity with democratic defection in the Argentine case. First, the government that the military deposed was of highly questionable democratic pedigree and character. Isabel Perón's presidency was an inheritance, not an entitlement. She had no political base of her own when she took office and no possibility of building one as time passed. More important than this, however, was her reliance on advisors (most notably López Rega) who were boldly and actively anti-democratic themselves.[151] A broad range of newspapers criticized Isabel's entourage as being "contemptuous of political parties and democracy in general."[152] Rampant and credible charges of corruption eroded the government's association with legality even further. To equate a defection from this particular government with a defection from democracy seems unwise.

It also seems unwise for us to assume, in retrospect, that ordinary Argentines were making correct predictions about the type of regime that the military would install. Their most recent experience with military government had ended with the calling of elections.[153] How was any ordinary civilian to predict that this would not happen again?

---

[150] Edward Gibson writes that this was a coup against Argentine political and civil society—and not just a coup against Isabel Perón. It was the first time in history that the military ruled without civilians. Gibson, *Class and Conservative Parties*, 79.

[151] López Rega was widely known as "El Brujo" ("The Witch"). His use of astrology and his control over Isabel Perón made him a Rasputin-like character. Worse than this, though, was Isabel's willingness to use state resources "to isolate and terrorize political opponents." James, *Resistance and Integration*, 246. This repression had no place in a democracy.

[152] The phrase is from an article in the left-wing Peronist newspaper *Mayoría*. It was quoted in *Review of the River Plate*, 27 February 1976, p. 258.

[153] In addition to being short-lived, the military government had also been a "dictablanda," meaning a "relatively mild" authoritarian regime. McGuire, "Political Parties and Democracy in Argentina," 216.

Even highly placed civilian elites were misled by the patterns of the recent past.[154] Ricardo Balbín, "like most of the country," believed it was a "temporary intervention motivated ultimately by the desire to restore and regularize democracy."[155] Francisco Manrique expected that the coup would bring to power "a military government with widespread civilian participation" and that he would personally "play a major role in the regime."[156]

The proclamation that the military issued at 3:40 A.M. on the morning of the coup reinforced benign illusions by giving a deceitful picture of what was to come. Argentines woke up that morning to read and hear that the military actions were "directed only toward those who have committed crimes or abused power," that the coup did not "presuppose any discrimination towards any civic movement or any social sector whatsoever," and that the new regime would "respect the rights and dignity" of all Argentines.[157] These reassurances were no doubt designed to maximize passivity. We know now that they were tragically false. Though we might fault ordinary people for believing these reassurances, there is still a vast difference between the silence born of ignorance and the silence born of support. The story of ordinary people in the breakdown of democracy in Argentina and elsewhere cannot be understood without this simple distinction.[158] What the story of ordinary people means for our understanding of polarization, parties, and the consolidation of democracy is the subject of the final chapter.

[154] Just days before the coup, the majority of the CGT directorate voted against a statement supporting the Peronist government and the constitutional order. They thereby implicated themselves in the coup itself. It is hard to imagine they would have voted this way if they had guessed that the coup would bring to power a fiercely anti-labor regime. McGuire, *Peronism without Perón*, 170.

[155] Acuña, *De Frondizi a Alfonsín*, 210.

[156] Gibson, *Class and Conservative Parties*, 84. Manrique's reference point was the 1955 military government that had overthrown Perón and had invited a large number of anti-Peronist civilian elites to share power.

[157] Kandel and Monteverde, *Entorno y Caída*, 223–26.

[158] To the credit of Argentines of all sorts, the coup-makers did encounter some opposition when the illusions of the coup's early days had dissipated. Scattered strikes broke out, and newspapers such as *La Nación* (4 April 1976) and *La Opinión* wrote editorials critical of the regime. The *Review of the River Plate* published an editorial on 9 April 1976 stating, "Men at arms do not know how to govern." By 22 April 1976, its editorialists were writing, "The rapid reduction in absenteeism and strikes has been achieved by . . . armed men [and] police methods have forced down quotations in parallel markets. [It is wrong] to believe that the underlying problems that provoked this behavior have been resolved" (p. 515). On strikes, see Ruth Collier, *Paths toward Democracy* (New York: Cambridge University Press, 1999), 15. Edward Epstein reports that there were 89 strikes between the coup and the end of 1976 and 100 strikes in 1977. "Labor Populism and Hegemonic Crisis in Argentina," in *Labor Autonomy and the State in Latin America*, ed. Edward Epstein (Boston: Unwin Hyman, 1989).

7

POLARIZATION AND THE IGNORANCE OF ELITES

WHEN I STARTED THIS PROJECT I intended to use the basic polarization model as a ready-made platform from which to launch an argument about why ordinary people chose extremism. Yet, when I moved from the abstractions of political science to the histories of real actors in real polities, I realized that the platform I had chosen to enhance my view obscured it instead. Despite undeniable incentives to behave differently, many people failed to polarize and failed to defect from democracy. I decided to make them a focal point of my study and to analyze stability as well as change. In so doing, I learned that our thinking about polarization was in need of refinement. I also learned that the culpability for democracy's demise lay overwhelmingly with political elites. I analyze the substance and the implications of these lessons below.

Rethinking Polarization

As I stated in the opening pages of this study, the general concept of polarization is of great and lasting utility. When political actors polarize, the common ground required for democratic procedures and policy-making erodes. Even deeply rooted institutions can find themselves listing unsteadily as the political ground beneath them begins to shift. The histories recounted here are replete with examples of monarchies, militaries, and long-established political parties that toppled democracies by leaning too far to the Right. Ordinary people sometimes threw democracies off balance too, but only rarely with their votes. The polarization model obscures this fact, though it captures a part of the breakdown dynamic. The concept of polarization should remain in our diagnostic toolkit, but it can be better used if we revise our thinking about how it works. Three cautions should be kept in mind as we think about polarization in the future.

People or Particles?

The first caution is that we must beware of taking our scientific metaphors too seriously. "Centrifugal" and "centripetal" forces move particles, but they do not move parties, voters, or party systems. If parties or party systems change, it is only because human beings change them. Focusing on ordinary people and the political elites who seek their support (or acquiescence) enables us to keep this simple truth in mind. It also enables us to focus on the concrete factors that constrain and promote changes in mind and behavior. The ordinary citizens, civilian elites, and military officials who peopled the democracies studied here had the capacity (denied to particles) to calculate the costs and benefits of any political action. Their calculations often led them in directions the polarization model would not predict.

Party elites did not, for example, group themselves in unity around the Left and Right poles of the political spectrum—even at the moment when democracies collapsed. A quick review of what types of government were toppled makes the point. With the exception of Poland, each of the many democracies studied here fell to forces who were decidedly on the Right, but the democracies they displaced were of varied hues. Predictably, some of the casualties were governments of the Left (as in Spain and Chile) and others were governments of a more populist coloration (as in Bulgaria and Brazil). But most of our casualties were governments of the Center-Right and Right. In a most diverse range of cases, from Italy through Austria, Estonia, Latvia, Greece, Uruguay, and Argentina, right-wing dictatorships replaced right-wing elected governments.[1] Why would the Right topple regimes that were themselves associated with the Right and why would this happen so often? An obvious answer is that "the" Right itself was highly diverse and that the "centrifugal forces" intrinsic to the polarization metaphor did not work as predicted. They did not unify "the" Right against "the" Left because a whole range of other identities complicated people's calculations about who was an enemy and who was an ally.

The behavior of ordinary people at the polls seems to have been even less affected by centrifugal forces than the behavior of elites. There were a few cases where anti-democratic movements became electorally successful political parties, but in the vast majority of our cases, voters did not choose dictatorship at the ballot box. Even in the case, of Italy, where a highly visible Fascist movement emerged and the Center clearly collapsed among parliamentary elites, the Center "held" among the people at the polls.

Some readers will find this story of steadfastness too romantic to be believed. For the skeptical, I emphasize that habit is more important

---

[1] The Argentine reference is only to Isabel Martínez de Perón's government and not to those of Juan Perón or Héctor Cámpora, or to the Justicialista Party more generally, which is too heterogeneous to classify.

here than heroism and that the power of habit in politics elsewhere is amply documented. A number of classics in the literature on party politics in the United States make the point that party identification is not easily changed. Angus Campbell found it "remarkably resistant to passing political events" and argued that it typically remained "constant" throughout one's life.[2] Donald Stokes argued that party identification is of "great psychological convenience," that it "performs an exceedingly useful evaluative function," and that even wars, scandals, and recessions would "not change the votes of more than some."[3] If party identity has staying power in a system (such as that of the United States) where the parties are so similar, would it not have at least the same (if not more) power in systems where party differences are more marked?

Observations about the stability of party identification seem not to be limited to a peculiar time or place. In the U.S., Larry Bartels's study of over a century of presidential elections shows that party identification is as strong today as it ever has been.[4] In Western Europe, Bartolini and Mair found that the mean volatility in party loyalty during "the supposed" era of dramatic change differed from "the period of steady-state politics" by just 0.01 percentage points.[5] In a study of twenty-nine democracies on four continents, G. Bingham Powell found that "the accumulation of memory, organization and issues that accompany the formation of a major contending party resist dissolution," and that, as a consequence, party systems often "change more slowly than the conditions that helped shape them."[6] In all of these studies, continuity is the norm and not an aberration. Even in relatively new party systems, such as those in contemporary Eastern Europe and Russia, partisan identities seem strong among certain kinds of voters.[7] A comparative

[2] "Voters and Elections: Past and Present," *Journal of Politics* 26 (November 1964): 747.

[3] "Party Loyalty and the Likelihood of Deviating Elections," in *Elections and the Political Order*, ed. Angus Campbell et al. (New York: John Wiley and Sons, 1966), 126–27.

[4] "Electoral Continuity and Change, 1868–1996," *Electoral Studies* 17, no. 3 (1998).

[5] Stefano Bartolini and Peter Mair, *Identity, Competition and Electoral Availability: The Stabilisation of European Electorates* (Cambridge: Cambridge University Press, 1990). The authors studied 303 elections in thirteen West European countries between 1885 and 1985. The periods referred to are 1965–1985 and 1945–1965, respectively.

[6] G. Bingham Powell, *Contemporary Democracies: Participating, Stability and Violence* (Cambridge: Harvard University Press, 1982), 105.

[7] Joshua Tucker explains that in the new democracies of the post-Communist world, people's ideological position is often fixed quite early in the transition process and that variation in voting is a reflection of the variation in the parties or party leaders that claim to represent this fixed position. Personal communication, Princeton University, 30 March 2001. See also Ted Brader and Joshua Tucker, "Let's Get This Party Started! Russia's New Partisan Voters," paper prepared for the Annual Meeting of the American Association for the Advancement of Slavic Studies, Washington, D.C., November 2001, available at http://www.wws.princeton.edu/%7Ejtucker/pubs.html.

perspective thus helps us see that at least part of the story told here is mirrored in other, very different political systems.[8]

A comparative perspective also helps us understand the irony of continuity during crisis. Changing one's party preference (and thus moving anywhere on a political spectrum) has costs under any conditions. While it is not unreasonable to argue that a citizen who is struggling to survive amid economic chaos and chronic public disorder might be mobilized (and polarized) more easily, one can make the opposite case as well. Several scholars have done precisely this, illustrating that "economic problems both increase the opportunity costs of political participation and reduce a person's capacity to attend to politics."[9] Might not the struggle for survival under conditions of scarcity and turmoil make the costs of switching parties too high? Vote switching seems to be correlated with high levels of information,[10] but the costs of securing new and credible information are surely higher under conditions of crisis than under conditions of calm. The subject clearly requires more research, but the puzzle of continuity during crisis may not be as perplexing as it initially seems.

One Dimension or Many?

The second caution to keep in mind regards the spatial metaphor that lies at the base of the polarization model. Sartori offers us a unidimensional image with a Left and Right pole. The relational aspects of this image do resonate with an important aspect of political life in the democracies that collapsed. Parties of the Right (seeking to conserve preexisting hierarchical orders) and parties of the Left (seeking to chal-

---

[8] Philip Converse discusses the links between the passage of time and party identification in his "Of Time and Partisan Stability," *Comparative Political Studies* vol. 2 (1969). His argument and the ones I summarize here explain only part of the story because the party systems in many of the interwar cases were relatively new and therefore historically different from the systems about which these generalizations were made. For the new systems I look at here, I submit that the longstanding nature of other identities based on religion, ethnicity, and economic position might have served to reinforce continuities too, as these were molded into political parties. My hunch derives, of course, from the now classic work of Seymour Martin Lipset and Stein Rokkan, *Party Systems and Voter Alignments* (New York: The Free Press, 1967).

[9] Steve Rosenstone, "Economic Adversity and Voter Turnout," *American Journal of Political Science* 26, no. 1 (1982): 25. See also Richard Brody and Paul Sniderman, "From Life Space to Polling Place: The Relevance of Personal Concerns for Voting Behavior," *British Journal of Political Science* 7 (March 1977): 337–60.

[10] Philip Converse, "Information Flow and the Stability of Partisan Attitudes," in A. Campbell et al., *Elections and the Political Order*, 156. See also W. Phillips Shively, "From Differential Abstention to Conversion: A Change in Electoral Change, 1864–1988," *American Journal of Political Science* 36, no. 2 (1992) 309–30.

lenge hierarchies of all sorts) certainly existed in the periods on which we focus. The tension between these poles was real (even deadly), and it increased dramatically after the triumph of the Bolsheviks in 1917 and the triumph of Castro in 1959. Sartori's model is simple, elegant, and undoubtedly useful in that many political parties in most of the democracies that collapsed can be located somewhere on a unilinear bipolar spectrum. But the unilinear, bipolar schema fails to capture two important and recurrent aspects of the systems we have reviewed. The first is their multidimensionality. The second is their opacity.

Donald Stokes made a cogent argument for the multidimensionality of party systems long ago. In a critique of the unilinear model of Anthony Downs and its relevance for the United States, he concluded that the "conception of a single dimension of political conflict . . . is false to the realities of two-party systems."[11] He suggested that unilinear models were even less appropriate in multiparty systems. The multidimensional aspects of political cleavage in our failed democracies verify his intuition. The political history of the interwar years illustrates the multidimensionality of political conflict in dramatic tones. Ordinary people, and the parties they supported, often identified themselves as leftists or rightists—but other identities were of equal if not greater importance. Many of the largest and most consequential parties of the interwar period simply cannot be easily placed on a Left-Right spectrum. Confessional parties, agrarian parties, regional parties, ethnic parties, and personalist parties loomed large on Europe's interwar political landscape.

The utility of the unidimensional bipolar spectrum was hardly greater in the failed democracies of South America. In Chile, the fit was best. In Brazil and Argentina, the largest parties in the political system were decidedly populist. They had broad Left-Right divisions *within* them and were therefore impossible to place on a Left-Right spectrum. The bipolar model was ill suited to Uruguay too: first, because its two major parties hid Left-Right spectrums of their own; second, because the independent Left pole of the unilinear spectrum had no institutionalized counterpart on the Right. There was no right-wing party that juxtaposed itself to the Left. There was no significant right-wing party that countered an extreme Left in Argentina either.

If we must use spatial imagery to capture the essential conflicts of political life in the societies studied here, our imagery must convey the

---

[11] Donald Stokes, "Spatial Models of Party Competition,"in Campbell et al., *Elections and the Political Order*, 165. Stokes was not the only scholar to draw our attention to the limitations of a single left-right continuum. G. Bingham Powell does this in "Extremist Parties and Political Turmoil: Two Puzzles," *American Journal of Political Science* 30, no. 2 (May, 1986): 374.

existence of multiple polarities on multiple dimensions. It must also convey the pervasive opacity of polar strength and support dynamics. The unilinear model that lies at the foundation of our current thinking on polarization is profoundly misleading in this respect as well. It gives us the impression that political actors see more than they do. Sartori's linear model gives us the illusion that the popularity of different positions on a bipolar spectrum is transparent and that elections enable actors to assess the weight of "the" Left or "the" Right with certainty. Its emphasis on centripetal and centrifugal forces gives us the impression that even the *dynamics* of public opinion (and elite behavior) can be assessed with accuracy through a Left-Right lens.

Even a brief review of our failed democracies shows that the meaning of elections was far from transparent. Electoral alliances embracing parties with radically different ideologies (or no consistent ideology at all) made the interpretation of particular votes extremely difficult in countries ranging from Italy and Poland to Brazil, Argentina, and Uruguay. Clientelism, and the exclusion of particular parties from open competition, also made the contours of public opinion much more opaque than the unilinear model allows. The fact that electoral laws were often in a state of fluidity added another dimension of opacity to these systems. Elites were not simply uncertain about how people would vote. They were often uncertain about who would be voting. If we must have a spatial model of party systems, it must allow for opacity and thus make uncertainty more explicit.

When Stokes argued against unidimensional models, he argued against spatial models in general. "Most spatial models," he wrote, "have a very poor fit with the evidence about how large-scale electorates and political leaders actually respond to politics."[12] The histories related here suggest that his skepticism is well placed. If there is an image—rather than a model—that depicts the party systems of failed democracies more accurately, it is the sphere, not the unidimensional line. Most of the systems reviewed here had multiple axes, joined together in the shared political space of state boundaries. The spherical image conveys the fact that many parties contain Left-Right spectrums of their own and that the most relevant coordinates of political life might shift. The spherical image also allows for alliances based on various "proximities"—not simply positions on a Left-Right dimension but proximities based on region, cronyism, or, as often happened, hostility to a third party. Finally, the spherical image is superior to the unilinear one in that it allows for opacity. Spheres are never fully visible, and

[12] Stokes, "Spatial Models," 161.

the weights of different groupings in the party systems of failed democracies were never fully visible either.

I emphasize that this is merely a metaphorical image and not a model, for it has no intrinsically dynamic elements and no pretensions to being predictive. It does convey the complexity and opacity of the party systems confronting ordinary people and political elites in failed democracies and in this sense is an improvement on the unidimensional bipolar image we have worked with thus far.

Polarization in Multiple Arenas

I argued above that polarization takes place along multiple dimensions. The histories of failed democracies show that polarization takes place within multiple arenas as well. This is a third caution we have to keep in mind. Though polarization is often discussed as if it were a "condition," it is also (even principally) a process. In the context of this study, it is a process involving the growth of mutually antagonistic, self-identified political groups who compete for scarce resources in the same political system and have public and fundamental disagreements about how their shared system should be structured. The antagonistic political groups are "extremist" in the sense that Bingham Powell uses the term. They "offer the promise of radical change in the social, economic and political fabric" of the existing system.[13] The polar extremes are distinguished from one another less by the scope of the changes they advocate than by the nature of the changes themselves.

If we conceive of polarization as a process and not merely a property of party systems, we can better appreciate the multiplicity of the arenas in which it takes place. Our case studies have enabled us to draw analytic distinctions between different processes of polarization: in public spaces, at the polls, in public opinion, and among political elites. Making these distinctions and tracing the trajectories of different polarizations in different arenas is of great importance for our understanding of democratic breakdowns.

Why? As a number of leading theorists have pointed out, democracies are themselves composites of multiple arenas. Philippe Schmitter, for example, conceives of democracy not as "*a* regime" but as an interdependent "composite of 'partial regimes' each of which is institutionalized around distinctive sites" for representation.[14] Linz and Stepan

---

[13] Powell, *Contemporary Democracies*, 42.

[14] Philippe Schmitter, "Interest Systems and the Consolidation of Democracies," in *Reexamining Democracy*, ed. Gary Marks and Larry Diamond (Newbury Park, Cali.: Sage, 1992), 160–62.

remind us of the composite nature of democracy as well. Like Schmitter, they emphasize that "democracy is more than a regime." They argue instead that it is "an interacting system" composed of five interrelated arenas, including political society, civil society, economic society, the rule of law, and the state apparatus.[15]

Because the arenas, or "partial regimes," within democracy *are* so interrelated, polarization in one realm inevitably has implications for other realms. The longevity of any democracy depends on what these implications are, that is, on how the actors in one realm respond to what the actors in another realm seem to be doing. I use the phrase *seem to be doing* quite deliberately here, because perceptions are more important than objective realities as determinants of individual behavior. Our case studies show that elite perceptions were especially important in the drama of democratic failure.

Our case studies also show that elite perceptions were often formed in ignorance, that is, with seriously inadequate or distorted information. Elite ignorance was exacerbated by the real opacity of party systems, but it was also exacerbated by the illusory transparency of civil society. Elected elites in political society often mistook the preferences of polarized forces in civil society for the preferences of larger constituencies. Acting on the (usually false) assumption that polarization in the streets was an accurate reflection of popular preferences in general, elected elites often exacerbated polarization in political society. Thinking that their representative functions (and future careers) required nothing less, politicians in the legislative and the executive sectors of political society continued to demand both increased concessions for the mobilized and extended toleration of disruption (and lawlessness). When pendular mobilization set in, the set of politicians making demands grew.

As polarization in political society increased, selected elites in military society[16] began to consider intervention. This development exacerbated divisions in the military itself. These divisions, in turn, caused further polarization among political elites as antagonistic forces of different extremes laid claim to protection from different sectors of the armed forces. By seeing polarization as a process that occurs in differ-

---

[15] Juan J. Linz and Alfred Stepan, *Problems of Democratic Transition and Consolidation: Southern Europe, South America, and Post-Communist Europe* (Baltimore: Johns Hopkins University Press, 1996), 13–14.

[16] This term is my own, but it derives from Alain Rouquié's vision of the *l'état militaire*, or "military estate." See his *The Military and the State in Latin America* (Berkeley: University of California Press, 1987). For me, military society is the complex set of social, professional, and political networks defining the armed forces as an institution set apart from political society.

ent arenas at different times, we are able to appreciate its profoundly contagious quality.

By examining more closely the arenas in which polarization occurs, we are able to appreciate why elite perceptions were often so distorted. The term "civil society" is used as a singular noun, but it should not be seen as a singular entity, either by scholars or by politicians. The term hides very different forms of associational life, including organized interest groups, religious groups, and social movements. Some were intensely polarized, others were moderately polarized, and some were not polarized at all. A review of our cases shows that democracies were most often disrupted when preexisting groups in civil society transformed themselves into social movements. When student organizations transformed themselves into student movements, or when labor unions transformed themselves into labor movements, public space changed character. When several movements joined in concert, the change became especially threatening. Often, these organizations were joined primarily at the top, by activist elites who were not fully representative of ordinary people in general, or even of the ordinary people at the organization's base. Yet, because these organizations were themselves opaque, outsiders could not judge the depth of activist support. Activists of all sorts contributed to outsiders' ignorance, for it was in their interest to exaggerate both the strength of their adversaries and their own support.

These "movement groups" drove public polarization and were mistaken (by both politicians and military elites) for the public as a whole. To understand this phenomenon and to understand why elites overlooked the moderate forces in the voting public, we must think harder about the dynamic of social movements themselves. Happily, other scholars have done much of the labor already.

By unpacking the term civil society and looking at social movements within civil society instead, we solve several perplexing puzzles about both polarization and the breakdown of democracy. These relate to timing, intensity, and saliency.

TIMING

Why did so many democracies enter into crises simultaneously? In other words, why are our cases clustered not only geographically, but temporally? Careful scholars have suggested that the answer is rooted in economic factors—factors related to the Depression in the interwar years and to the crisis of import substitution in South America in the 1960s and 1970s. Economic factors certainly contributed to system crises, and it is surely significant that none of the seventeen cases reviewed here suffered a regime change during an economic boom. But the standard economic approaches to the breakdown puzzles leave puzzles of their own. Six of the thirteen cases of interwar breakdown occurred before the Depression.[17] At least three of the democracies that broke down after the Depression were in better condition by standard measures than many of the democracies that survived.[18] The average rise in unemployment was actually lower in the European democracies that collapsed than in those that did not, and most of the democracies that broke down experienced no hyperinflation at all. German and Austrian democracies actually survived for ten years after horrendous bouts with hyperinflation.

In South America, economic scarcity was surely a factor that worked to the advantage of anti-democratic forces, but the dramatic differences within the set of economies that fell to dictatorship make all but the most general propositions hard to sustain. The Uruguayan economy was vastly different from the Brazilian economy, which was, in turn, different from the Chilean and the Argentine.[19] The Argentine case offers us the clearest evidence that anti-system groups and economic crises followed separate trajectories. The survival of South American electoral democracies in the context of grave economic crises in the 1990s provides further evidence that the relationship between economic crisis and the rise of dictatorship is far from direct. Hard times are not necessarily times of dictatorship.[20]

---

[17] These cases were Italy, Bulgaria, Poland, Lithuania, Portugal, and the Kingdom of the Serbs, Croats, and Slovenes.

[18] These cases were Greece, Romania, and Spain. The Netherlands, Belgium, and France had deeper economic crises than most of the democracies that collapsed. For the data I use to make these comparisons, see Dirk Berg-Schlosser, "Crisis, Compromise and Collapse: Social and Political Reactions to the Great Depression," unpublished manuscript presented to the ECPR workshops in Madrid, 19–21 April 1994. For more recent work, see Dirk Berg-Schlosser, "Conditions of Authoritarianism, Fascism and Democracy in Interwar Europe: A Cross-sectional and Longitudinal Analysis," *International Journal of Comparative Sociology* 39, no. 4 (Nov. 1998) and Dirk Berg-Schlosser and Jeremy Mitchell, eds., *Conditions of Democracy in Europe, 1919–39: Systematic Case Studies* (New York: St. Martin's Press, 2000).

[19] Many of these differences are introduced in David Collier's *New Authoritarianism in Latin America* (Princeton: Princeton University Press, 1979).

[20] As Larry Diamond argues, "Political experience with democracy and alternative regimes, and how well a formally democratic regime functions to deliver the 'political goods' of democracy, have sizeable independent effects on political attitudes and values, often overpowering . . . those of the regime's economic performance." "Political Culture and Democratic Consolidation," CEACS Estudios/Working Papers, 1998/118, June 1998, p. 3. In a similar vein, José Maria Maravall has argued persuasively for "the autonomy of political legitimacy"—meaning that legitimate democratic governments have a certain insulation from the results of poor economic performance. People can and do blame poor

The social movement literature offers us an alternative answer for the timing question. It teaches us that social movements emerge (and thus contribute to public polarization) when there are changes in political opportunity structures. These are defined by Tarrow as "dimensions of the political environment which either encourage or discourage people from using collective action." The changes in opportunity structure that are most salient for Tarrow are those resulting from "the opening up of access to power," "shifts in ruling alignments," "the availability of influential allies," and "cleavages within and among elites."[21]

The timing of the public polarization that looms so large in our case studies was directly related to changes in opportunity structures. The success of the Bolshevik revolution gave leftist movement entrepreneurs in Europe new and highly "influential allies." The restructuring of Europe in the aftermath of World War I (with monarchies, borders, and electoral restrictions falling overnight) caused immediate "shifts in ruling alignments" and opened up "access to power."

The success of the Cuban revolution gave leftist movement entrepreneurs highly "influential allies" in Latin America. The U.S. reaction to the revolution gave the same boost to anti-leftist groups. A variety of forces, including the Catholic Church, the Alliance for Progress, and groups of economists in ECLA and CEPAL, made the early 1960s a

---

economic performance on things other than democracy itself, including capitalism, the international economy, trade unions, etc. Even when people blame a particular government, democracy allows them to choose another government rather than force a regime change. See José Maria Maravall, *Los Resultados de la Democracia* (Madrid: Alianza Editorial, 1995), 254–55. Limongi and Przeworski have found that a democracy had a 73% chance of surviving three years of negative growth while an authoritarian regime had only a 33% chance. Maravall and Przeworski have shown that poor economic performance in Spain's new democracy had little role in the shaping of even *partisan* attitudes, much less overall attitudes, toward the new regime. They found instead that "political reactions to the economy are mediated by political loyalties and by ideology" and "that partisan attitudes were stable, whatever the conditions of the economy." These points support the argument for a preference towards stability that emerges in my case studies. See José Maria Maravall and Adam Przeworski, "Political Reactions to the Economy: The Spanish Experience," CEACS Estudios/Working Papers, 1998/127, December 1998, p. 42

[21] See Sidney Tarrow, *Power in Movement: Social Movements and Contentious Politics* (New York: Cambridge University Press, 1998), 18. The literature on political opportunity structures is vast. Among the many other authors making contributions to my thinking on these points are Charles Tilly, *From Mobilization to Revolution* (Reading, Mass.: Addison Wesley, 1978); Herbert Kitschelt, "Political Opportunity Structures and Political Protest," *British Journal of Political Science* 16 (1978); and Doug McAdam, *Political Process and the Development of Black Insurgency 1930–1970* (Chicago: University of Chicago Press, 1982). I strongly agree with McAdam when he emphasizes that changed opportunity structures do not in themselves produce social movements but just the "structural potential" for action. "Mediating between opportunity and action are people and the subjective meanings they attach to their situations." *Political Process*, 48.

period of intense social, political, and economic reform throughout the southern cone.[22] The resultant expansion of universities, industries, cities, and electorates opened "access to power," created "shifts in ruling alignments," and changed opportunity structures for a broad variety of groups. Economic crises stimulated polarized social movements too, but this was due, in large part, to the fact that crises exacerbated "cleavages within and among elites." Where elites stood united and formed pacts, economic crisis did not contribute to a regime change.[23] The coincidence of profound changes in opportunity structure in the interwar years in Europe and in the 1960s and 1970s in South America help us understand the timing of public polarization.

INTENSITY

A second insight from the social movement literature helps us understand the intensity of public polarization. Our historical comparison shows that public polarization varied in intensity and political content across cases. In most cases of breakdown, ordinary people did not mobilize for dictatorship in any significant number. Yet, there were exceptions to the peripheral scenario. Germany, Austria, and Romania exemplify a different and profoundly disturbing pattern where the "suspect" citizen identified in my opening chapters really does emerge. Curiously, these exceptional cases emerge precisely where many of the theorists quoted in the introductory chapters would least expect them. "Suspect" citizens emerged most often where civil society was relatively *dense*. There is a vast literature on the density of organizational life in Weimar Germany.[24] Likewise, interwar Austria was said to have the most densely organized society in Europe.[25] Italian civil society was extensively developed in the country's north, as Putnam points out, but this is precisely the region that proved most susceptible to Fascism. In Romania, where the density of associational life was relatively weak in the aggregate, the Iron Guard still drew most of its resources from universi-

---

[22] Victor Bulmer-Thomas, *The Economic History of Latin America since Independence* (Cambridge: Cambridge University Press, 1994), 318. The reference to the church is mine, not the author's.

[23] Dirk Berg-Schlosser provides clear evidence of this point in "Conditions of Authoritarianism," 360–61.

[24] See the recent work of Peter Fritzsche and Larry Jones for examples, as well as Berman, "Civil Society and the Collapse of the Weimar Republic," *World Politics* 49, 1997.

[25] See Walter Simon, "Democracy in the Shadow of Imposed Sovereignty" in *Europe*, ed. Juan Linz and Alfred Stepan (Baltimore: Johns Hopkins University Press, 1978); also Charles Gulick, *Austria from Hapsburg to Hitler* (Berkeley: University of California Press, 1948).

ties, veterans' organizations, and Christian religious groups—precisely the sectors of society which were organized best.

Situating our cases of intense anti-democratic polarization in the social movement literature helps explain the curious association between civic density and democratic collapse. Social movements are always based on preexisting social networks. "The denser" these networks are, "the more likely movements are to spread and be sustained."[26] Anti-democratic movements thrived most where history had left a strong base of social networks that could be captured and mobilized for collective action. In nations such as Portugal and, to a lesser extent, Poland, these networks were weak on the eve of democratic collapse. In nations such as Austria and Germany, they were stronger.[27] Throughout our cases, the mobilization and conversion of preexisting networks depended on the skill of entrepreneurs and the accidents of history. In Romania, for example, where social networks were less dense, Fascism got off to a slower start. It was not until the early thirties, after Hitler furnished "an influential ally" in Germany and an influx of mostly Jewish refugees from Russia had entered the country, that the Iron Guard was able to use student, veterans,' and religious networks as solid bases for anti-Semitic movements. The social movement literature helps us understand the when and where of what we have observed.

SALIENCY

The final puzzle that the social movement literature helps us solve relates to the issue of saliency. Why was it that public polarization was so often mistaken for the public will? Why was it that political elites so often failed to recognize (or, more important, act upon) the distinctions (and moderation) uncovered in our case studies? The simple truth is that elites were forced to get their readings on the public in public space itself. Social movements dominated this space, and since social movements by definition "have no certain size or clear membership,"[28] their true popularity was impossible to judge. The fact that these movements often claimed to be "representing new or unrepresented constituencies"[29] left their boundaries even harder to trace. It was in the interest of movement elites, of course, to maximize this uncertainty and to exaggerate their movement's support. Risk-averse political elites (whether friends or foes) obligingly took the bait and thought in maximum terms

[26] Tarrow, *Power in Movement*, 1.
[27] See Berman, "Civil Society," 419–29, for a discussion of how the Nazis used preexisting networks for the expansion of the NSDAP.
[28] Tarrow, *Power in Movement*, 15.
[29] Ibid., 4.

themselves. Elections gave a more accurate reading of public preferences, but these were only occasional. Social movements engaged in "*sustained* sequences of interaction with opponents [and] authorities,"[30] and thus gave elites a continuous (though inaccurate) reading of popular preferences. Joining a revised conception of polarization to what we know about social movements helps us understand much more about how, when, and where democracies break down.

Polarization and the Culpability of Elites

To understand who was ultimately responsible for the breakdown of democracy, we have to recognize the limits of polarization's effects. Even profound polarization—in both public and private space—is never, in itself, a sufficient condition for regime collapse. Democracies will only collapse if actors deliberately disassemble them and the key actors in this disassembling process are political elites. With the possible exception of Germany, ordinary people never opted for dictatorship at the polls. Mobilized groups contributed mightily to their democracy's demise when they launched violent assaults on public officials or beat and murdered ordinary citizens from rival camps. But there is little evidence that the majority of ordinary people supported these extremist actions.[31] On the contrary, we learned that in the last moments of German and Uruguayan democracy, both the Nazis and the Tupamaros *lost* support when the scope of their violent actions began to expand.

Moreover, there is little evidence that the individuals who engaged in violence or even in disruptive demonstrations were representative of their ordinary compatriots—in the sense of being either "typical" or "freely chosen." In Italy and Germany, Fascist thugs were younger and less educated than the rest of the population. In Romania, the Fascist Iron Guard emerged from elites in universities.[32] In Argentina, Chile, and Uruguay, the violent forces on the far left emerged from universities too and were substantially younger than their compatriots. In most countries, ranging from Latvia to Brazil, violent groups were nonexistent or very small, but where they did emerge, they were never a cross-

---

[30] Ibid., 2.

[31] My generalization about support applies only to the period before the democracies actually collapsed. What people did after the Nazis became hegemonic is detailed in Daniel Goldenhagen, *Hitler's Willing Executioners: Ordinary Germans and the Holocaust* (New York: Alfred A. Knopf, 1996).

[32] See Irina Livezeanu, *Cultural Politics in Greater Romania: Regionalism, Nation Building and Ethnic Struggle, 1918–1930* (Ithaca: Cornell University Press, 1995) 245–96.

section of their societies. Extremist groups were never "representative" in the second sense either. Rather than being legitimately elected to speak and act for a particular sector of society, extremists typically fought their way into leadership positions—sometimes in a literal sense. Even among highly mobilized (as opposed to overtly violent) groups, organizational democracy was rare.[33] Ordinary people were not blameless in the stories told here, but those who were most guilty were also extraordinary.

Ordinary people generally *were* guilty of remaining passive when dictators actually attempted to seize power. In Spain the citizenry fought the onset of dictatorship at horrific cost, and in Uruguay people mounted strikes and street protests shortly after the military seized power, but in other countries open resistance was minimal. Though ordinary people generally did not polarize and mobilize in support of dictatorship, they did not immediately mobilize in defense of democracy either. This last, incontrovertible fact sets the limits of the argument presented here but does not undercut it. Passivity is not synonymous with support for dictatorship. Three contextual factors need underscoring to make the point.

First, in the majority of cases where people remained passive, no one (except, perhaps, the dictators themselves) knew what would transpire after the seizure of power. In many cases, the men who toppled these regimes portrayed themselves as the salvation of democracy. Much of the public believed these statements, as did sectors of the political class. In these cases, people remained passive because they assumed that the new regime would simply restore order and hold new elections.

In other cases, those who seized power portrayed themselves as the only alternative to totalitarian dictatorship. In Austria, Estonia, and Latvia, for example, the civilian leaders who engineered executive coups claimed they acted only to prevent the victory of fascism. People believed this argument too. Even Sigmund Freud, along with many other Austrian Jews, supported the coup by Dollfüss.[34] Citizen passivity in the face of dictatorship was not an indication of a defection from democracy, or an indication of hostility either. Passivity was often rooted in uncertainty and ignorance, instead.

---

[33] The absence of real democracy within far-right groups and some trade unions is well known, but some far-left groups were sites of internal authoritarianism too. See, for example, Astrid Arrarás, "Armed Struggle, Political Learning and Participation in Democracy: The Case of the Tupamaros," (Ph.D. dissertation, Princeton University, 1998). See also María Matilde Ollier, *La Creencia y la Pasión: Privado, Público y Político en la Izquierda Revolucionaria* (Buenos Aires: Ariel, 1998).

[34] Payne, *A History of Fascism*, 250.

Citizen passivity was also rooted in fear. The second contextual factor we have to keep in mind relates to the effects of coercion. Those who dare to mobilize against dictatorship risk jail, torture, and even death. Under these conditions, passivity cannot be understood as either support for authoritarianism or defection from democracy. State coercion forces people to conceal their true preferences, and the regimes that replaced failed democracies were certainly highly coercive.[35] Strictly speaking, the fact that ordinary people did not rise up in defense of a particular elected government tells us only that they were not willing to risk their lives in defense of a particular set of rulers. In the Kingdom of the Serbs, Croats, and Slovenes, or in Isabel Perón's Argentina (and in other cases), we can justifiably ask whether the regimes under assault were still democracies at all. But even if we argue that resistance would have saved democracy per se, popular passivity only allows us to infer that people's preference for democracy ranked lower than their preference for life or physical security. We cannot infer that people preferred dictatorship over democracy.

On the contrary, popular resistance to dictatorship manifested itself in all these cases whenever the two constraints outlined above were absent. This is the third fact we have to keep in mind as we analyze the meaning of passivity. In Spain, the resistance was immediate because Francisco Franco's anti-democratic plans were unambiguous and because the resistors had substantial coercive force of their own. With control of at least a section of the armed forces, as well as the central government, Spaniards fought the onset of dictatorship because they had some hope of victory. In Uruguay, the plans of the coup-makers were ambiguous at first, but when they became clear, resistance (led by the national labor federation) gathered broad support and only collapsed when state forces fired on demonstrators and raised the level of fear. In our other cases, open resistance emerged as soon as the ruling elite liberalized and sent signals that it would tolerate dissent. In some countries, this process took decades. In some, it took defeat in war. In Eastern Europe, people had to endure dictatorships of the Right and of the Left, but whenever these states let up on coercion, people mobilized protests. The outcomes of mobilization varied and were sometimes disastrous, but ordinary people did fight dictatorship openly when they could and with clandestine weapons when they

---

[35] For a compelling analysis of the connection between dictatorship and the falsification of political preferences, see Timur Kuran, "Now out of Never: The Element of Surprise in the East European Revolution of 1989" in *Liberalization and Democratization: Change in the Soviet Union and Eastern Europe*, ed. Nancy Bermeo (Baltimore: Johns Hopkins University Press, 1992), 7–48.

could not.[36] These facts too must be kept in mind when we read negative meaning into citizen passivity.

Though citizen passivity made the dismantling of democracy easier, it is undeniable that the democracies studied here were brought down by their own political elites. Elite actions followed a range of trajectories. At one extreme, politicians (and sometimes monarchs) chose dictatorship deliberately. They either became dictators themselves, or they knowingly made anti-democratic figures head of government. At another extreme, political elites brought on dictatorship through their own ineptitude: they made a series of errors that produced a coup coalition. Their errors were surprisingly similar, despite the great variation in our cases: they always produced a coup coalition including military elites. This is highly significant.

The polarization model leaves the armed forces off-stage, but the drama of democratic collapse never comes to an end without them. Of the seventeen failed democracies studied here, a full nine ended with military coups. A tenth, the Spanish, ended with a coup that became a civil war. In the remaining cases democracy ended with the blessing of the military. The military was especially important in Germany, where officers-turned-politicians dealt democracy its final blows.

No matter how we refine it, our understanding of polarization will never add up to an understanding of democratic collapse until we can relate the processes of polarization to the interests of the military. How polarization affects the perceptions of military elites is key. When military elites come to believe that elected civilian elites are incapable of handling polarization in an orderly way, the core of a coup coalition will form. The original conspirators will often meet with resistance from within the armed forces itself, but this will be overcome if the conspirators can convince their colleagues that civilian polarization is affecting the military as an institution. Civilian radicals often *do* target the military as an institution. In so doing, they unwittingly unify the single force that is essential—and sufficient—for the installation of dictatorship. Capitalists can destabilize democracies, but without the cooperation of armed force they cannot topple them.

What sorts of structures might block this path to breakdown? The question brings us back to the beginnings of this study and to our discussion of political parties. Our opening overview of the literature highlighted some classic arguments about "strong" parties being the principal means of controlling the disruptive and polarized forces of

---

[36] James C. Scott, *Weapons of the Weak: Everyday Forms of Peasant Resistance* (New Haven: Yale University Press, 1985).

civil society. Our case studies do not contradict this basic argument. Indeed, by exposing the culpability of elites (mostly party elites), these histories help to confirm the view.[37] More importantly, though, our case studies help us clarify what *sort* of party strength is required for destabilizing polarization to be held in check. Surprisingly, strength defined as "institutionalization" is not sufficient for the task. By standard measures, Chilean and Uruguayan parties were highly institutionalized—yet their democracies failed anyway. Strength defined as "popularity," that is, in purely electoral terms, seems not to have been sufficient either. The Peronistas had an overwhelming electoral majority from 1973 through 1976, but Argentine democracy failed anyway. Strength derived from a particular sort of party system seems not to have been decisive either. Our cases of failed democracies embrace the whole range of party system types: from modified two-party systems (as in Uruguay) to systems with over a dozen parties (as in Poland).[38]

What sort of strength *was* key? The strength that most of the major parties in all the failed democracies lacked was what we might call *distancing capacity*. By this I mean the strength to distance a party and its members from acts of violence and lawlessness. This distancing involves condemning and prosecuting all those who engage in violence, even when they present themselves as current or potential party allies. The act of distancing serves as an antidote to the contagion of polarization. If parties can muster this sort of strength, they show themselves to be solutions to the problem of disorder and not contributing factors. They thus deprive anti-democratic forces in the military and elsewhere of their most powerful argument for intervention.[39] Over time, they probably lower the level of violence itself, for they lower its pay-offs and raise its costs.

---

[37] In so doing, I confirm the sentiment of a number of leading Latin Americanists today who argue that the neglect of parties in Latin American studies has been highly detrimental. See for example, Jorge Domínguez, "Samuel Huntington's Political Order and the Latin American State" in *The Other Mirror: Grand Theory through the Lens of Latin America*, ed. Miguel Angel Centeno and Fernando Lopez-Alves (Princeton: Princeton University Press, 2001).

[38] Democracy has failed and succeeded in a variety of party systems, suggesting that system type is not a decisive determinant of success. This latter point has been made eloquently by Scott Mainwaring and Timothy Scully in *Building Democratic Institutions*, 34.

[39] It is important to emphasize how divided the armed forces often are on the issue of intervention. This division provides opportunities for political crafting that civilian elites often miss. Even in Argentina, where the ruthless nature of the last dictatorship gives the opposite impression, the lust for rulership cannot be assumed. For elaborations on this point, see Alain Rouquié, *Poder Military y Sociedad Política en la Argentina* (Buenos Aires: Emecé, 1982), 2:379. Huntington makes a similar point about militaries in general. See Huntington, *Political Order*, 409–11.

Ideally, distancing action should be taken early, so that movements do not gather momentum. The tragic consequences of delaying distancing are illustrated by a diverse range of governments: Giolitti, Papen, Allende, Campora, and others proved either unable or unwilling to punish violence and impose the rule of law. Their failure to punish the perpetrators of violence raised citizen fears, energized pendular mobilization, and provided the rationale for the suspension of democratic freedoms.[40]

It is important to note that distancing capacity does not derive from the will of party leaders alone. Their political will is essential for the condemnation of lawlessness, but the actual capacity to punish wrongdoers and remove them from society depends on the political will of other elites in other institutions. Elites in the police forces and in the judiciary must cooperate with elected leaders and mete out justice without political bias if political distancing is to work. The histories of failed democracies are replete with examples where police and judicial elites failed to punish lawlessness and thus encouraged citizens to take the law into their own hands.

Because this project focuses on failed democracies, the evidence it has offered on "distancing capacity" has thus far been only negative: the parties discussed in the preceding chapters lacked the precise type of strength I suspect is essential. But positive evidence (meaning evidence about successful parties in democracies that survived) is available too. The conclusion of G. Bingham Powell's major, crossnational research project on democracies and violence was that "democratic processes continued unchecked ... in countries where the major parties presented a united front against violence and kept themselves and their supporters from engaging in it."[41]

A diverse range of cases suggests that Powell is right. Where major parties succeed in distancing themselves from violence, electoral democracy is much more likely to survive. This distancing has taken many different forms, but it appears consistently across a broad range of cases, from Finland to Czechoslovakia to Venezuela.

Finnish political parties were able to distance themselves from violence in the 1930s and deter a serious threat from the extreme-right Lapua movement. Finnish democracy triumphed against the odds for, like many of the states where democracy collapsed, it was a new de-

---

[40] When intellectuals are slow to distance themselves from violence, the results are especially tragic. Guillermo O'Donnell does us a service by pointing out this failure in Argentina, but it is a phenomenon we see in many of our cases including Germany, Italy, Romania, Chile, and Uruguay. See O'Donnell, *Y a Mi, Que Me Importa? Notas Sobre Sociabilidad y Política en Argentina y Brasil* (Buenos Aires: Estudios CEDES, 1984), 23.

[41] *Contemporary Democracies*, 168.

mocracy born from the remnants of a disintegrated empire. It was ranked with Romania in terms of education, urbanization, wealth, and division of labor,[42] and its Communist Party (with as high as 14.8 percent of the vote) was as large as any in Europe.[43] Most ominously, the Communists and Nationalists were still recovering from fighting a brutal civil war when the effects of the Depression began to be felt. When anti-Communist farmers rioted in the town of Lapua in 1929, an extreme-right movement swept the country and made the breakdown of democracy "a real possibility."[44]

At first, political elites made concessions to the group: a new parliament arrested Communist deputies, passed anti-Communist laws and sometimes allowed extreme-right lawlessness to go unpunished. Politicians rationalized these concessions as moves "to prevent the growth of anti-parliamentary feeling,"[45] but by the autumn of 1930, concessions gave way to open conflict. The courts began to crack down on movement violence and even convicted the movement leader's son of "political murder." Politicians of all sorts condemned the movement publicly and issued calls for order.[46] Most importantly, the nation's major parties formed a Lawfulness Front to bring an immediate end to "the law of the Lapua" and curtail the movement's growth.

The Lapua movement's attacks on the moderate Social Democratic Party provided a major catalyst for the policy change because they made politicians realize that the movement was a threat to parliamentary government itself. The "boundaries within the political Right

[42] Risto Alapuro, "Students and National Politics: A Comparative Study of the Finnish Student Movement in the Interwar Period," *Scandinavian Political Studies* 8 (1973) 113.

[43] Marvin Rintala, *Three Generations: The Extreme Right Wing in Finnish Politics* (Bloomington: Indiana University Publications, 1962), 19–20; Daniele Caramani, *Elections in Western Europe since 1815: Electoral Results by Constituencies* (New York: Grove's Dictionaries, 2000), 267–70.

[44] Risto Alapuro and Erik Allardt, "The Lapua Movement: The Threat of Rightist Takeover in Finland, 1930–32," in Linz and Stepan, *Europe*, 125. For a more recent discussion of the Finnish case, see Lauri Karvonen, "Finland: From Conflict to Compromise," in Berg-Schlosser and Mitchell, *Conditions of Democracy in Europe*.

[45] Rintala, *Three Generations*, 167.

[46] The Social Democratic leadership had condemned violence since the civil war. Indeed, the widely publicized last will and testament of party leader Eetu Salin pleaded for the rejection of "all extra-parliamentary methods and violence," even if they emanated "from the Ghost of Father Marx himself." Rintala, *Three Generations*, 20–21. The cabinet in power when the Lapua movement first marched on Helsinki issued an official statement insisting, "Mob action must be ended for the good of the fatherland" (p. 178). Even when the first president of the republic was kidnapped by the Lapua movement, he insisted that "a legal order in a democratic state" was the best way to ensure "an orderly, peaceful and successful Finland" (p. 174).

began to crystallize" as differences between "conservatism and fascism began to emerge."[47] The conservative Agrarian Union Party turned decisively against the movement in 1930 and allied with the Social Democrats, the National Progressives, and the majority of the Swedish People's Party. The resulting Lawfulness Front enhanced each party's distancing capacity by effectively ending any competition for the votes of the violent.

When Lapua leaders organized an armed march on Helsinki in 1932, they inadvertently brought about the movement's demise. The conservative president P. E. Svinhufund declared a state of emergency, demanded the arrest of movement leaders, and made a personal radio appeal asking the movement's rank and file to go home. As a well-known Nationalist hero from the civil war who had once had the electoral backing of the Lapua movement leadership, Svinhufund might have played a role like that of von Hindenburg. Instead, he called out the army to block the march and outlawed the movement altogether. The commanding general of the armed forces, the minister of the interior, and the minister of defense gave these initiatives their full support.[48] The fact that these key elites proved steadfast in their opposition to the extreme Right enhanced each party's distancing capacity, since it meant that violence and lawlessness would be curtailed and not merely verbally condemned. Distancing capacity was also enhanced when the movement lost the support of figures from the commercial and industrial elites, because this meant that condemning the perpetrators of violence came at no economic cost.[49] The Finnish political elites effectively "clipped the wings of the Lapua movement" and kept Finnish democracy alive.[50]

The Czechoslovakian case provides another example of a political elite that succeeded in distancing itself from anti-system forces. Yet their task, like that of their Finnish counterparts, was far from easy. Czechoslovakia was "an artificial creation," cobbled together from "bits of other states."[51] Its political elites had to accommodate at least five distinct nationality groups (Czechs, Slovaks, Germans, Hungarians, and Ruthenians) with very different histories. It also had to cope with a division between secular forces (which were especially strong in the Czech lands) and Catholic forces (which were especially strong

---

[47] Alapuro and Allardt, "The Lapua Movement," 135.
[48] Rintala, *Three Generations*, 133 and 194–95.
[49] Alapuro and Allardt, "The Lapua Movement," 133.
[50] Ibid., 139.
[51] Gordon Craig, *Europe since 1815* (New York: Holt, Reinhart and Winston, 1971), 596.

in Slovakia).[52] The state's diversity was reflected in its parliament, which struggled with a series of coalition governments and sometimes contained as many as thirty political parties.[53] Czechoslovakia had the advantage of a "relatively highly developed economy at the outset of its existence,"[54] but the nature of its industrial development made it especially susceptible to the effects of the Depression.[55]

Czechoslovakia's political elites faced foes from subnationalist groups of varied sorts, but the parties on the extreme Left and the extreme Right posed especially potent threats. The Communist Party garnered 13 percent of the national vote in its first election in 1925, and though its share of the vote dropped to only 10 percent by 1935, its internationalist character gave it a constituency in all the different regions of the country and made it Czechoslovakia's third largest party.[56]

The support for the extreme Right was diffuse, consisting mostly of tiny personalistic movements around different regional identities, but in the German-speaking regions (known as the Sudetenland) the extreme Right had deep roots. Paramilitary groups had emerged as part of a network of nationalist organizations in the region as early as 1918, and the German Nazi Party had sent funds and organizers to help the local Nazi Party for years before the Depression.[57] Despite outside assistance, the party gained control of only 2.7 percent of all lower-chamber seats at its peak in 1929. Unfortunately, this did not prevent its leadership from conspiring to overthrow the government through force.[58] The democratic government banned the Czechoslovak Nazi

---

[52] Jan Havránek, "Fascism in Czechoslovakia" in *Native Fascism in the Successor States, 1918–1945*, ed. Peter F. Sugar, (Santa Barbara: ABC-Clio, 1971), 52.

[53] Vera Olivová, "The Czechoslovak Government and its Disloyal Opposition, 1918–1938," in *The Czech and Slovak Experience*, ed. Jahn Morison (New York: St. Martin's Press, 1992), 89.

[54] Sharon L. Wolchik, *Czechoslovakia in Transition: Politics, Economics and Society* (London: Pinter, 1991), 2–3.

[55] Craig, *Europe since 1815*, 596–97.

[56] Bruce Garver, "Václav Klofáč and the Czechoslovak National Socialist Party," in Morison, *The Czech and Slovak Experience*, 110. The Communist Party often used "non-parliamentary means to further their cause," according to Wolchik, *Czechoslovakia in Transition*, 6. The party's leader, Gottwald, was particularly aggressive in Parliament, arguing that the party was "taking lessons from the Bolsheviks" on how to "wring your necks," Olivová, "The Czechoslovak Government," 95.

[57] Joseph Zacek, "Czechoslovak Fascisms," in Sugar, *Native Fascisms*, 57; Olivová, "The Czechoslovak Government," 100, and Josef Korbel, *Twentieth-Century Czechoslovakia: The Meanings of Its History* (New York: Columbia University Press, 1977), 118.

[58] Giovanni Capoccia, "Legislative Responses to Extremism: 'The Protection of Democracy' in the First Czechoslovakian Republic (1920–1938)" *East European Politics and Societies* (forthcoming), manuscript, available from www.europanet.org/conference2002/papers/g3_capoccia.doc.

Party in 1933, but the party's core simply transferred its activities to a new group known as the Henlein Party. This group renamed itself the Sudeten German Party in 1935 and, after Hitler's victory in Germany, gained a full 63 percent of the vote in the Sudetenland.

The political parties running the democratic government in Prague used a variety of means to distance themselves from the destabilizing forces on the extreme Right and extreme Left. One of their most successful means was through national legislation. The banning of the Nazi Party was only one of many instances in which the political elite used existing legal structures to demarcate intolerable behavior. Czechoslovakia's president, Tomas Masaryk, spoke openly and often of the threats to Czech democracy and instituted what he called a "strong hand democratic programme" to ensure that "Czechoslovakia would remain a pluralist, parliamentary [regime]."[59] The program was constructed incrementally around a series of repressive measures against extremist groups and parties. Its "pervasiveness and the harshness of the sanctions that it entailed . . . had few equals."[60] One of the most important of these legal measures was the 1921 Law against terror, which provided immediate arrest and non-jury trials for anyone engaging in political violence. A law passed in 1923 prohibited "the incitement of hatred against specific categories of people," "the causing of disaffection among the armed forces," and "the public approval of criminal acts." All citizens were put under legal obligation to inform public officials if they heard of any planned subversion, and state officials were required to denounce subversive acts. A 1933 law held that anyone drawing a salary from the state (including professors, teachers, clerics, and members of the armed forces) would be prosecuted for "the propagation of facts that were apt to undermine public confidence in legal institutions." A second 1933 law allowed for the permanent dissolution of any party, group, or movement if it endangered "the independence . . . the integrity, the democratic-republican form or the security" of the state. A final major law prohibited the use of uniforms or symbols indicating either affiliation with a banned group or extreme hostility to the constitutional order.[61]

These laws were not merely symbolic gestures. The "strong-hand democratic program" was enforced throughout the presidency of Masaryk, from 1920 through 1935, and throughout the presidency of his

[59] Olivová, "The Czechoslovak Government," 98–99.

[60] Capoccia, "Legislative Responses to Extremism," 10.

[61] This section draws heavily on Capoccia, "Legislative Responses to Extremism," 14–18. For a detailed comparative analysis of the Czech laws, see Karl Loewenstein, "Legislative Control of Political Extremism in European Democracies" pt. 1, in *Columbia Law Review* 38, no. 4 (April 1938); and pt. 2 in vol. 38, no. 5 (May 1938), esp. 607–12.

friend and successor Eduard Beneš, from 1935 until 1939. Continuity of executive leadership—and Masaryk's immense personal prestige—enhanced the distancing capacity of all the country's democratic parties, but institutional factors helped as well. The government in Prague had "inherited a competent civil service from the Austrian empire." It thus proved more able to implement reforms of all sorts and to take the action that distancing required.[62] The country's court system was successful in bringing extremists on the Right and the Left to justice,[63] and social status did not buy impunity. Members of Parliament and even generals were punished for anti-democratic activities[64] and their fate discussed widely in the press. The heterogeneity of the state's police system was used to advantage as well: when it was necessary to crack down on extremist activity in the Sudetenland, police from the Czech lands were sent in to do the job.

Early and successful efforts to control violence from the Communist Left had long-term implications: in 1920, the government implemented a harsh crackdown on radical attempts to seize the property and presses of the Social Democratic Party. It then proved willing to shoot rioters and arrest over three-thousand workers during a general strike. These actions alienated members of the Left, but firmly established the "authority of the government"[65] and deprived the Right of a ready rationale for vigilante action.

State structures were used with efficacy because a critical mass of Czechoslovakia's political elite united against extremism. This elite allied in what was called the Petka, an association of the five largest democratic parties in Parliament. This alliance met behind closed doors before any important policy decision came before the cabinet or national assembly. It worked out consensual positions before any public debate and thus presented a more united front to the public and to the parties on the political extremes.[66] In this case, as with Finland, an inclusive party alliance bolstered distancing capacity.

[62] Craig, *Europe since 1815*, 596–97; Otto Friedman, *The Break-up of Czech Democracy* (London: Victor Gollancz, 1950), 51. The successful implementation of reforms included a successful land reform, the institution of an eight-hour workday, and the extension of autonomy in language and schooling policy to the country's varied ethnic communities.

[63] Olivová, "The Czechoslovak Government," 98.

[64] David Kelly, *The Czech Fascist Movement, 1922–1942* (New York: Columbia University Press, 1995); see Capoccia, "Legislative Responses to Extremism," 39 n. 43.

[65] Victor S. Mamatey, "The Development of Czechoslovak Democracy, 1920–1938," in *A History of the Czechoslovak Republic, 1918–1948* ed. Victor S. Mamatey and Radomír Luza, (Princeton: Princeton University Press, 1973), 105–6.

[66] Vaclav Beneš, "Czechoslovak Democracy and Its Problems, 1918–1920," in Mamatey and Luza, *A History of the Czechoslovak Republic*, 97–98.

Distancing capacity was also enhanced by another association founded by Masaryk, called the Castle Group. This brain trust, composed of intellectuals and business leaders of all nationalities plus democratic politicians from the Czech, Slovak, and German communities, provided a lasting network to counter anti-system forces of all sorts. The Castle Group was also the source of the nonpartisan leadership that occupied ministries and even the prime minister's office when politically difficult policies had to be undertaken.[67]

A final factor that enhanced distancing capacity was the fact that Czechoslovakia's major parties were relatively hierarchical. They were even "less influenced by the rank and file" than parties in Anglo-Saxon countries,[68] and a body called the Electoral Court had the power to deprive politicians of their parliamentary seats if they broke party discipline.[69] A strong internal hierarchy meant that distancing directives were more likely to stick. As Daniel Miller noted, "The Petka functioned efficiently because each party enforced strict discipline."[70]

Party elites' ability to unify in opposition to extremism was exemplified after the electoral success of the extreme Right in the Sudetenland. Rather than polarizing, party elites of the most varied political hues (including Communists and Slovak Nationalists) united behind the presidential candidacy of Eduard Beneš and concentrated on containing the threat from German-speaking extremists. Their joint efforts succeeded, at least temporarily, for the far-right party "faced a profound crisis by the spring of 1936."[71] Czechoslovakian democracy endured until Hitler's invasion in 1939.[72]

A third and very different example of distancing emerged in Venezuela after the Pérez Jiménez dictatorship was ousted in 1958. The inchoate democracy that took its place had to counter strong historical and regional crosswinds in its attempt to stabilize a new regime. Venezuela had had a long history of military dictatorship. Indeed, Simón

---

[67] Economics ministers were routinely recruited from this group, as was Prime Minister Cerny, who had no party affiliation and implemented the 1920 crackdown—saving the political career of the moderate Social Democrat who preceded him.

[68] Friedman, *The Break-up of Czech Democracy*, 51.

[69] Kelly, *The Czech Fascist Movement*, 10.

[70] *Forging Political Compromise: Antonín Švehla and the Czechoslovak Republican Party 1918–1933* (Pittsburgh: University of Pittsburgh Press, 1999), 119.

[71] Beneš got the support of Republican parties from the German, Czech, and Slovak regions, plus the support of Slovak Nationalists and even the Communist Party. Together, these parties placed so many limits on the extreme Right in the Sudetenland that the party was in chaos by 1936, Olivová, "The Czechoslovak Government," 100.

[72] For a cogent, recent analysis of the Czech case, see John Bradley, "Czechoslovakia: External Crises and Internal Compromise," in Berg-Schlosser and Mitchell, *Conditions of Democracy in Europe*.

Bolívar proved prescient in describing his homeland as a "barracks," for the country had suffered under a series of authoritarian "general-presidents" since the nineteenth century.[73] Threats of an alliance between the military and the extreme Right were still in evidence when a freely elected government took office in 1958, but the strongest opposition to the new order was to come from the extreme Left. By the early 1960s, Venezuela faced what was then "the largest guerrilla movement in Latin America."[74] A double threat from the Right and the Left made Venezuelan democracy similar to many other democracies in the region that were to suffer collapse. Yet Venezuela would buck the regional trend. Though the first president of the new democracy ruled "in the midst of the most extreme social and political tensions,"[75] Venezuela was deemed "the most governable country in Latin America" by the 1970s.[76]

Oil revenue helped ensure the survival of the new democracy, but as the histories of Nigeria and other oil-rich states indicate, oil revenue is not a sufficient condition for democratic stability.[77] The deliberate actions of Venezuela's political elites were key to the democratic outcome. Like their counterparts in Finland and Czechoslovakia, party leaders in Venezuela took a variety of measures to counteract threats from violent forces of all sorts.

Their most consequential action was the signing of a party accord called the Pact of Punto Fijo in October 1958. The accord committed the three largest parties in the nation to "cooperation in defense of the democratic system."[78] Concretely, this meant a promise to honor elec-

---

[73] John D. Martz, *Acción Democrática: Evolution of a Modern Political Party in Venezuela* (Princeton: Princeton University Press, 1966), 299.

[74] Terry Lynn Karl, "Petroleum and Political Pacts: The Transition to Democracy in Venezuela," *Latin American Research Review* 22, no. 1 (1987): 86.

[75] Daniel H. Levine, *Conflict and Political Change in Venezuela* (Princeton: Princeton University Press, 1973), 50.

[76] Michael Coppedge, "Prospects for Democratic Governability in Venezuela," *Journal of Interamerican Studies and World Affairs* 36, no. 2 (Summer 1994): 39. Venezuelan democracy is far from calm today. Difficulties began in the 1980s when charges of corruption and economic mismanagement combined with a slump in oil revenue and a revitalization of some of the forces excluded from the bargains forged in the late 1950s.

[77] For a well-argued and lengthy discussion of the connection between oil and democracy in Venezuela, see Terry Lynn Karl, *The Paradox of Plenty: Oil Booms and Petro-States* (Berkeley: University of California Press, 1997).

[78] Martz, *Acción Democrática*, 105. Though the pact was formally signed only by leaders of the three major parties, representatives of the Business Association, the Labor Association, student groups, and the Junta Patriotica were invited to witness the event. Labor and student representatives objected to the exclusion of the Communist Party, foretelling future divisions. Miriam Kornblith, "The Politics of Constitution-Making: Constitutions and Democracy in Venezuela" *Journal of Latin American Studies* 23, no. 1 (February 1991): 70.

tion returns, to adhere to a common basic program, and to establish a government of national unity whereby cabinet positions would be divided equally among the three parties, regardless of which party won the upcoming election. Rómulo Betancourt of the center-left Alianza Democrática (AD) won the presidential elections that followed the signing of the pact and duly set up a multiparty government. Though the ideologically heterogeneous URD abandoned the government in November 1960, and factions of the AD itself defected to both the radical Left and the democratic opposition, the center-right COPEI remained loyal to the pact "in word and deed."[79]

The AD-COPEI alliance enabled the new democracy to cope with potentially destabilizing forces on the Right and Left. Forces on the Right were appeased by COPEI's presence in key government positions and by the government's promise to ensure labor peace.[80] The Right was also deprived of its traditional allies in the military, for Betancourt made successful efforts to ensure that the armed forces would remain loyal to electoral democracy. He purged right-wing interventionist officers immediately and staved off revenge attacks by promising legal amnesty for those associated with the previous dictatorship.[81] He also improved military salaries, expanded educational and weaponry support, and "did his utmost" to assure the armed forces of his personal loyalty.[82]

The support of the military was essential to the neutralization of extremists on the Left as well. The new democracy initially allowed the Communist Party to operate legally, but the AD and COPEI leadership were vociferous in their criticism of the party and unapologetic about excluding the party from the founding pact. These distancing moves alienated both the URD and many younger members of the AD itself. They eventually caused the latter to form a far-left party called the MIR, but the ruling coalition remained steadfast in refusing to cooperate with the far Left. Communists and MIRistas engaged in a massive campaign to destabilize the regime through bombings, kidnappings, and assaults on embassies and multinationals in the years that followed the first elections. The ruling coalition acted with restraint at first and waited twenty-one months before cracking down on violent

---

[79] Robert J. Alexander, *The Venezuelan Democratic Revolution: A Profile of the Regime of Rómolo Betancourt* (New Brunswick, N.J.: Rutgers University Press, 1964), 84–87.

[80] Coppedge, "Prospects for Democratic Governability," 44.

[81] Daniel Levine, "Venezuela since 1958: The Consolidation of Democratic Politics," in *Latin America*, ed. Juan Linz and Alfred Stepan (Baltimore: Johns Hopkins University Press, 1978), 97; and Karl, "Petroleum and Political Pacts," 83.

[82] Edwin Lieuwen, *Generals and Presidents: Neomilitarism in Latin America* (New York: Frederick A. Praeger, 1964), 87–88.

dissent, but the fourth in a series of deadly riots provoked the cabinet to declare a state of emergency in November 1960. In addition to calling out the regular army to quell disorder, the coalition government revoked a number of constitutional guarantees involving detention, privacy, freedom of speech, and the right to assembly.

The government's show of force evoked "the respect and the loyalty of the military"[83] but failed to bring immediate results. Revolutionary forces continued bombings and other acts of terrorism, attempted two military insurrections in the spring of 1962,[84] and launched a deadly campaign to sabotage the scheduled 1963 elections. The coalition government reacted to the tenacity of the revolutionaries with strengthened resolve. The government banned the revolutionary parties, arrested Communist and MIRista representatives in the legislature, and detained hundreds of citizens suspected of participating in extralegal political activities. By the mid-1960s guerrilla activity had been crushed. Constitutional guarantees were not suspended again until February of 1989.[85]

The distancing capacity of the AD-COPEI government was enhanced by at least three factors. The first was the breadth and nature of ruling party support. Both parties—and especially the AD—had been successful in penetrating key groups in civil society. Party influence was "so pervasive that it helped to moderate behavior and keep social peace."[86] The AD had strong support among the peasantry, a slight majority among organized workers in general, and very strong support among oil workers.[87] Whereas in Chile the president had to battle against unions and against the workers in the key export-commodity sector, in Venezuela the president enjoyed union leaders' support. AD labor leaders were virulent in their opposition to the revolutionary Left and were among the first groups to urge suspension of constitutional guarantees.[88] The business community cooperated with the government as well, because of longstanding links to COPEI and because the coalition managed to keep its promise of ensuring labor peace.[89]

[83] Coppedge, "Prospects for Democratic Governability," 45.

[84] Frank Bonilla, *The Failure of Elites* (Cambridge: MIT Press, 1970), 306.

[85] Kornblith, "The Politics of Constitution-Making," 74.

[86] Jennifer L. McCoy and William C. Smith, "Democratic Disequilibrium in Venezuela," *Journal of Interamerican and World Affairs* 37, no. 2 (Summer 1995): 122.

[87] Alexander, *The Venezuelan Democratic Revolution*, 76.

[88] Martz, *Acción Democrática*, 272.

[89] After 1958 and lasting at least until 1973, the control of strikes seems to have been a special priority during election years. Legal strikes always decreased at election time, though illegal strikes began to rise in 1973. See the data in Argelia Bravo, *Crisis, Elecciones y Violencia* (Caracas: Editorial Ruptura, 1978), 49.

Labor peace was ensured, in part, by the fact that the AD had majority support in most trade unions, but the maintenance of support depended on two other factors. One involved informal and formal tripartite commissions in which labor, business, and government brokered cross-class agreements to preempt strikes. The other involved the revenue from oil exports that helped pay for these agreements: labor kept strikes to a minimum in exchange for higher social spending and advantageous legal changes regarding health, education, and social security.[90] The dynamic was the same in the countryside. Rural voters remained loyal to the government (and almost impervious to the revolutionary Left) in exchange for increased social welfare spending and major land reform made possible by government financed compensation. The breadth of the governing parties' support from key economic actors made the crackdown on the Left less risky politically.

Distancing was facilitated by the nature of internal party governance as well. Both AD and COPEI "imposed an iron discipline on their members"[91] and eventually commanded what at least three scholars deemed "the most extreme example of a centralized party system" in any Latin American or European democracy.[92] With solid ties to key social sectors and control of the economic resources that financed a vast network of political exchange, Venezuela's ruling parties "acquired an autonomous position with respect to any single sector."[93] It was this sort of autonomy that enabled Rómulo Betancourt to distance his administration from violent social forces in unambiguous terms, as in the following speech:

> The thesis that the streets belong to the people is false and demagogic. . . .
> The people in the abstract does not exist. In modern, organized societies,
> . . . the people are the political parties, the unions, the organized economic
> sectors, professional societies, university groups. Whenever any of these
> groups seeks authorization for a peaceful demonstration . . . there will be
> no difficulty. . . . But whenever uncontrolled groups jump into the streets,
> under whatever pretext, they will be treated with neither softness nor lenience for . . . behind these groups work . . . totalitarians of all stripes.[94]

[90] The commissions were the fruit of a cross-class pact called the Worker-Employer Accord, which mirrored the Pact of Punto Fijo. Karl, *The Paradox of Plenty*, 99–100.

[91] Coppedge, "Prospects for Democratic Governability," 42.

[92] McCoy and Smith, "Democratic Disequilibrium," 122, quoting Coppedge.

[93] Levine, "Venezuela since 1958," 102 n. 36.

[94] Rómulo Betancourt, *Tres Años de Gobierno Democrático, 1959–1962*, (Caracas: Imprensa Nacional, 1962): 245. He precedes this passage with a list of other countries that will not allow demonstrations without permits.

The hierarchical structure of Venezuela's parties and, more specifically, the deference accorded party leaders, made "changes in elite norms particularly important." The "rank and file accept[ed] new patterns of action because of a general faith in the leadership."[95] A broad spectrum of the political leadership communicated their changed norms in the clearest of language, and this was the third asset in the distancing process. In democracies that broke down, democratic elites often fed public polarization by engaging in harsh criticisms of one another and by taking ambiguous (or even openly supportive) positions on anti-system parties and activities. The core of the Venezuelan political elite behaved differently. Recognizing the need for interelite consensus, the parties signing the Pact of Punto Fijo "committed themselves to avoiding harsh inter-party antagonism" during elections,[96] and then sustained this commitment, for the most part, after the elections were over. The leaders of the UDN were harshly critical of the other ruling parties when they left the government, as were the political figures who split off from the AD, but key political elites avoided exploiting divisions at pivotal moments in the consolidation process. Three examples make the point: (1) When a popular military challenger to Betancourt won a landslide victory in Caracas during the presidential elections, many feared the elections would be questioned or even overturned. Instead, the Caracas victor (named Wolfgang Larrazabal) got on television and radio, declared his support for Betancourt, and asked for immediate compliance with the national results.[97] (2) Whenever there was an attempt at a military coup, observers feared defections in the high command. Instead, the highest military officers consistently made statements in support of the elected government and against the coup-makers.[98] (3) When the AD-COPEI coalition decided to crack down on revolutionary parties, many expected the democratic opposition to exploit the opportunity to question the democratic credentials of the ruling coalition. Instead, even the arrest of Communist and MIR congressmen "aroused no opposition" among competitive democratic elites.[99] Democratic parties of all sorts remained united against anti-system groups of all sorts.

[95] Levine, "Venezuela since 1958," 84–85.

[96] Kornblith, "The Politics of Constitution-Making," 70.

[97] Martz, *Acción Democrática*, 106. Since Larrazabal had helped drive Pérez-Jiménez from power and gained a broad following in the capital as head of a caretaker government, he might well have been a powerfully divisive figure—but he played a conciliatory role instead.

[98] Alexander, *The Venezuelan Democratic Revolution*, 108–9.

[99] Ibid., 130.

Betancourt, unlike his counterparts in systems that broke down, left no ambiguity about his toleration of lawlessness. It was predictable that the center-left leader would rail against the anti-democratic Right, but he also railed against revolutionary parties of the Left. His virulent criticisms of revolutionary Communism (which began on the day he returned from exile and continued throughout his presidency)[100] made him dramatically different from João Goulart and Salvador Allende. This, plus his insistence on maintaining public order even at high cost, eventually made the far Right superfluous and the far Left impotent.

Venezuela, Czechoslovakia, and Finland differed markedly in their institutional, social and economic structures, yet they shared at least three qualities that enabled their democracies to survive grave threats. The first involved their party alliances. In each of these cases, party elites exhibited a commitment to democracy that led them to overcome interparty differences and form broad alliances against anti-democratic groups. Elite decisions to establish Finland's Lawfulness Front, Czechoslovakia's Petka, and Venezuela's Pact of Punto Fijo proved pivotal in protecting each democracy from collapse. Party alliances enabled each democratic government to pass laws controlling anti-democratic activity, to institute reforms that coopted the issues of their anti-democratic opposition, and to govern with relative efficacy. This last achievement, plus the presence of conservative parties in the coalitions, staved off serious defections from capitalists and the military. It is highly consequential that all of these alliances managed to placate these two forces.[101]

The second quality these diverse cases shared related to party structure. The main parties in all these alliances were extremely hierarchical. Thus, decisions by party elites were highly and immediately consequential. Finally, each of these systems was headed by a charismatic leader who wielded a clear leadership mandate. Masaryk was Czechoslovakia's founding father. Svinhufund was a hero from the civil war. Betancourt took on heroic stature during his exile under the years of

---

[100] See Martz, *Acción Democrática*, 99; and Alexander, *The Venezuelan Democratic Revolution*, 77 and 90. In addition to distancing himself from the revolutionary Left, Betancourt downplayed the threat that revolutionaries could pose—and thereby emphasized the efficacy of the democratic regime. In this, too, he differed from the leaders of many failed democracies. See, for example, Betancourt, *Tres Años*, 121.

[101] Dirk Berg-Schlosser's broad comparative history of interwar Europe adds further evidence to my argument about the importance of party alliances and distancing. In every democratic regime that survived, he found a "broad democratic coalition." In none of the regimes that broke down was such a coalition forged. See Berg-Schlosser, "Conditions of Authoritarianism," 360–61.

dictatorship. Their capacity to lead their parties—and their party's allies—was heightened by their personal histories and their decisive electoral victories. Many of the leaders of collapsed democracies had neither of these advantages, and this weakened their distancing capacity.

Though the point needs more evidence and refinement, distancing capacity does seem to distinguish failed democracies from successful ones. Distancing capacity is a mixed blessing, for it obviously sets limits on just who has access to democratic rights. The trade-offs intrinsic to distancing capacity should be the subject of further research and debate (as should the origins of distancing capacity), but it is surely as important a quality in today's struggling democracies as it was in the historic cases analyzed here.

The mention of today's struggling democracies brings us full circle, back to the images with which this study began: the heroic images of ordinary people taking extraordinary risks to bring new democracies into being. How these democracies function and how long they last will have much to do with how popular preferences are understood and ranked by political elites. Democracy, as Lijphart reminds us, is not only rule *"by* the people but rule *for* the people, that is, *rule in accord with people's preferences."*[102] As long as the path to rulership depends on elections, elites will be mindful of what popular preferences are. The histories related here suggest that people's preferences were more supportive of democracy than elites recognized. Leaders who recognized these preferences and who distanced themselves from anti-democratic forces might well have kept their democracies alive.[103]

In emphasizing the culpability of political elites, the story told here has backward and forward linkages. Looking backward, it has a clear connection with one of the central insights of Juan Linz and Alfred Stepan in *The Breakdown of Democratic Regimes.* Writing in the 1970s, at a time when the breakdown of democracy was often attributed to immutable "structural strains," Linz and Stepan thought it important to question assumptions about the "virtual inevitability" of particular breakdowns and to ask how the behavior of "incumbent democratic leaders . . . contributed to the breakdown" process.[104] My

---

[102] Arend Lijphart, *Democracies* (New Haven: Yale University Press, 1984), 1. Lijphart is, of course, drawing on Lincoln here.

[103] The older literature on consociationalism pointed out the importance of elite conviction and cooperation in the face of divisive threat. The classic here is Arend Lijphart's *Democracy in Plural Societies: A Comparative Exploration* (New Haven: Yale University Press, 1977).

[104] These quotations are from the editors' preface and acknowledgments in Linz, *Crisis, Breakdown, and Reequilibration,* ix.

research question focuses on the behavior of citizens as well as elites, and on leaders of all sorts, whether incumbents or not, but my conclusion about elite culpability is very much in keeping with their theme that poor leadership "can be decisive."[105] The story I tell about the failure of leadership differs from what has been written before, however, in specifying that elite failure derived from a misreading of popular preferences rather than from a desire to cater to truly polarized polities.

In highlighting the failures of political elites and their decisive role in the breakdown process, my argument also links up with current themes in the literature on democratic consolidation. This is its most obvious forward linkage, but the parallels between the historical cases analyzed here and the cases we confront today must be drawn with caution and a sensitivity to changes as well as continuities. Four changes seem especially noteworthy.

First, the continuities in party preferences we traced in the past may now be harder to sustain. Dictatorships and development have transformed many of the social networks that reinforced continuities in the past; the collapse of the Soviet Union has weakened parties of the Left and shaken old polarities; eased access to information from the expansion of mass media makes vote switching less costly; and parties built around media figures have made even long-established party systems more volatile.

Though party preferences may become more fluid, political preferences in general are less likely to be misread by political elites. Extensive opinion polling, universal suffrage, and improved communication of all sorts give today's leader better information about the public will. This is a second, important change.

A third, related change regards the expansion of civil society. Ordinary people are better able to organize and express their preferences through associations of all sorts. The rise in literacy and urbanization, the growth of international civil society, and the use of the internet mean that public space is filled more easily and with a more diverse range of actors.

Fourth, and finally, what these actors chose to do (or not to do) is affected by their past experience. Most countries have now had some meaningful experience with both competitive and noncompetitive regimes. Ordinary people and political elites are better able to compare dictatorship to democracy, and, happily, the comparison generally fa-

---

[105] Ibid., 5.

vors democracy. Despite undeniable performance failures in the economic realm, democracy has more support today than ever before.[106]

All but the first of these changes suggest that the breakdown of democracy should be less likely in the twenty-first century than in the twentieth. More people prefer democracy to dictatorship, a strengthened civil society is better able to express these preferences, and political elites have better information about just what people's preferences are. However, caution and vigilance are still very much in order. The expanded mass media can be used for ill purposes as well as good;[107] anti-democratic leaders can replace Left-Right polarities with religious, ethnic, and regional polarities instead; the embrace of democracy is very far from universal, and our more densely organized civil societies can still contain fundamentally anti-democratic elements. Most consequentially, the preferences of ordinary people can be ignored if political elites decide that free elections are no longer a viable formula for deciding who rules.

This last point brings us to the single most important continuity between the frail democracies of the past and our frail democracies today. In contemporary times, as in times gone by, it seems that democracies do not break down unless political elites deliberately destroy them. The key elites today, as in the past, seem to be men in uniform. I use cautious language here because only speculations are possible without

---

[106] A study of over 10,000 people conducted in six African countries in 1999–2000 found that respondents "overwhelmingly support democracy and reject authoritarian regimes," and that a full three-quarters of respondents identified themselves as "supporters of democracy." Michael Bratton and Robert Mattes, "Africans' Surprising Universalism" *Journal of Democracy* 12, no. 1 (January 2001): 108–112. In all but one post-Communist regime in Eastern Europe, "a clear majority" reject all the alternatives to democratic government. In the single exception, Lithuania, respondents lean toward the ambiguous category of "strongman rule." See Richard Rose, "A Diverging Europe" *Journal of Democracy* 12, no. 1 (January 2001): 99. In South Korea and Taiwan, too, majorities agree that "democracy is always preferable" to dictatorship, though the margin is not high—55% and 54% respectively. See Yun-han Chu, Larry Diamond, and Doh Chull Shin, "Halting Progress in Korea and Taiwan," *Journal of Democracy* 12, no. 1 (January 2001): 125. In Latin America, opinion was "conflicted" in the year 2000, but *Latinobarometro* surveys revealed that, in most of Latin America, "majorities of the public accept democracy as the best form of government." See Marta Lagos, "Between Stability and Crisis in Latin America," *Journal of Democracy* 12, no. 1 (January 2001): 137.

[107] The mass media may, alas, have a detrimental effect on political parties and even the quality of democracy. Citing examples from Brazil, Peru, and Argentina, Edward Gibson writes of the "growing substitution of the mass media for party structures" and notes that most of the New Right electoral movements in Latin America have "risen to prominence not by the strength of party organization, but by the power of the mass media." "Conservative Electoral Movements and Democratic Politics," in *The Right and Democracy in Latin America*, ed. Douglas A. Chalmers, Maria do Carmo Campello de Souza, and Atilio A. Borón, (New York: Praeger, 1992), 30.

systematic research. But it appears that democracies still do not die at the hands of ordinary people, even in times of severe economic crisis. Mass mobilizations may temporarily force specific elected executives from power, as happened in Venezuela in 2002. They may even force the permanent ouster of freely elected heads of state, as happened in Ecuador in 2000.[108] These mobilizations represent vivid illustrations of the continuing ambiguities of civil society and of the many different visions of what democracies should provide.[109] But they also illustrate that democracy itself will not be swept away unless the armed forces seek to either seize power themselves or stand in unity behind a civilian with the same goal. The armed forces in Ecuador and Venezuela eventually took the side of the existing democracy, and thus these crises stopped short of full-blown changes in regime. When the armed forces make the opposite choice, democracies collapse. Larry Diamond records that there were four blatant reversals of democracy in countries with populations over twenty-million in the last twenty years of the twentieth century.[110] Each one of these reversals was led by military

---

[108] Venezuela's president Hugo Chavez was forced out of office for two days in April 2002, after the national guard and his personal gunmen fired on a crowd of anti-government demonstrators. The demonstration was led by a coalition of business leaders and trade unionists protesting corruption, economic mismanagement, and restrictions on democratic freedoms. At first the high command of the military supported an interim government led by Pedro Carmona, the civilian head of the national business federation. Though Carmona promised to call new elections, popular and international pressures against the interim government led General Efrain Vasquez to withdraw support in a matter of days. Carmona resigned immediately, and Chavez was restored to power. In Ecuador, in January of 2000, thousands of mobilized Indians took control of the national legislature, demanded the resignation of the elected president Jamil Mahuad, and attempted to instate a three-man junta including the leader of the indigenous movement. Under national and international pressure, the military soon turned power over to Gustavo Noboa, Mahuad's vice president. It is highly significant that both of these attempted coups were condemned by the OAS. It is also significant that the successful executive coup led by Alberto Fujimori in Peru had military backing, while the unsuccessful executive coup led by Jorge Serrano in Guatemala failed to marshal military support. For more on these cases, see Maxwell A. Cameron, "Self-Coups: Peru, Guatemala and Russia," *Journal of Democracy* 9, no. 1 (January 1998): 125–39. The military's decision to stand by President Juan Carlos Wasmosy, the legitimately elected president in Paraguay, prevented a coup in April 1996. See Arturo Valenzuela, "Paraguay: The Coup That Didn't Happen," *Journal of Democracy* 8, no. 1 (January 1997): 43–55.

[109] For a stimulating discussion of how indigenous movements have brought collective rather than individual views of citizenship into democracies in the Andean countries see Deborah Yashar, *Contesting Citizenship: Indigenous Movements, the State, and the Post-Liberal Challenge in Latin America* (Cambridge: Cambridge University Press, forthcoming).

[110] Larry Diamond lists these as the 1983 coup in Nigeria, the 1989 coup in Sudan, the 1991 coup in Thailand, and the 1999 coup in Pakistan. For more detail see "Is Pakistan the Reverse Wave of the Future?" *Journal of Democracy* 11, no. 3 (July 2000): 91–92.

elites and each produced a military dictatorship. This is probably not coincidental, but it is decidedly reminiscent of the patterns we traced in earlier periods.

The preferences of ordinary people are important to the quality of democracy, and they are certainly important when civilian and military elites calculate the costs of intervention. But, as Valerie Bunce puts it, the "termination of democracy is very much a matter of what elites choose to do—and not to do."[111] Advances in communication give today's political elites better capacities to understand and to shape the preferences of ordinary people. History gives elites the capacity to learn from the deadly mistakes of the past. Whether elites use these capacities in the interests of democracy may depend as much on strength of conviction as on economic strength or on any other measure of performance. Where the experience of dictatorial rule has strengthened elite convictions about the merits of democracy, there is reason for hope. Where dictatorship has had other effects and where elected elites still fail to distance themselves from anti-democratic actors, ordinary people may once again be caught up in the drama of democratic breakdown.

---

[111] "Comparative Democratization: Big and Bounded Generalizations," manuscript, 27 September 1999, 14. The paper is now available in *Comparative Political Studies* 33, 6 (August 2000).

INDEX